EUROPE SINCE
THE SEVENTIES

EUROPE SINCE
THE SEVENTIES

JEREMY BLACK

REAKTION BOOKS

For Peter Hennessy

Published by Reaktion Books Ltd
33 Great Sutton Street
London EC1V 0DX
www.reaktionbooks.co.uk

First published 2009

Printed and bound in Great Britain
by MPG Books Ltd, Bodmin, Cornwall

British Library Cataloguing in Publication Data
Black, Jeremy
    Europe since the seventies. – (Contemporary worlds)
    1. Europe – History – 1945 –
    I. Title
    940.5'5

ISBN: 978 1 86189 424 3

Contents

Preface

This book breaks the mould by starting at 1970 and not, as a number of excellent works do, 1945. This choice is deliberate because our perspective is now that of the twenty-first century and, for the young, including the bulk of the electorate across Europe, 1945 is fairly distant, if not ancient, history. Furthermore, beginning in 1945 means a focus on post-Second World War recovery, on the Cold War, not least its early stages, and on the establishment of the European Economic Community, the basis of the modern European Union. In contrast, starting at 1970 offers very different possibilities, and this is particularly true if the view is from the late 2000s when, for many readers, the Cold War is a dimming memory. Those born after 1975 have scant recollection of the period. Their perspective tends to be underrated by historians, which is paradoxical as this is very much an age of changing views, but scholars all too often learn little from their children or their students.

As a result of focusing on the post-1970 period there is also a clear difference in coverage and therefore theme. The years 1945–70 not only take us back to the Second World War, and its legacy in the shape of the stark divisions of the Cold War, but also deal with the prolonged post-war period of economic recovery and growth. This growth was important to social shifts and to a more general sense of improvement and prospects, contributing, more than its advocates realized, to the exuberant optimism and cultural and social experimentation known as the 1960s. More specifically, economic growth in France, West Germany and Italy helped fuel not only the optimism of the early stages of Western European integration, but also other European changes including the building of key features of a road network and the massive expansion of tertiary education.

Starting in the 1970s, however, takes us in different directions. For the political dimension, indeed, the focus is on the dissolution of the divisions that had characterized the previous quarter-century. This dissolution of divisions was a matter not simply of East–West *détente* in the 1970s, which attracted much contemporary attention, but was in some respects a false dawn for the later, and very different, largely peaceful collapse of Communist rule in 1989–91. A more immediate dissolution of divisions in the 1970s was provided by the lasting collapse of right-wing authoritarian regimes in Greece, Portugal and Spain. The importance of this collapse tends to be underplayed due to the concentration on the conventional agenda of the Cold War, but this Mediterranean shift was a crucial aspect of the new politics of Europe. It transformed economic opportunities, challenged social, cultural and political norms in Catholic and Orthodox heartlands, and altered the European Union. The fall of these regimes indeed prefigured the changes that accompanied, and followed, the collapse of Communism. The aftermath in Mediterranean Europe also showed that such a transformation could last, and instructive comparisons can be drawn with later developments in Eastern Europe.

At the same time there was also, from the early 1970s, a challenge to the previous period of economic expansion. This challenge was a product not only of the major oil price shock following the 1973 Arab–Israeli Yom Kippur War, with the significant impact this had on inflation, growth and economic optimism, but also of serious fiscal and economic problems in the international commercial system, not least those that led to the end of the Bretton Woods fixed-rate exchange currency system. These problems prefigured both the subsequent decades of often troubled economic growth and severe difficulties that persist today.

More particularly, a growing sense of Europe as relatively less prominent and successful at a global scale became readily apparent.

This sense was pushed to the fore by Japanese and, later, Chinese imports, and by an awareness among policymakers that growth opportunities were no longer focused on Europe. The global scale is important in the judgment of European developments, while particular episodes take on more meaning in an international context. The use of the word 'globalization' to describe this process can obscure this, as globalization is so often seen in terms of broad-brush trends and developments. Instead, it is necessary to consider both the extent to which these trends and developments take (and will continue to take) on meaning and bite in specific circumstances, and also the degree to which the detailed chronology of this period in European history, particularly, but not only, its political and economic history, was interwoven with issues and events elsewhere, from the anxieties of American geopolitics to the investment strategies of particular conglomerates.

This book follows my *Britain since the Seventies* (2004) and *Altered States. America since the Sixties* (2006). In preparing it I have benefited from lecture invitations that in 2005–8 gave me opportunities for travel to Denmark, Estonia, Finland, France, Germany, Greece, Ireland, Italy, Malta, the Netherlands, Norway, Portugal, Russia, Slovenia, Spain, Sweden and Switzerland. I have profited greatly from the advice of David Ellwood, Bill Gibson and Michael Leaman on an earlier draft, and thank Simon Barton, Tim Black, Michael Bregnsbo, Tom Buchanan, Bruce Charlton, Edward Corp, Olavi Fält, Maria Fusaro, Jan Glete, Nicholas Kyriazis, Wayne Lee, Karl de Leeuw, Thomas Otte, Stephen Richards and Arno Richter for their comments on particular sections.

This book is dedicated to Peter Hennessy whom it is a great pleasure to know as much for his warm and engaging personality as for his acute and critical mind. Peter has been a great help, always offering pertinent and thoughtful advice. That his company is a great delight is an additional boon.

Chapter 1

Introduction: Europe 1945–70

A continent in ruins in 1945, Europe was subsequently on the frontline of the Cold War, and gave the name to the Iron Curtain. Moreover, as a result of the Cold War, Europe's recovery from the Second World War was a divided and divisive one. In essence, there were three major zones in post-war Europe, and these were to be important to the continent's subsequent history.

EASTERN EUROPE

The first zone, Eastern Europe, was an area of Communist one-party states with government control and oversight of all areas of life. This was a zone dominated by the Soviet Union, which had conquered most of the region in 1944–5, defeating Nazi Germany and its allies. It is indicative of the major changes that have occurred in Europe since 1989 that it is necessary to treat the Soviet Union as an aspect of history that requires explanation. It was the state created as the result of the Communist revolution in Russia in 1917 and the subsequent success of the Communists in the Russian Civil War. This state controlled most, but not all, of the former Russian empire, including Ukraine, Belarus and the Caucasus, though not Finland.

In turn, in 1939–40 Soviet expansionism in concert with Nazi Germany led to the seizure of the independent republics of Estonia, Latvia and Lithuania, as well as of territories from Finland, Poland and Romania, all of these territories at some point part of the Russian empire overthrown in 1917. At the close of the Second World War the Soviets retained these gains and added, from Germany, what is now the Kaliningrad enclave (formerly part of East Prussia), as well as part of Czechoslovakia that had been annexed by Hungary in 1939. The city of Königsberg was renamed Kaliningrad, a German name marking royal power replaced by a Russian one honouring Mikhail Kalinin, who had been President of the Presidium of the Supreme Soviet. The Soviet drive for territorial gains was in part fuelled by paranoia and fear of the West.

In Eastern Europe the destruction of earlier political structures in the Second World War, the 'liberation' by the Red (Soviet) Army in 1944–5, and the subsequent establishment of Soviet hegemony and Communist rule cleared the way for the economic bloc of Comecon (1949) and the security bloc of the Warsaw Pact (1955). Although they were far from similar to the European Economic Community (EEC) and the North Atlantic Treaty Organization (NATO) in Western Europe, there were instructive parallels.

The Soviet Union tried to integrate the Eastern European economies, although it was handicapped by the inherent weaknesses of Communist economic management, and also resisted by attempts by national governments, conspicuously those of Yugoslavia, Albania and Romania, to retain and assert control. Yugoslavia under Josip Tito and Albania under Enver Hoxha broke from the Soviet bloc in 1948 and 1960–1 respectively, while Romania, from which Soviet forces withdrew in 1958, followed an increasingly independent line from the 1960s.

A key political structure that had been destroyed was Germany. It was divided after the war between a Soviet zone of occupation, which became the German Democratic Republic, East Germany, a Communist dictatorship, and American, British and French zones, which became the Federal Republic of Germany, West Germany, a democracy. There was therefore a parallel founding of two very different states. One was democratic, market economy-based, and Western, with a constitution focused on the idea that 'Bonn [the capital of West Germany] is not Weimar [the fragile German democracy of the 1920s]', while the other laid claim to being anti-Fascist, anti-imperialist and Socialist. The 'German question' remained open in terms of foreign policy and international law. Germany was the key country or would-be country in the entire Cold War in Europe, from beginning to end.

Poland and, to a lesser extent, Russia gained much of pre-1938 Germany and, in 1945–6, 9 million Germans fled west from these territories, but also from pre-1938 Czechoslovakia, Poland and other countries. This flight was an aspect of the widespread displacement that the war had brought and that continued after its end. Whereas the population movements within Europe in the 1950s and 1960s were primarily of labour (with families sometimes following), those in the late 1940s were mostly of entire families as an aspect of what would later be termed 'ethnic cleansing'.

Eastern Europe was dominated by the Soviet Union. There were client states in Poland, East Germany, Czechoslovakia, Hungary and Bulgaria. Romania, Yugoslavia and Albania were each Communist one-party states but by 1970 they had gained a degree of independence from Soviet direction, with Yugoslavia under Tito following an independent international line from 1948. Albania was sponsored by China, which from 1960 was an ideological rival of the Soviet Union within the Communist world. Romania under Nicolae Ceauşescu, General Secretary of the Communist Party from 1965 and President of the State Council from 1967, became a maverick member of the Warsaw Pact, winning American Most-Favored-Nation status in 1975 as it followed a 'Romania-first' approach. Nevertheless, the difficulty of gaining a degree of independence was underlined in Hungary in 1956 and Czechoslovakia in 1968 when Soviet forces intervened to suppress attempts to provide a degree of liberalism and autonomy. Yet alongside the drive for conformity there was, even among those states closest to the Soviet Union, a variety in political culture that reflected earlier differences.

Although Russian nationalism and geopolitics also played a major role in Soviet behaviour, these invasions underlined the ideological nature of the Cold War: it was more than a confrontation between great powers with differing political systems. The character of these systems was also a crucial issue. In the Communist states, terror and force were routinely used to maintain control and to implement policies, although terror was not the sum total of rule, and there was a process of 'negotiation' at the local level through which the diktats of the system were implemented. Nevertheless, like other totalitarian regimes, Stalinism, the system of ideology named after Joseph Stalin, Russian dictator from 1924 to 1953, worked in part by creating an all-pervasive sense of surveillance and fear, as well as of monolithic support by the 'people' which could not be opposed. The Soviet regime was felt but could not be seen: prison camps existed, but few knew their location or extent. Terror worked on ignorance, on the ungraspable nature and undefined scope of the oppressor. For this reason Communist states controlled information and made major efforts to block radio transmissions from the West. In Czechoslovakia the suppression of the reform movement in 1968 was followed by the reimposition of a police state.

European Communist regimes after the Stalin era did not routinely execute, still less slaughter their citizens for political crimes, but the terror state remained in place. Those regarded as unacceptable were readily incarcerated, sentenced to internal exile or committed to psychiatric clinics where they were deliberately driven mad. Work camps could be – in effect – a death sentence. The fate of dissidents tarnished Communist claims on political virtue and compromised Western European supporters; while the exposure of Communist policies made acceptance of the Communist bloc through normalization sinister. Similar critical remarks about the attempt to render the Communist bloc acceptable can be made about some overly favourable modern scholarship on East Germany.

SOUTHERN EUROPE

The second zone in Europe was composed of the authoritarian right-wing dictatorships of Mediterranean Europe, Portugal, Spain and Greece. The first two had become dictatorships in the inter-war period, Spain after a bitter civil war in 1936–9. Greece had had such a dictatorship in the late 1930s but was a democracy after the Second World War, before the military seized power in a coup in 1967, 'the colonels' retaining control until 1974. This zone is discussed at greater length in the opening section of Chapter 7.

WESTERN EUROPE

The third zone was that of most of Western Europe. This zone was defined by democratic political systems. After the Second World War Italy became a republic, while in France the Third Republic, discredited by defeat, and brought to an end by the collaborationist Vichy regime in 1940, was replaced by the Fourth Republic, the constitution of which was backed by a referendum in 1946. West Germany's democratic constitution defined it as part of Western Europe.

In terms of power politics, however, there was far greater variation in democratic Europe than in Eastern Europe, not least with the contrast between powers that were joined in NATO, formed in 1949 to resist Soviet expansionism, and states that were, at least ostensibly, neutral in the Cold War, principally Austria, Finland, Ireland, Sweden and Switzerland. NATO included the USA, Canada, Britain, Norway, Denmark, the Netherlands, Belgium, France, Portugal, Italy and Luxembourg. Greece and Turkey joined NATO in 1952, which represented a major expansion of the containment of the Soviet Union into the Mediterranean. West Germany followed in 1955, with the rival Warsaw Pact being formed ten days later. The rearmed Bundeswehr (West German army) was very important to NATO strength in Europe, while the inclusion of the East German National People's Army in the Warsaw Pact forces sealed the international division of Germany.

Replacing the idea of a Western European 'Third Force', and in the absence of a European solution to the German question or to domestic British and Western European security issues, NATO reflected the willingness of the USA to avoid the temptations of isolation, but also the military weakness of the Western European states in the face of Soviet strength and expansionism. There was a psychological dimension, with a widespread assumption in 1950 that the Soviets could and would invade. The fear of this was manipulated on both sides of the Iron Curtain and on each side of the Atlantic. Fear of atomic war was important to the foundation of NATO, as was the discovery of just how like the Soviet Union was to Nazi Germany.

In military terms Western Europe was under American guardianship. The breaking of the Soviet blockade of West Berlin in 1949 fostered a sense in West Germany of belonging with regard to the USA and the West. The construction of the Berlin Wall in 1961 and the invasion of Czechoslovakia in 1968 served to underline the apparent threat from the Soviet Union. These were both key episodes in the 1960s.

THE 'LONG BOOM'

The Second World War had ended with America the dominant economy in the world. Germany had been hit hard by bombing, Britain had large debts, many to the USA, and the Soviet economy had been devastated, while France and Italy had been greatly affected by defeat, occupation, bombing and being the site of conflict. The new economic order was established by the Americans. The international free trade and capital markets that had characterized the global economy of the 1900s, and subsequently been wrecked by the First World War, were slowly re-established.

The availability of American credit and investment was very important. Among the major powers, only the USA enjoyed real liquidity in 1945. Under the Bretton Woods Agreement of the previous year, American-supported monetary agencies, the World Bank and the International Monetary Fund (both of which had American headquarters), were established in order to play an active role in strengthening the global financial system. The General Agreement on Tariffs and Trade (GATT), signed in 1947, began a major cut in tariffs that helped trade to increase. From 1945 to 1973 there was what was subsequently to be termed the 'long boom' or the *Trente Glorieuses* (Thirty Glorious Years), a period of rapid economic development. This boom had a number of interrelated causes, and played out differently in various parts of the world, but the net effect was a synergy in which free trade and readily available investment encouraged profitable interaction. West Germany, which became the leading European economy, was a major exporter benefiting from free trade. Economic growth in Europe owed much to the application of new technology in manufacturing and agriculture, which resulted in important productivity gains. In agriculture mechanization led to a movement of workers from the land, especially in France and Germany. The process was already far advanced in Britain. In manufacturing the employment of mass-production in new purpose-built plants permitted a more effective introduction of new technology and organizational methods. American investment, and the catch-up factor of applying advanced, mostly American, technology and production methods, were significant in Western European growth.

The political economy of the countries of Western Europe varied greatly. Britain, France and Italy developed mixed economies that included much state planning and nationalization, in Britain as a result of the policies of the Labour governments of 1945–51. West Germany grew faster. This owed something to American aid, although its role remains controversial. It was not that much – just over $1.4 billion and was mostly used to deal with bottlenecks. American aid was spent in West Germany on industry, not arms, but growing global demand, not least the Western economic boom due to demand at the time of the Korean War (1950–3), was at least as important as this aid. So also was the national focus in West Germany, during the 'Chancellor Democracies' of Konrad Adenauer and Ludwig Erhard, on economic activity, especially at the expense of politics. The economic liberalization, especially in foreign and domestic trade, pushed by Erhard (who directed economic policy from 1948 to 1963 and was Federal Chancellor from 1963 to 1966) and other leaders was also important to growth. This liberalization was a major break from the cartels characteristic of earlier German history. Influenced by liberal-minded economists, the Christian Democratic West German governments followed pro-competition policies and fostered currency stability, although, until it adopted the Godesberg Programme in 1959, the left-wing SPD (Social Democratic) opposition favoured state planning. Furthermore, the

West German economic and financial system contrasted with the nationalizations and state control seen in France and Britain.

West Germany also benefited from the skill of its engineering industry and from more harmonious labour relations than those in Britain. The latter was an aspect of West German corporatism, which encompassed government, business, banks and trade unions. In turn, this corporatism rested on the social cohesion that the exclusion of the far left and far right from politics helped encourage. Prosperity and consumerism lessened tension, although both were to lead to criticism from the young in the 1960s.

Economic growth in West Germany had an impact elsewhere, not least because the male German labour force had been hit by heavy war losses. As a result, prefiguring the periphery-to-core movements that were to be important in Europe later in the century, notably after the Iron Curtain came down in 1989 (see pages 70–73), there was a major population shift to West Germany. Prior to 1961 when the Berlin Wall was built, millions of East Germans went west in a fundamental rejection of the East German system. They went in search of jobs and economic liberty, and what they could produce, as much as for political freedom. The Socialist planned economy with the 'New Economic System' in East Germany did not arrive at the same standard of living and prosperity as the concept of the 'Social Market Economy' closely associated with the 'Economic Miracle' in West Germany.

MIGRATION

There was also an important migration from Mediterranean Europe, particularly from Italy, Yugoslavia and Turkey, but also from Greece, Portugal and Spain. As a result, by 1973 12 per cent of the West German labour force was foreign, while the foreign workforce in France was 11 per cent, many of them from Portugal. This migrant flow was as important a social transformation as the cultural shift of the 1960s that more generally attracts attention. The flow had a major impact on both sending and receiving areas and, in the latter, helped transform significant sections of the working class. Due to their being recent migrants, important sectors of the blue-collar workforce were now poorly integrated into established patterns of social and political relationship in the areas in which they settled, and this helped lessen the general political significance of this sector of the workforce. As such, the situation prefigured the consequences of the crises in traditional heavy industries later in the century as they confronted international competition and structural change.

At the level of the poor this migration, which was at a particularly high rate in the 1960s, created an experience of Europe or, at least, of a Europe defined by both birthplace and destination. The migration also entailed a major exposure to foreignness, both for the migrants and for the host communities. Of course, migration, short- or long-term in search of work, had been common in Europe over the last century and, indeed, had been facilitated by the extent to which it had been ruled by empires. Thus, Poles from the German-ruled part of Poland had moved within Germany to work in the industries of the Ruhr, while there had been large-scale movements within the sprawling Austro-Hungarian empire. There had also been migration across international borders. This 'cost' the receiving state less than was to be the case in the late twentieth century due to the far lower availability of social welfare, although conscription systems created a problem.

Migration outside Europe had also been very common and this remained the case after 1945. In part this was a response to the earlier lack of opportunity for emigration due to the war and in part a response to post-war disruption. For example, committed to a White Australia policy and anxious about the demographic strength of Asia, Australia encouraged British and Dutch immigrants, although post-war displaced persons from Eastern Europe were also significant. In Canada Britain remained the largest individual source of immigrants in the 1950s, although by then it was considerably less significant than the remainder of Europe combined. From the 1970s former British colonies, particularly Australia, became more open to immigration from elsewhere, especially Italy and Greece, and this openness in turn became part of the history of Europe.

Movements within Europe after 1945 began in large part for political reasons and this element remained significant, receiving a fresh burst from Hungarians fleeing the reimposition of Communist tyranny in 1956. Scenes of people fleeing across the frontier and the establishment of large refugee camps in Austria testified anew to the fragility of peace. About 200,000 Hungarians fled, and this is now a major theme in modern Hungarian discussion of recent history. The exodus of Hungarians has attracted cultural attention, for example in film, as in Andrew Vajna's *Children of Glory* (2008), a Hollywood film by a Hungarian-born producer.

Yet by the mid-1950s the prime reason for movement was the combination of poverty and under-employment on the periphery, with opportunity and lack of labour in the core. As such, this movement was a crucial aspect of the move from agriculture and the land, which gathered pace across Europe as mechanization removed rural opportunities, while rural life failed to satisfy the expectations of the young. Moreover, for many young males, service in the war (in the military or in factories) had broken the hold of village life, and the return to it proved suffocating.

Large-scale migration from Mediterranean Europe was a key aspect of the relative failure of the South, one that was also expressed politically by its lack of a major role in political structures: Italy might be in the EEC, but that was because of the role of northern Italy, the economic and political powerhouse of the country centred on Milan and Turin, and not of the poor south. Throughout the period southern Italy was seen by Italian governments and the EEC very much in terms of failure, being identified more as a problem society than as a zone of economic under-performance. With much of their population leaving for work elsewhere, Portugal, Spain, Greece and southern Italy could not expect much political weight whatever the nature of their constitution. Emigration from the Mediterranean worked as a safety valve for these countries, since it lowered their unemployment and so decreased social tensions. Further, remittances from the workers to their families remaining behind helped the latter increase their incomes and living standards. These transfers also helped ease the trade balance deficits that Mediterranean countries had, particularly as far as Germany was concerned.

Within Western Europe there was a process of political transformation from 1943 as first Fascist Italy and then the Nazi empire collapsed. Those states defeated in the war (France, Italy and Germany) experienced political and institutional change on the domestic and international level. Political structures had been found inadequate, creating a situation of political and governmental fluidity, and leading to a sense that change was necessary.

The establishment in 1958 of the EEC was part of a process in which the political structures and party politics of France, Italy and Germany were transformed between 1945 and 1958. The EEC was to be the basis of the modern EU. The reaction against nationalism and the memories of 1930s beggar-my-neighbour policies were important to European integration, but so also was American support, which was intended to try to anchor Western Europe in the Western system.

With the right in large part discredited by its association with Nazi Germany, most of Western Europe swung very strongly to the left after the war, and most of the public demanded and got some form of welfare state. Ideology was also important. Few Continental Europeans supported the free market to the extent that was still regarded as normal in Britain (and even there it was greatly constrained by the policies of the Labour governments of 1945–51). Even when Europeans said they backed the free market, their behaviour suggested otherwise, as was seen with the monopolistic practices of big corporations. There was much denunciation in Western Europe in the late 1940s and 1950s of the alleged evils of the free market, private enterprise and economic individualism. Instead there was considerable backing for a state-regulated and directed mixed economy, a drive that led toward the EU.

Political parties on the right, moreover, were discredited by the events of the 1930 and 1940s, both Fascism and collaboration with Germany. These parties would be reborn in the different form of Christian Democracy, which became a continuing tradition that contrasted with that of British Conservatism. Christian Democracy was more corporatist and more ostentatiously concerned with social welfare, and also looked to roots in Catholic political activism. Indeed, in West Germany Christian Democracy was consistently stronger in Catholic than Protestant areas, for example in the Palatinate (the base of Helmut Kohl, who became chancellor in 1982), rather than Bremen, Hamburg and Lower Saxony. The Christian Democratic Union (CDU), though cross-denominational and a deliberate attempt to unite both Christian denominations in the political middle and thus rectify a weak aspect of the politics of Weimar Germany, took over the mantle of the Centre Party (dissolved in 1933) as the representative of Catholic political interests. Many former Centre politicians, the principal example being Konrad Adenauer, and many leading Catholic clerics, such as Archbishop Frings of Cologne, endorsed the new party. The Centre Party was refounded after the war but rapidly sank into insignificance.

At the same time the CDU's independent sister-party in Bavaria, the more right-wing CSU (Christian Social Union), while based on the solid support of the Catholic bulk of the population, also benefited from its ability to win backing in the Protestant areas of northern Bavaria, round, for example, Bayreuth and Ansbach. More generally, the movement for Western European unity owed much to the growth of Christian Democratic parties, including in Belgium, Italy and the Netherlands as well as Germany.

Britain was separate from this process of transformation. On the Continent, the disastrous experience of war, which for France was underlined by the serious post-war failures in resisting insurgency in the key colonial territories of IndoChina (Vietnam, Cambodia and Laos) and, from the mid-1950s, Algeria, lent energy to the idea of European union. Furthermore, on the Continent, although less so in France, a sense of problems, if not of failure, encouraged a willingness to surrender some of the powers and prerogatives of the nation-state to supranational bodies, especially the EEC, in part in order to provide an institutional constraint on political extremism, of left or right, in any one country. Thus, at the same time that the EEC helped democracy in the member states, especially Italy, it was also designed to counteract what were seen as the potentially baleful consequences of the popular will.

In modern terms this ensured that a deliberate democratic deficit was built in as a structural part of the EEC. Such a process was easier for societies that were undergoing considerable centrally driven change, and whose political structures were being similarly transformed, than it was for Britain, Denmark, Norway and Sweden, and this process also seemed less necessary for the latter. The EEC indeed was a creature of the era of economic planning, which applied wartime nostrums to peacetime life and assumed that the state had a duty and a responsibility to control employment, inflation and growth, and had the instruments to do so. In the era of growth, a concept very much coming from America, politics became economics, and expectations of what the state could do went skywards. The meaning of democracy was changed to mean equal access to goods, opportunities and aspirations, all expressed in terms of material goods.

A key stage toward the EEC was taken when the European Coal and Steel Community (ECSC) was agreed by the Treaty of Paris in 1951. The ECSC was to be the direct precursor to the EEC, with the same six members: France, West Germany, Italy, Belgium, Luxembourg and the Netherlands. Britain refused to join: to do so would have meant handing over control of nationalized industries to an international body. This decision proved to be the first of a long, and not always sensible, series of British 'nos' toward options for European integration. For France, modernization of the economy required planned co-operation with West Germany in the key sectors of coal and steel. These sectors were regarded as crucial to manufacturing, specifically heavy industry, which attracted the attention of most economic planners and trade unionists. For France and West Germany to get together like this so soon after the war seemed revolutionary.

The ECSC was followed by the establishment of the EEC in 1958 as a result of the Messina Conferences of 1955 and 1956 and the Treaty of Rome of 1957. West German willingness to accept the concessions France required helped lead the latter to back the scheme. France wanted the ECSC and the EEC to help its modernization, but also to control West Germany, and wished to control West German independence so much that it was worth some loss of sovereignty to achieve this vital national aim; a national interest which the British did not share to the same extent. West Germany and Italy wanted the EEC to root and safeguard their democracies (although this had largely been done by 1957), again a need Britain did not share, but one that was crucial later to Spain, Portugal, Greece and Eastern Europe. This argument of the need to safeguard democracy is currently employed by supporters of the expansion of the EU to include the Balkans, Turkey and Ukraine.

Despite the arguments of the enthusiastic federalists of the period, few of the Continental leaders of the 1950s saw the EEC as likely to replace the nation-states, and it was not clear that it was political, social or cultural in intent. In a Europe suffering from devastation, political dislocation and international division stemming from the traumatic events of the 1940s, the EEC, however, offered a means to create space for development. It also provided a way to organize the huge boom in intra-European exports which had taken place in the 1950s, a boom that was an aspect of post-war recovery and was part of the post-imperial adjustment in Europe as markets within Europe were sought. France had found her empire a disappointing economic resource, which encouraged the focus on Europe.

Although the Treaty of Rome pledged to work for 'an ever closer union of the peoples of Europe', it lacked the utopianism seen with some earlier discussion of European federalism and, instead, focused on practical issues of economic transformation. The treaty provided that tariffs within the EEC were to be removed within twelve to fifteen years, which in the end meant by 1968. Furthermore, the tariffs levied on imports from outside the EEC were to be harmonized at the average level in 1958. The fall, and then removal, of internal tariffs led to a further rapid growth of trade within the EEC. This integration of markets within the EEC created major problems of adaptation for producers, but it also brought significant benefits. Growth enhanced profitability and encouraged investment, resulting in renewed expansion within the context of competitive pressures. In the first fifteen years of the EEC, West Germany had an average annual growth rate of 5 per cent, France, from a lower base, an average annual growth rate of 5.5 per cent, and Italian industrial exports also boomed, helping produce significant growth and optimism in northern Italy.

France had to dismantle a protectionist economic system in order to integrate and, in return, it insisted that the EEC adopt an agricultural system that served its farming interests. To protect them from the effect of the free market the Common Agricultural Policy (CAP), which, after hard negotiations, was finally agreed in 1962, provided both price guarantees and income support. These, however, entailed heavy taxation that represented a transfer of wealth from town to country which was (and remains) a key aspect of the fiscal politics of the EEC. It is also a drag on the more productive sectors of the European economy. In Britain, as in the rest of the modern EU, farmers receive large sums of EU money.

More positively, the CAP performed a vital political goal of reducing the rate of rural depopulation and easing social tensions at a time of rapid agrarian change. Yet, although funds were made available for 'structural change', there was to be less concern for areas of heavy industry when they experienced even greater rates of decline. Alongside creating a system that was to be associated with waste and corruption, the CAP was an important aspect of the way in which France successfully pressed for a form of European integration designed to advance its own interests. The horse-trading that was to be so important in recent European history, or, looked at differently, the institutionalized corruption, was there from the inception of the EEC. Equally, the 'pork system' in the USA can be seen as institutionalized corruption, and the EEC spoils system is not generally as personalized as the American one.]

The creation of the EEC was to be crucial, but it was not an end to the process of seeking to establish new organizations to transform Europe. In 1957 the British floated the idea of an International Free Trade Area, which answered British goals, not only in that the focus was on free trade, but because Britain would have played an equal role in its formation. As West German economics minister, Ludwig Erhard was sympathetic to the idea, but Charles De Gaulle, who grasped power in France in May 1958, persuaded Adenauer, the chancellor, to overrule Erhard and reject the proposal.

The British, instead, inspired a European Free Trade Association (EFTA) of countries not in the EEC. Established in 1960, it initially included Britain, Portugal, Norway, Denmark, Sweden, Switzerland and Austria. Finland became an associate member in 1961. Britain also made a free trade agreement with Ireland, which joined EFTA. Britain sought to lead EFTA, just as France dominated the EEC project. By the end of 1966 mutual tariffs within the EFTA area had been ended, but growth did not compare to that in the EEC. EFTA was also deliberately restricted to commercial matters and lacked the idealistic and federalist flavour of the EEC. In this, EFTA did not represent opposition to Europe but, instead, a different type of European identity, and one that tends to be neglected in accounts of recent European history.

The existence and goals of EFTA were apparently a clear constraint on the possibility that the EEC would serve as the basis for a supranational Europe. This constraint, however, was undermined by the apparent success of the EEC and by the sense in Britain and most other EFTA states that they could achieve their goals only through membership of the EEC. That EFTA did not include any major economies (or large populations), other than Britain, weakened it, as did an absence of geographical cohesion. A lack of political and economic co-operation capable of promoting economic growth was a key flaw in EFTA, but such co-operation would have meant becoming and acting like the EEC, which had the head start in this race.

The British government's wish in the 1960s to join the EEC, like that later of Portugal, was an aspect of a focus on growth rates which were seen as a substitute for empire, and also as a way to satisfy domestic political pressures and thus ensure stability. Moreover, support for joining the EEC became more widespread as it became clear that the organization would be more than short-term; indeed, that it would be a success in terms of the level of economic growth enjoyed by the member states. Any further delay in entry risked leading to eventual entry on worse terms.

THE USA AND WESTERN EUROPE

International pressures were also important and, indeed, the consolidation of the EEC was an aspect of the Cold War and of the American influence that was crucial during it. Ironically, in light of subsequent tensions, the USA had supported European integration long before the Cold War: the Americans looked with contempt at how the Europeans had messed up the Peace of Versailles of 1919 and its aftermath and had then compounded the 1930s Depression. American analyses of Europe produced during the Second World War expected integration, if not federalism, and in the 1950s the USA saw the EEC as a way to stabilize Western Europe in the non-Communist world, and as a counterpart to its membership, through NATO, in the anti-Communist one.

In particular, there was the issue of imperial succession: the American government was keen to encourage Franco–German reconciliation as an aspect of a necessary European self-reliance, to ensure that the EEC was pro-American, and to press for Britain to join the EEC, which was an aspect of the long-term American strategy to move Britain from imperial power to the supporter of, indeed voice for, American interests in Europe. The British had earlier assumed that the USA would be happy to co-operate with Britain separately and closely, but this proved unfounded. Indeed, it was one of the fantasies of British politics that has been persistently confounded by reality. The Americans showed no sympathy for any idea of an exclusive economic relationship with the British. Instead they wanted Britain to play a strong role in the EEC. The British could not afford to sustain an independent nuclear capability and thus a special strategic relationship with the USA, while the Suez Crisis of 1956 had revealed that it was impossible to rely on the USA to support Britain's global role.

The first bilateral meeting of American and Soviet leaders in 1959 showed that Britain could be left out of international power politics. In 1961 Britain under Prime Minister Harold Macmillan applied to join the EEC, in part because he thought the Americans wanted a stronger Western Europe and feared that, if he could not ensure entry, Britain would find it harder to win American support for its interests. President John F. Kennedy indeed pressed Macmillan to join the EEC because he feared, correctly, that De Gaulle had ambitions to lead a Europe separate from American interests, and that the EEC might prove the basis for this Third Force. Indeed, from 1944, European integration was increasingly seen by its European supporters as the best hope of defence against the weight of the two new superpowers.

There were also issues of economic management. A lack of confidence in free-market mechanisms affected many British policymakers, and there was a widespread belief that corporatism was the best way to ensure economic modernization and social equity. French-style planning was particularly influential. France in the 1960s benefited from economic growth and restructuring and from an ability to control inflation, all of which seemed enviable to British commentators. France also developed a closer relationship with West Germany, leading to the Elysée Treaty between the two in 1963.

In return for the political weight West Germany gained from French support the West German government was willing to make economic concessions to France, and to accept the French verdict on excluding Britain from the EEC. This agreement represented the basic axis of the EEC and prefigured the closeness between the two powers in opposition to Britain during the Mitterrand–Kohl and Chirac–Schröder partnerships, one that is now challenged by less warm relations between Sarkozy and Merkel. With the Fouchet Plan, pushed from 1961, De Gaulle envisaged a European Political Union but in practice this French-dominated proposal rested on De Gaulle's relationship with Adenauer. In the event the USA was opposed to De Gaulle's envisaged alliance with Adenauer, and the Fouchet Plan failed because of opposition from the Netherlands.

In 1963, notwithstanding the support for British entry from the other five members of the EEC, France vetoed the British application, De Gaulle declaring at a press conference, 'England is insular . . . the nature and structure and economic context of England differs profoundly from those of the other states of the Continent'. He saw Britain as an American Trojan horse and Atlanticism as a threat to Europe. Indeed, De Gaulle, who thought that everyone's defence was in the end national, did not believe that the USA would risk its own destruction by fighting if the Soviets invaded Europe but did not attack the USA. De Gaulle's assault on, and response to, American hegemony took many forms. For example, while De Gaulle did not care for economics, he understood the importance of growth and was anxious to make sure France 'modernized' in whatever way it took to help ensure it.

A difference between French and American political cultures had certainly been demonstrated in October 1962, when Georges Pompidou, whom De Gaulle had appointed as prime minister that April, was immediately reappointed after his defeat in the National Assembly on a motion of no-confidence had led to his resignation. He remained prime minister until 1968. De Gaulle's attitude towards both the National Assembly and ministerial appointments reflected at once an autocratic manner that helped foster a democratic deficit, and his rejection of the political culture and structure of the Fourth Republic, a rejection deliberately intended to achieve this authoritarian goal. Indeed, the Fifth Republic he established in 1958, and which was endorsed by a referendum in October 1962, was more presidential. As eventually settled, the president was to be directly elected by the electorate, rather than chosen by the National Assembly, the power of the latter was reduced, which also cut that of the political parties, and the president emerged as a key figure in a strengthened executive. This situation gave the president particular control in the field of foreign policy where De Gaulle was determined to reverse French decline and instead to affirm and demonstrate national greatness. In 1962 he cut France free from its most onerous colonial commitment, that to Algeria, which rescued the state from a very heavy financial burden, and the political system from a most divisive issue that was challenging its capacity to produce results. Two years earlier most of French Africa had been granted independence.

De Gaulle presented France as necessarily the leader of Europe, and this as a political and cultural mission (he was far less interested in the economic, let alone fiscal, dimension) for France. The Fifth Republic enjoyed considerable support within France because the Fourth Republic had provided no stability and, indeed, had been discredited in the 1950s by the way the political parties dominated and ruined it, much like Italy today. As a reminder of the role of contingency De Gaulle, however, failed to win an overall majority in the first round of the French presidential elections held in December 1965, and was forced into a second-round run-off with the Socialist François

Mitterrand in which De Gaulle won with 55.2 per cent of the votes cast. Moreover, in the first ballot of the French National Assembly elections held in March 1967, the Gaullists and their allies won only 38.45 per cent of the vote.

ENLARGEMENT AND THE EEC

De Gaulle's rigid interpretation of French interests, and his unwillingness to compromise, helped ensure not only that Britain did not join the EEC, but also that the EEC did not develop, either in terms of new members or with reference to greater integration. Concerned that French interests might be subordinated as a result of the latter, De Gaulle made clear his hostility to further integration. Instead he proposed what was to prefigure later British aspirations: co-operation within a looser 'Europe of the Nations'. French obduracy led to the Luxembourg compromise of 1965, under which an effective veto existed for member states in many fields of EEC activity, and this continued to be the case until 1986. Moreover, no new states joined the EEC while De Gaulle was president.

De Gaulle was also responsible for withdrawing France from NATO's integrated military command in March 1966 and for blocking a renewed British application to join the EEC in November 1967. That month he argued that there was scant place for Britain outside the EEC 'in face of the great movements which are now sweeping the world', which were itemized as 'the huge power of the United States, the growing power of the Soviet Union, the renascent power of the Continental countries of Europe, the newly energizing power of China'.

The situation, however, changed in the late 1960s. De Gaulle's resignation in 1969, after the French government had lost a referendum on relatively minor constitutional changes, was crucial. His successor, the chain-smoking Georges Pompidou, president from 1969 until his early death in 1974, was concerned about growing West German strength and the need to balance it and not, as De Gaulle had been, about the challenge from Anglo-American links. He was also more committed to the EEC than De Gaulle, and therefore more willing to respond to his partners' pressure for enlargement. An important shift was when the Social Democrats (SPD), under Willy Brandt, came to power in West Germany in 1969 as a result of the Free Democrats swapping over from supporting the CDU. In 1970 the EEC invited four applicants, Britain, Ireland, Denmark and Norway, to resume negotiations. Enlargement was now definitely on the agenda.

A clear path might seem to be drawn from this decision to the far larger European Union of the present day. This can then be linked to a host of current conditions and issues that had already been clearly anticipated in the late 1960s, such as concern about the environment. Yet it is also necessary to place due weight on the extent to which developments were unpredictable. The overthrow of Greek democracy in 1967, when power was seized by the Greek army, was a dramatic display of this, not least because, after the Second World War, this was the first (and so far only) European democracy overthrown outside the Communist sphere. Furthermore, the new Greek regime acted rapidly in order to introduce not only an authoritarian style but also a conspicuously conservative social agenda that markedly contrasted with the liberalism seen across most of Western Europe, especially Protestant Europe. A pluralist society was corralled by repression, with secret policemen following on from tanks on the streets.

The thwarting of reform Communism by the overthrow of the Prague Spring was another marked break with any optimistic account of improvement. The earlier inability of the Czech Communist system to deliver much economic growth had helped to discredit the authoritarian government, and its unpopularity was accentuated by the economic stagnation that prevailed there by 1963. Moreover, the intelligentsia had become disenchanted with traditional Communism. The combination of discontents led to an attempt at reform Communism, but this proved unacceptable to the Soviet Union, which, with the support of Bulgaria, East Germany, Hungary and Poland, invaded and repressed the reform movement in 1968. The public response (especially in Bohemia though less so in Slovakia) was hostile, but avoided the violence that would have triggered the bloody use of force seen when Hungarian independence was crushed in 1956. As an example of the use of divisive paranoia for political ends, some Warsaw Pact troops were told that they were being deployed into Czechoslovakia in order to stop a NATO invasion.

The combination of Greece and Czechoslovakia served to underline the extent to which the 1960s were still as one with the 1930s in seeing liberal democracy struggle in Europe with both right-wing and left-wing authoritarian movements, and without any clear sense that liberal democracy would triumph. This can be all too readily forgotten in the 2000s. Nevertheless, whereas democracy was discredited in many countries in the 1930s, in the 1960s it had plenty of defenders, including NATO, the EEC and all the Western European governments bar Portugal and Spain. In contrast, Czechoslovakia was behind the Iron Curtain, while Greece seemed a marginal country. The role of both right and left in the post-war struggle for dominance in Greece is a reminder that the Cold War went on not just between the USA and the Soviet Union, but also within countries, particularly Greece, France and Italy. The USA played a major role in these internal struggles, especially in Greece.

RADICALISM AND '68

An alternative route of development had also been suggested in 1968 with a major upsurge in radical action, particularly, but not only, in France. Student protest proved a key element, with the students moving to the left, but to a left not of Communism, but of a direct action through Maoism (modelled on the Revolutionary Guards of Mao Tse-tung's China) and anarchism. Student activism in Italy and France in 1967 was followed in May 1968 by demonstrations and violence in Paris. A brutal response by the riot police there led to a consolidation of support around the students, including a general strike followed by more sustained trade union action. Assured of military support if necessary, De Gaulle, however, regained the initiative, encouraged by a mass demonstration by his supporters in Paris. In June De Gaulle's followers won an overwhelming majority in elections, while the student movement collapsed due to divisions as well as a fall in worker and popular support.

In Italy crises of student and worker disaffection persisted into 1969, with the 'hot autumn' leading to major concessions to the trade unions in 1970. Violence by right-wing extremists and by left-wing anarchists became more sinister, each aiming to overthrow a democracy they despised. In West Germany student activism had fewer links with the trade unions, which, in turn, were less radical than in France or Italy. More generally, the '68 movements touched all Western European countries (including Britain) in many ways and had as their basic cause anti-authoritarianism, specifically the clash between young people, with new purchasing power and expectations, and gerontocratic power structures, including the family, school, business (presented as capitalism) and government (seen as the authorities). There was also an echo of these movements in Eastern Europe.

The radicals in Western Europe failed to appreciate that in criticizing and seeking to demolish allegedly or apparently ossified systems such as the nuclear family there was frequently nothing much to take its place. On the one hand the movements were too successful in discrediting those institutions and established social practices but, on the other, more positively, there was an extension of democracy in many ways, with much more power given to young people and women.

The short-term political repercussions of '68, to use the disruption and aspirations of that year in order to sum up a very varied movement which defies ready summation, were in fact limited, which encouraged some to resort to more radical ideas and a few to more violent means. The institutional expression of the demand for change had proved weak and far from durable. Demonstrations were no way to challenge the police when the latter enjoyed the acceptance, if not backing, of much of society. Moreover, radicalism in the military was limited, unlike in Russia in 1917 or Portugal in 1973. Partly as a result, Portugal, where the longstanding right-wing dictatorship was overthrown, was to witness more radical change than France, Italy or West Germany. Furthermore, although, across Western Europe, a radical fringe lent support to terrorism, the ability of terrorist movements to radicalize the working class or to turn the fears and sense of menace they conjured up into a transforming crisis was limited. As a result, although they were very important in Italy, the attention devoted to these movements elsewhere is often disproportionately high.

More pertinent was the extent to which many of the attitudes expressed in '68 affected the next generation of left-wing politics, as feminism and environmentalism became more topical, while respect for authority and age was challenged. From that point of view the 1960s proved a watershed in values. This watershed was very much apparent, especially in Britain where there was a sort of cultural revolution, much more so than in Continental Europe where the issues were more political. Across much of Western Europe a huge expansion of higher education came after the student revolts as a panic response by the authorities. Entry to university, however, was freed up without the provision of equivalent resources.

Those engaged in the challenge to established values were mistaken in the sensation that the entire world was changing, and that this was the way things were certainly going to be, and as a result were not prepared for what turned out to be a 1970s ebb. Moreover, a shift in values was scarcely on the terms of radicals disappointed that Pompidou succeeded De Gaulle, that the SDP in West Germany distanced itself from progressive causes, that the established order remained in power in Italy, that the Conservatives under Edward Heath won the 1970 election in Britain, and that Richard Nixon had won the 1968 presidential election in the USA. Indeed, in many respects, if '68 was pregnant with possibilities for change, these changes should be seen both as coming some time later and as a consequence of other developments.

In particular, the tendency to emphasize the transforming nature of new values via liberal legislation needs to be matched by an awareness of the role of economic growth and the extent to which this provided wealth and thus purchasing power for individuals. Encouraging their role as consumers helped bring a practical independence to many; it also owed something to the extent to which new jobs and new houses meant that a large number of Europeans prospered away from where they had grown up. The 'long boom' was crucial to this independence, but so also was the extent to which it permitted the development and pursuit of increasingly ambitious social programmes without expropriatory levels of taxation. Economic growth indeed allowed a balance to be struck between collective and private consumption without conflict, which was a fundamental necessity of social democratic government in all forms, and a major reason why European governments have since been desperate to return to this situation. Much of the shock experienced in the 1970s was due more to the earlier experience of recovery and growth. The position varied by country, but people as purchasers, rather than the state as spender, was an important dynamic not only economically but also socially and politically. This dynamic was true not only of Western Europe, but also to an extent further east. Consumer choice also built up a potent sense of entitlement. As a result of this, an important chronology was provided by economic growth, which was to encounter difficulties across much of Europe in the early and mid 1970s.

A TIME OF CHANGE

An either–or approach is unhelpful, but there is a tendency to emphasize demonstrators and popular action, in 1989 as in 1968, and to underplay the role of socio-economic developments. The latter were certainly crucial to the subject of the next chapter, the transformation of the environment. That transformation indeed showed that the collective pressure resulting from individual actions, such as buying and driving cars or installing central heating, could have a greater impact than the collectivist aspirations for control located within the political process. At the same time there are links between the two. In part this is a matter of a reaction by each against the other, but there are also less antagonistic relationships. For example, a drive to express through consumption, understood as capitalism, is not necessarily separate from one to express through a new lifestyle, understood as radical. Moreover, democratization – the assumption that institutions should respond to the popular will – could be part of the same process and, at once, conservative or radical in tone and content.

The common theme was one of change. That may not seem to have required the radicalism of '68, but although the economy changed very rapidly during the 'long boom' many institutions and social practices did not, and a measure of radical change was necessary in this sphere. Nevertheless, change was already present – in new constitutions and political practices, economic growth, and a transformation of the European space through new organizations. Underlying all was the pace of environmental change.

Chapter 2

Environment Transformed?

The valleys of the Adda and Po in northern Italy, October 2005. The water levels are low, very low. The conversation is on how there is far less snow on the Alps, on how it is not so cold in the autumn, on change. A sense of unease: water is of life; change seems out of control.

The European environment, of course, has never been constant. There was no primitive or latter-day state of perfection, rudely shattered by human action, nor a holistic balance subsequently destroyed by industrialization, however much such beliefs have played a role in the discussion of environmental history. Nevertheless, the human impact on the European environment in recent decades has been especially striking. Not only has the context within which humans live and operate changed greatly, but all the other species living in Europe have also been affected. Furthermore, the environmental movement has testified to the growth and extent of public awareness, an awareness that is the very opposite of triumphalist about the future of mankind. Instead, there is widespread and deep concern. Moreover, a new and troubling sense of where human history will lead, or indeed end, has developed. This sense has resulted in a new apocalypticism, one without the consolation of a messianic conclusion.

Anxiety is a result of the extent to which greater knowledge of the environment served two different, but related ends: its utilization and yet also its protection. Both of these ends were pushed with great energy in Europe. A greater understanding of the issues present in the protection of the environment helped to clarify the damaging extent of the utilization of its possibilities. Some of the damage was short-term in scope, and reversible, and led to considerable activity, for example in landscaping coalmining waste tips, but much of the damage was long-term and cumulative. This long-term damage helped to make it difficult subsequently to effect any radical improvement in particular localities.

GLOBAL WARMING

Alongside this damage to particular locations, global climate change has been an issue for Europe, with major climate episodes attributed to this change. This emphasis on climate change at once underplays the extent to which the climate is never constant and overplays the human contribution to climate change, but also captures an important development in the tendency of variation: the trend in temperatures has been upward, with important rises from 1980 and, even greater, from 2000. When periodic falls in temperature occurred after 1980, for example in 1999, in every case they were to a higher level than the temperature in 1980. Furthermore, this rise in temperature is an accelerating process, and has registered figures apparently higher than in any period of human habitation. It is also a year-long process. Winters are becoming less cold, and feel warmer, and summers are, and seem, hotter.

These figures are set to continue rising as the process becomes self-sustaining. The shrinkage of the Arctic ice as a consequence of global warming will ensure that the Arctic will warm up more quickly, because open water absorbs more solar heat than ice, which reflects it. The summer melting period is getting longer by about five days per decade; the sea ice has thinned by about a half from 1950 to 2005 and, on present trends, there will be none at the North Pole by the summer of 2080. In 2005 the ozone level over the Arctic thinned to its lowest level since records began. This process will greatly affect water levels, winds and temperatures further south in Europe.

Warming ensures that climate zones move both geographically and in terms of the terrain: more northerly and higher regions both became warmer. There was also significant desertification in southern Spain, with greater heat and aridity linked to a change in vegetation types. More generally, water levels were severely hit by drought, as in France, Greece, Italy and Spain in 2005-6. This drought had serious consequences for agriculture, which was heavily dependent on irrigation across much of southern Europe as well as, for some crops, further north. A combination of lower rainfall with less surface and subsurface water placed many challenges on irrigation systems, at the same time that it increased the need for irrigation. In the winter of 2007-8 Spain again had severe drought, with Catalonia and Valencia having less rain than at any time since 1912, although the situation on Spain's Atlantic coast is much more benign. The more persistent differential availability of water led to schemes to move water, but they were perceived through the prism of politics, especially those of regional preference. In the early 2000s the prime minister, José Maria Aznar, proposed to take water from the River Ebro to arid regions on the Mediterranean including Valencia, Alicante and Muria, only for the plan to be scrapped by his successor, José Luis Rodríguez Zapatero, in 2004. In 2007-8 Aragon rejected Catalonia's plan to divert water from the River Segre, a tributary of the Ebro, to supply Barcelona.

Simultaneously, the climate has appeared to become more volatile, as with the major floods in Germany, Austria and Hungary in 2002, and in Britain in 2007. The damage done by these and other large-scale floods ensured that they posed political issues, although public and political attention focused on government responses rather than the underlying causes.

Summer heat waves attracted even more attention as they more clearly fitted in with public anxiety about global warming. There were direct economic consequences of such heat waves with serious issues of water availability for agriculture, for example in France, but the immediate results in terms of health and fire were more dramatic. During the hot summer of 2004 large numbers of the elderly, in particular, were affected by heat-related conditions, and many died as a result. In France 14,000 people died prematurely. There were also fatalities in 2006, and even more in 2007, not least in Bulgaria, Hungary and Romania, although, conversely, snow in Athens and Jerusalem in

February 2008 attracted almost no coverage. In 2007 temperature records were set in Bulgaria (44°c) and Greece (45°c), while Hungary had its hottest weather for a century (41.9°c). Moreover, Albania, Bosnia and Macedonia (Former Yugoslav Republic of) declared states of emergency in the face of the large numbers of heat-related conditions. In Romania at least 19,000 people were admitted to hospital as a result of such conditions.

The combination of heat and an absence of rain also encouraged forest fires, as in Serbia, where over 2,000 fires were reported in 2007. Yet, as a reminder of the complexity of causation, such conditions are particularly serious if they follow heavy rainfall, as the latter encourages vegetation growth. In turn, environmental practices are an issue as fires are more likely if the vegetation has not been burned off earlier in a controlled fashion.

It is all too easy to abstract environmental pressures and developments from socio-political issues, but this is unhelpful, not least because it leads to an underplaying of human agency, or at least role, in these pressures. Moreover, there can be a failure to note the extent to which these developments throw light on other aspects of recent history. In the case of France, it was argued, with cause, that the deaths of old people through heat-related conditions reflected not only the poor state of governmental care for the elderly, but also the breakdown of social cohesion, as adult children left the responsibility for their aged parents to the state and, instead, went on holiday. At the level of public provision, health-care systems, of which France was justly proud, did not extend to the long-term care required for effective social welfare. The pressures caused by the marked rise in the number and percentage of the elderly (see next chapter), a large percentage of whom lived on their own, were also highly significant.

In 2007 the focus, instead, was on the collapse of social cohesion reflected in the role of arsonists in causing forest fires, as in Italy. In Greece and Italy, this was given an added twist as it was argued that the arsonists were working for property developers determined to see land cleared for development whatever the attitude of officials. It was also claimed that the latter were bribed as part of the process, in order to ensure acceptance once land had been cleared. In Greece, where building is not supposed to take place in forests, they were reclassified as farmland once they had been cleared by fire. As a result of development, whether or not assisted by arsonists, in the mid 2000s, central and southern Greece lost much of its forest cover. Thus in 2007 the planned development of a road along the coast of the western Peloponnese was linked to arsonists concerned to acquire land cheaply so that they could subsequently resell it at a profit. The Greek government's failure to devise a fire-prevention strategy contributed to the crisis, as did global climate change in the shape of hotter summers and drier winters. A lack of space interacted with climate change, and each reinforced the other. Satellite photographs of the fires, the smoke of which was readily visible from space, provided the European public with a lurid reminder of vulnerability and one that was readily reproduced in newspapers and on television. As a further reminder of the need to focus on human agency, arson in some areas, for example Provence in France in the early 2000s, was traced to boredom and alienation among part of the population.

HUMANS, ANIMALS AND RUBBISH

The changes in habitats stemming from human development also affected other species. It has been easier to chart the process for larger animals, especially land mammals, than, say, for amphibians, let alone insects, and it is likely that the impact on smaller animals has been considerably underrated. The challenge to animal habitats also engaged imaginative attention. The great expansion in population, and in man-made environments and products, ensured that animals that benefited from contact with humans increased in numbers. In part this was a matter of animals that Europeans wished to have around, such as farm animals and pets, but other animals, for example rats, also benefited greatly.

The human impact on the environment also had unintended consequences for animals. Global warming affected their habitats and breeding patterns, greatly in some cases, and may have been beneficial for some species. Birds and fish, both sharks and jellyfish, appeared in more northerly latitudes as aspects of widespread shifts in migration patterns. At a more local level, wastewater emissions from power stations and factories raised water temperatures, and led to greater animal and plant activity nearby. Animals were also affected by human activity that removed predators.

In urban and suburban environments, rats, cockroaches and other wildlife benefited considerably from the growth in the volume of rubbish. This growth owed much to the greater unwillingness to reuse material, and was a product of rising affluence and of the transformation of material culture, including major changes in packaging, notably the greater role of plastic. The resulting pressure on local government provided a topic for politics, most dramatically so in the Campania, the region round Naples in Italy, where by December 2007 the local rubbish dumps were all full, and rubbish collection ceased. If the role of organized crime in the Campania, in rubbish-related racketeering, was relatively unusual, this crisis also reflected more widespread pressures, not least opposition to incinerators and dumps near settlements. In turn such opposition is a product of greater knowledge of, and concern about, toxic emissions and run-off, as well as of the risks posed by some of the garbage. In the Campania the criminals created space in their dumps for fresh rubbish by paying boys to set light to it, although this produced highly dangerous fumes. Research published by the University of Pisa in 2008 suggested that pollution, especially dioxins, from the Campania dumps was an aspect of a wider pollution-linked crisis in the sperm-levels of Italian males, with sperm-counts dropping from the 1970s most notably in urban areas and least in remote rural ones such as Puglia. This pollution also seriously affected cheese production in the Campania in 2008.

Illustrating the linkages seen throughout the book, the rubbish crisis in Campania can be directly related to the corruption that is presented, in Chapter 6, as a major pressure on European business. The situation also raises deeper questions about the quality of the national and local ruling classes in Europe, a question posed again in a big way in Eastern Europe from 1991. The situation then in Yugoslavia was the starkest warning of what could happen when developments went as wrong as they could do.

Across Europe animals such as squirrels, seagulls, foxes, deer and bears altered their activity patterns in order to exploit sites of rubbish accumulation and disposal, for example near fast-food restaurants. Indeed, all these animals became increasingly urban, a process partly caused by the abandonment by farmers of economically marginal farmland, which lessened the buffer between towns and woodland, while the advance of suburban areas was also an important factor in ensuring that humans and animals shared habitats. Seagulls were affected by the change in fishing practices towards a 'factory' process that left fewer fish-parts in the wake of boats. Instead, the seagulls moved inland, to feed on rural seed corn and urban rubbish. In a different sphere the widespread increase in sewage levels meant that bacteria found in human waste, such as faecal coliforms, thrived.

The period certainly witnessed an accelerating race between humans and animals for profit from what Europeans saw as their habitat but which was also, of course, that of animals. Rabbits, for example, were seen as a particular problem by farmers in France by the mid-2000s due to the amount they ate. Europeans used animals of their own in the contest with animals. Hunting dogs helped shooters, while cats were still employed against rats and mice. These, however, were traditional responses of diminishing consequence. On the whole the remedy to animal competition was chemical, in both houses and fields. Unfortunately there were unwanted side-effects, as some chemicals also affected humans. The DTT used against malaria-carrying mosquitoes was a particular hazard. In some cases, moreover, as in the battle against rats, there were also signs of increasingly limited success, since the animals began to develop immunity to chemicals.

AGRICULTURE

The chemical offensive was also employed in agriculture. The monoculture that came from an emphasis on a few high-yield crop strains, such as maize, and from a pressure for intensive specialization in order to ensure competition, lessened biodiversity and also provided a food source for particular pests that were countered with chemicals. In this and other ways agricultural demands were frequently environmentally hazardous. Thus the emphasis in southern Europe on early ripening varieties of avocados and strawberries, which enjoyed a big profit margin in urban shops, especially in northern Europe, led to the removal of soil-retaining tree crops, such as olives, from slopes.

More generally, as a result of agricultural practices, the organic matter in soil was widely degraded. Thanks in part to the removal of hedgerows associated with farm consolidation from the 1960s, cultivated land left without a protective cover of vegetation suffered from the large-scale erosion of soil by wind and water. This contributed to soil degradation in, for example, the Welsh mountains, which played a role in flooding in Gloucestershire in 2007.

Soil degradation, in turn, encouraged the application of unprecedented levels of fertilizer. Fertilizers, herbicides and pesticides, however, increasingly affected the crops that were grown and the food thereby consumed. There was also a major impact on water resources as fertilizers ran off into rivers with groundwater, or were transferred into the water system through leaching into the soil (affecting well-water), or evaporation and then distilling out in colder air. Decreases in the water supply, moreover, accentuated concentrations of pollutants. The widespread application of nitrogenous fertilizers also had an effect on global warming as nitrogen evaporated from soils.

A focus on particular crop strains was a result of the role of standardization and scale in European economies increasingly driven by mass-consumerism. As with the standardization in manufactured goods, supermarket chains insisted on certain types of agricultural produce and emphasized specific physical characteristics, especially colour, shape and size, as supposedly betokening wholesome produce. What they advertised and displayed shaped as well as reflected public assumptions. The role of supermarkets in food sales affected not only societies where purchase in markets had long been subordinated to the role of shops, for example Britain, but also more conservative shopping environments, such as Greece by the 2000s. Thus travel patterns in Thessaloniki were clearly influenced by the opening of suburban supermarkets. There were class and spatial dimensions, with more affluent consumers switching to supermarkets and driving to do so, while poorer and older consumers walked, or went by bus, to city-centre markets.

Public policy was also an issue in agriculture. Here, the key was the CAP (see Chapter 1) which was designed to prevent international competition directing the content and pace of agricultural change. The CAP was an aspect of a more general growth in governmental intervention in rural areas, rather than the more established commitment to regions of industrial unemployment. Rural poverty and depopulation encouraged such intervention, but it led to disproportionate expenditure on agricultural subsidies, an encouragement of production when and where global trading conditions were unfavourable, and the destruction of resulting food surpluses in order to keep prices high.

This situation remains the case as, in 2002, France and Germany, ignoring a critical Britain, reached a bilateral agreement over the future of farm support payments, which then became the basis of EU policy. Under this agreement the CAP was to remain unchanged until 2012, despite the pressure on EU budgets and the likely consequences of Eastern European accession, notably that of Poland with its very large agricultural sector, much of which has not experienced the consolidation of holdings and reduction of the labour force seen widely in Western Europe.

In 2001 France received 22 per cent of CAP subsidies; Spain, Greece and Ireland were the other major beneficiaries. Far from preserving a way of life, however, subsidies in large part bolstered the already most prosperous and productive sections, as in France, with the large cereal producers of the prairies of the Ile-de-France, and the intensive poultry and pork farmers of the west, benefiting in particular. In effect, a guaranteed market and the certainty of high prices provided the security for mechanization and the large-scale use of chemical fertilizers, both aspects of what were increasingly agri-businesses, rather than farms. Politically, this constituency helped provide voting and financial support for major political interests on the right. Similarly, farmers in Bavaria, many of whom have small farms, some of which are ancillary to other jobs, have disproportionate political influence on the German right via the CSU.

Despite the support of the CAP, however, much of French agriculture proved uncompetitive. Indeed, there was a disjuncture between the heavily subsidized, large-scale French agri-businesses, which crucially competed with the USA in world markets, and small-scale producers who increasingly went bankrupt in the face of over-production. A similar contrast was seen elsewhere in the EU, although with a higher share for small-scale producers. The role of the farmer, nevertheless, remained important in France, even though the number of farms fell from about 1.6 million in 1970 to about 700,000 in 2005. As president from 1995 until 2007, Jacques Chirac, who had earlier been minister of agriculture, very much identified with his rural constituency in the Corrège, and presented the countryside in terms of an immutable Frenchness. His successor as president, Nicolas Sarkozy, 'Mr Bling Bling' to the critical French media, conspicuously lacks rural interests and has a metropolitan image, which does not play with traditional concepts of Frenchness.

The CAP also led to large-scale fraud (notoriously but predictably so in Italy), to a higher cost for food within Europe due to protectionism, to resulting problems in international trade, and to the moral issue outlined in the World Development Bank Human Development Report of 2003, in other words before the accession of twelve, mostly Eastern European, states to the EU in 2004–7. This report suggested that each EU cow was the subject of $913 of annual subsidies, a sum considerably greater than that spent on overseas relief to humans suffering malnutrition. At the same time the requirements of EU agricultural regulation were sufficiently stringent as to create problems in the 1990s and early 2000s for the agricultural interests in states that wanted to accede to the EU, such as the Czech Republic and Hungary. Criticism of the CAP, however, needs to address the extent to which much European agriculture either is subsidized or goes out of business. There is no perfect market solution for farming, but nor is it easy to provide subsidies as part of a widely accepted social policy.

Consumer pressure and technological enhancement also affected fishing. European waters were fished intensively by large boats, with Spain being particularly active and using the EU control of fishing outside narrowly defined territorial waters to dominate the industry. Outside the EU, Norway and Iceland preserved their national fishing industries with greater success. Large fishing boats consumed substantial quantities of energy and were equipped with sophisticated finding devices, and these industrial fleets hit fish stocks. The EU sought to redress the situation by setting fish quotas. Pressure on stocks, however, ensured that the situation could not be defined simply in terms of benign management. Instead, there was marked competition between different fishing interests.

An effort was also made to develop fish farming, notably of salmon and trout, which fitted the tendency to make the most intensive use possible of all land and water that could be utilized. Fish farming, however, also consumed resources, not least fishmeal, and led to a serious accumulation of waste and toxins, and to scandals over their dumping. Moreover, the crowded fish are subjected to fungal infections, while food colourants are used to make the flesh pink. At the same time globalization exposed European fish farmers to competition from warmer-water producers.

European agriculture and fishing are affected by climate change, which tends to be under-emphasized as the focus in scholarly discussion of agriculture is on public policy in the shape of the CAP, but in the long term climate change is more significant as it affects the parameters within which public policy can be framed. The impact on agriculture of climate change is an aspect of the sustained pressure on the environment already discussed. For example, increased extraction of water from rivers ensured that river levels dropped and, as a result, the volume of water reaching the sea declined. Rising consumption also led to the depletion of natural aquifers and to the movement of salt to the surface, which greatly affected soil quality and agricultural productivity. Little attention was devoted to such issues when considering agricultural subsidies. Water levels were also hit by drought. Furthermore, the decline in snowfall is an issue, as water availability from snow is more consistent than if it falls as rain: much of the latter becomes run-off that cannot be used so readily in the water system. As yet the impact of a rising sea level has not been felt greatly in Europe but, as the warming oceans expand when polar ice melts, it will become more of a feature, and this will threaten low-lying areas such as the English Fens and the Rhone delta.

Other environmental changes that can be measured include carbon-dioxide emissions and acid deposition, the former the result of burning fossil fuels, particularly coal, the latter a consequence of sulphur and nitrogen production from industrial processes. Carbon dioxide is a greenhouse gas, while acid rain damages woodland and hits both rivers and lakes. Pollution spread widely across Europe, for example from Britain and Germany to Scandinavia, and this spread helped ensure that environmental concern did likewise. The assault from pollution was also very varied and insistent. Lead emissions from traffic seriously affected air quality, particularly in cities, accentuating the appeal of suburban life, but car-borne suburban commuters then further damaged urban air quality, both in the suburbs and further afield. Moreover, transport-related carbon dioxide emissions in the EU increased by a third between 1990 and 2005.

The consumer society also produced greater and greater quantities of rubbish, much of it non-biodegradable and some of it toxic. The nuclear industry posed particular problems, which were highlighted with the disastrous incident at the Ukrainian nuclear power station of Chernobyl on 26 April 1986. A fire in the reactor that arose from poorly prepared tests lasted for weeks. In accordance with the usual Soviet preference for secrecy, there was no publicity, while contamination was treated in an incompetent fashion. About 600,000 people suffered as a result of radiation, and crops were affected over much of Europe, providing a bitter lesson on the continent's interconnectedness. There was also an upsurge in criticism of nuclear power, including in the Soviet Union. Indeed, the mass demonstrations that helped bring about the end of Communist rule included a big march through Kiev on the third anniversary of the Chernobyl disaster. This disaster also had cultural resonances, as in the German film *England* (2000) by Achim von Borrie, in which the protagonist is terminally ill as a result of working in Chernobyl after the accident.

Environmental damage as a consequence of accidents was not restricted to the nuclear industry. The transport of oil in tankers was the background for major disasters when they sank, as with the *Amoco Cadiz* off France in 1978 and the *Aegean Sea* off Spain in 1992, while discharges of oil from shipping were also a serious issue. The chemical industry was another major problem, not least when habitual dumping in waterways was exacerbated by accidents, such as the Sandoz chemical spill in the River Rhine in 1986.

Noise and light pollution have also become more serious and widespread, and the latter ensured that the view of the sky at night was increasingly affected. Light pollution might seem an affectation of recent decades, but it is readily apparent from the sky, and is brought home by night-time photographs of Europe over a long period of time. Street-lighting became more common, and was a clear index of prosperity, for example in Mediterranean Europe from the 1970s. More direct visual impact arose from industrial and mining activity.

A different form of visual impact arose from urban building. Surrounding rural areas were transformed by the rapid and large-scale spread of cities, often at an unprecedented rate, while in both Communist and non-Communist Europe the need for housing was in large part met by urban high-rises which were seen as the way to keep costs down. The amount of land that had to be allocated or obtained for them was modest, while mass-produced housing was cheaper to produce. Unfortunately, it often proved a poor and dispiriting urban environment, and this was a particular problem in Communist societies, where people were not given choice, as well as in public-housing systems in Western Europe, where poverty removed the element of choice. Yet mass-produced public housing was not inevitably of low quality, as a consideration of the situation in Scandinavia makes amply clear.

ENERGY

Across Europe, there was particular pressure on energy supplies. Paralleling the increased demand for water, for showers, dish-washers and washing-machines, rising energy needs reflected the enormous growth in both per capita and aggregate energy consumption, in response to developments in economic activity, social processes and living arrangements. The range of energy uses also increased. Oil-based additives became important in agriculture, while the spread of agricultural machinery increased demand for oil. From the 1990s the much greater use of computers and the Internet pushed up demands for electricity. The resulting supply system varied by state. The infrastructure was particularly poor in the Balkans, a poor region that (despite their claims) was left with limited social capital by the Communist regimes and that subsequently did not attract sufficient investment. Thus, Albania had a major lack of power generating-capacity. As a result of frequent power-cuts there in the 2000s, many companies and concerns acquired their own generators, although small-scale generation is a far less efficient system than its large-scale counterpart.

Energy use was linked to issues of finance and national security. Oil and natural gas imports put pressure on the balance of payments, hitting the ability of governments to pump-prime their own economies or to afford social welfare programmes. Abrupt rises in prices, as in the early 1970s, 1979 and 2007–8, had particularly savage consequences. These imports also led to a dangerous dependence on the politics of the Middle East and North Africa, and on the stability of particular regimes, with French concern about Algeria increased by its role as a major energy supplier. The politics of energy were also especially important in Eastern Europe, with Russia using the supply and pricing of its natural gas to put pressure on other countries, for instance Ukraine in 2006 and 2008, and Belarus in 2007. By then, Bulgaria, Estonia, Finland, Latvia, Lithuania and Slovakia were totally dependent on Russian gas, while Austria, Greece, Poland and Romania took 60–80 per cent of their gas from Russia, and Germany took 40 per cent. Linked to this politics came dissension over the routes of pipelines, as part of a geo-politics of favour, influence and control, for example the planned Russo–German Nord Stream gas pipeline, which projects a route under the Baltic Sea in order to avoid passage through Poland or the Baltic states. The Burgass–Alexandroupolis pipeline agreement signed between Russia, Bulgaria and Greece is a further example of energy politics.

Energy problems led to a continued interest in nuclear power, especially in France where a major share of power generation was provided that way, and thus found its way into electricity exports from France, notably to Britain. In Finland, by 2008, in order to secure more domestic energy, one nuclear power station was under construction and two more were planned. The availability of passive safety features, rather than those dependent on operators, suggests that any new nuclear reactors will be safer than hitherto. Vulnerability to terrorist attack, however, is an issue, as, more persistently, is the disposal of nuclear waste, which was a factor in the generally critical response to the government's decision in 2008 to press ahead with such power stations in Britain. Public hostility to nuclear power was particularly strong in Germany, and this resulted in a dependence on Russian natural gas. The contrast between France and Germany helped ensure that the idea of a EU energy policy based on shared supply assumptions was not viable.

Environmentalists thus preferred to press for other options but, given the very limited prospect of any reduction in energy use, and the lack of political support for restricted growth, they had to confront the problems posed by the various options for increased provision. Tony Blair's conversion to nuclear energy was paralleled by that of the environmentalist James Lovelock. Concern about fossil fuels and carbon emissions reduced the options, although coal remains a major source of supply in Poland. Wind turbines have become a favoured remedy in mostly coastal areas of northern Europe, as well as in Greece, but they prevent a powerful visual challenge to many sensibilities, while there is also concern about the impact on radar. Yet there are currently improvements in design that are intended to increase the turbines' yield and thus their value. There are also important experiments with creating commercially viable solar-energy plants in Spain. By 2007 the biggest such plant in the world had been established in Portugal, while the largest independent manufacturer of solar cells was located in Thalheim, in what was East Germany, where it was supported by the EU Regional Development Fund. Biofuels, such as ethanol, are seen as another solution. The European Commission set goals for such fuels: 2 per cent of EU fuel consumption by 2005 and 5.75 per cent by 2012, but so far these goals have proved very difficult to meet. Germany was most successful, obliging refiners to use a proportion of biofuels. Production of biofuels, however, reduces the amount of land available for food, and this became especially controversial in 2007–8 as world food prices rapidly increased.

Transport was a key development and a major issue in post-1970 Europe, linking energy use, pollution, land use and social amenity. On the world scale, much of Europe already had well-developed systems of public transport but, as an aspect of changing lifestyles and rising prosperity, the car was increasingly the dynamic hub at the intersection of a number of pressures and trends. Car use rose greatly, and the car had a major impact on lifestyles, design, architecture and the economy. This use rose even in countries with a good system of public transport. Thus, by 2006 270,000 cars were being sold annually in Switzerland, which has an excellent rail and bus system. In an abrupt demonstration of a changing society, Albania, which had no private cars under the Communist regime that ended in 1991, rapidly became a car society. Indeed, the spread of car ownership in Eastern Europe, in this case in the former East Germany, was partly responsible for the major increase in the German vehicle stock – to 48 million by 2001, compared to 35 million for France, 32 million for Britain and 27 million for Italy.

In many European states the position of car manufacturers, such as Citroën and Peugeot in France, Volkswagen, BMW, Porsche and Mercedes in Germany, Fiat in Italy and Volvo in Sweden, was seen as crucial to the economy, to the trade balance and to national prestige. However, a major part of the market was met by imports or by manufacturing within Europe by foreign companies, for example by Nissan and Toyota in Britain. Across Europe Japanese competition proved particularly effective.

The imprint of the car in social life was insistent, affecting a wide range of activities, including family relations, courtship rituals and shopping. It was also linked to changes in social style and image. For example, Communist Albania had been open to the influence of Italian television from across the Adriatic, and this encouraged a stylization of fashion in terms of Italian cafes and fashions. When Communist rule ceased in 1991, both became common in Albania's cities, while Mercedes cars did so on the roads.

Greater personal mobility for most, but by no means all, Europeans, enabled, and was a necessary consequence of, lower-density housing and a declining proportionate role for public transport, developments that were linked to changes in employment patterns and urban structures, not least the shift from manufacturing to the service sector. Furthermore, in place of factories, or mines, that had large labour forces, most modern European industrial concerns are capital-intensive and employ less labour. They are located away from the central areas of cities, with their problems of traffic congestion and the unavailability of uninterrupted space. Instead, these industrial concerns are on flat and relatively open sites with good road links. There was a comparable shift in docks, for example on the Elbe, Tagus and Thames, away from city anchorages to large, new, 'greenfield' container ports that employ far less labour, and are also far from the trade-union problems of established docks. Greenfield construction was also true of business, science and shopping parks. It was far easier to deploy new technology in new buildings, especially the multiple electric networks required by computers.

Related changes in location were also of great importance in such areas as education, health and leisure. Roads provided not only access, but also the flexibility lacking in rapid-transit systems; and this made low-density development possible and profitable. Cars organized time as well as space, the journey time by car becoming a prime unit of time and a way to organize people's lives. Satellite navigation systems, which became common in the 2000s, enhanced this process.

Yet, as more cars led to greater car use and to significant levels of congestion, so there was a need for more roads. Large amounts of money were spent on the road system, in response to the wish to create effective routes for freight, as well as to rising demand for transport by car. Road signs and travel controls became more important to the fabric of urban life and the topics of conversation. In turn, roads defined links and created physical barriers, producing a clear shaping of local environments that was often, as in Oslo and Paris, linked to ethnic and social divisions, both real and psychological. This local specificity, defined by transport, housing, ethnicity and class, was the background to urban life, as experienced by many urban Europeans.

Despite the emphasis on roads, much governmental effort was also put into encouraging other forms of transport. The public response to governmental support for public transport, however, varied, in part as a consequence of the cost and reliability of such systems, but also with reference to social and cultural ideas about transport and concerning public responsibility. This variation was seen, for example, in very different attitudes toward walking, cycling and using the bus. The strong commitment to cycling in the Netherlands remained important to its culture and was supported in public policy, while the situation in Italy was very different and this was not simply a matter of the more hilly terrain. In Italy prosperity led to an abandonment of cycling, whereas in the Netherlands this was not the case. The American model encouraged the appeal of the car, notably in Western Europe in the 1960s and early 1970s, but there was a widespread reaction to it in favour of public transport. In West Germany from the 1970s *Bürgerinitiativen* (citizens' initiatives) focused on the idea of the city as a livable community, and this led to numerous pedestrian zones and bike lanes.

Across Europe, and not only among policymakers, there was also widespread agreement on the social value of public transport. The British notion that public transport must make money was resisted across the Continent, where indeed, alongside the emphasis on public benefit, there was much investment in improving the rail system. In France, Germany, Italy and Spain national prestige was involved in the creation of long-distance rail systems. These were constructed in state-driven projects of affirmation and unification, although increasingly the EU goal of the creation of high-speed European international links became part of the dynamic. This goal was seen in the improvement of services between Paris and Brussels, but also in the attempt to link high-speed national systems, particularly those of France, Spain and Germany. Commercial considerations were very much secondary, although the high-speed trains do make money, which is one reason that the new systems are built. However, the rate of return in relation to the huge costs of building them requires time perspectives well beyond the horizons of private finance. Indeed, the new Milan–Turin line is built to last 200 years. The Italians in this are copying the French: the national rail company will run the profitable sections, while those who want local services will pay for them through local government.

The views of local communities, as well as traditional patterns of spatial organization, were very much subordinated in the planning process for high-speed rail networks. The views of the former about disruption had scant impact on routing, most obviously in France. Moreover, in France, the prestige TGV (*transport à grands vitesses*; high-speed travel) line between Paris and Lyons bypassed Dijon, a longstanding transport hub, which was thereby marginalized. Similarly, in Germany, a new high-speed line bypassed Kassel.

Social geography was also at stake. The southern extension of the French TGV service to Marseilles led to an expression of the social differentiation that was such a significant aspect of the period, as earlier divisions were expressed afresh in new forms but also remoulded. Big out-of-town stations on the new line were built to serve both Avignon and Aix. They ensured that these cities developed a new relationship with Paris. Wealthy Parisians acquired second homes either in the cities, principally in their attractive old quarters, leading to socially divisive urban regeneration, or in the surrounding countryside. Prices were driven up, hitting local purchasers keen to acquire property. Being out-of-town, the new stations were particularly convenient to those living in the surrounding countryside and driving to and from the station. Thus space was reconceptualized. Instead of the train being a central feature of urban life, with the station in the city centre, it became a key intermediary between the 'ex-urbs', or outer-town, and the wider world, and did so to the profit essentially of those who lived in the latter. The role of the train in the social dynamics of a world in which status and lifestyle were linked to second homes and related commuting patterns was also seen elsewhere. Long-range train commuting in Britain, Germany, Italy and Spain had a similar impact, not least with the middle class able to afford second homes and to structure a working week that included a long weekend.

More generally, the social politics of the high-speed train services were far more problematic than a stress on public transport, and thus communal good, might suggest. For example, pricing policies often ensured that these publicly financed projects were outside the scope of many of the poor. Instead, bus services or hired vans were much more significant for the latter. The immigrant flows in Europe in the 1990s and 2000s, for example of Poles and Slovenes to Western Europe, owed far more to buses than to the train.

Rail remained very significant for long-distance freight. Both rail and road transport adapted to the introduction of containers, which increased the speed, and cut the cost, of freight movements. Containerization was linked to the needs for labour productivity and product predictability, which played a more insistent role in the economy. Road and rail competed for freight, with government tending to favour the latter. Thus, in Finland, at present, the aim is to build more two-track railway connections and to decrease long-distance truck traffic.

Rail has also been important in politics, and, specifically, in the social politics of public expenditure and regulation. The dominant model in Europe has been state ownership, with this being seen as the best way to secure investment and social equity. The former may have been true of the post-war decades, when extensive rebuilding was required and private-sector liquidity was restricted, but became less the case as economic growth built up this liquidity and borrowing capability, while government finances, in turn, were put under pressure from the major growth in social welfare payments. However, public assumptions encouraged continued state ownership, not least the view that such ownership was the guarantor of a continued subsidy for uneconomic rail lines that should stay open as a public service.

A two-fold social politics was involved. The social investment of support for uneconomic lines was generally a frozen-case scenario of sustaining past commitments, not a progressive one of deciding that such lines should be constructed to face present and future concerns. In specific terms, lines in rural and upland areas used by relatively few were to be sustained rather than constructing similarly uneconomic, but new, schemes in urban areas, where public transport pressures were most acute. Thus the emphasis, seen in national and EU regional support policies, on rural areas, for example the Massif Centrale in France, was replicated in public transport. This was even more the case in Italy, where most of the local train system has been preserved. Yet, to complicate the situation, as populations shift outwards from the cities, Italian branch lines are being revived, if slowly, while, across Europe, there was also strong pressure from within the rail industry challenging the maintenance of underused rural lines, for example in France in the 2000s. In part this pressure was driven by regulation and the pressure for uniformity, for safety requirements ensured the need for significant investment if many of these lines were to remain open.

The second aspect of social politics was a marked preference for state control, in part reflecting distrust of market mechanisms and in part a sense that such control was more responsive to public pressure through the interest politics, or politics of horse-trading, that characterized so much governance. A lack of investment, nevertheless, was an issue, although EU infrastructure funds helped supplement national taxation. In the 1990s and 2000s there was a move toward rail privatization, most prominently in Britain, but also in Germany where the *Deutsche Bahn* was part-privatized in the late 2000s. This, however, was unacceptable to the left, not least because of the strong representation of rail workers in the trade union movement. The rail industry also reflected the range of pressures affecting environmental issues. The challenge of current environmental concerns, particularly pollution and energy use, has transformed the prospects for rail, although the British government is reluctant to admit this.

The role of the state in the rail industry serves as a reminder of the strong interconnectedness between politics and the economy in Europe in this period, an interconnectedness that became more insistent when state regulation was extended to prescriptive schemes of equity and public policy. If these were most associated with Communist Eastern Europe, they were also the case throughout the Continent. The relationship between these top-down attitudes and the individualism that was a stronger feature from the 1960s, not least with the rise of private wealth and consumerism, created a tension that was a suppressed narrative not only in politics but also in spheres such as environmental regulation. In the case of transport, this narrative was more than the simple dichotomy of car versus train, although that clash was a key element. In addition, the train itself, as already indicated, involved a series of competing social policies, and this was also seen in the 'spaces' of trains and train stations, as well as in arrangements for transfers with other traffic systems, particularly the choice of cars or buses. If great train stations, such as Amsterdam Central or Vienna Hauptbahnof, were major public spaces in which very different social groups rubbed shoulders, this was, neverthe-less, as part of a system in which travellers were explicitly divided by classes with contrasting facilities. That payment was the sole determi-nant of these classes meant that these divisions did not need to correspond with more general social differences, while there was noth-ing fixed about expenditure and some who travelled first class could also travel second, a point that was more generally relevant for social classifi-cation (see pages 89–93). Nevertheless, the issue serves as a reminder of the degree to which public provision did not mean uniform provision. Although the social politics were different, the same was true of health and education, with the catchment area of state schools defined often by social indicators and with this leading to contrasting cultures at the level of individual schools. There was a counterpart with the contrast between the equality of consumers (as opposed to citizens) and the reality that some consumers were more equal than others.

Yet, precisely because public provision did not assert difference, it enjoyed a wider popularity among policymakers than private provi-sion. That remark, however, has to be hedged with caveats not least because the Communist experiment (and indeed many episodes of state provision in the West) revealed the serious shortcomings of the system. Moreover, it is unclear how far those who did not benefit conspicuously from this provision shared the confident support expressed both by the providers of services and by those grateful for a safety net. The providers of services were important to the politics of Europe and represented a core constituency of the left. In doing so, they reflected its strength not only among the traditional working class, a group very much in decline, but also among white-collar work-ers: managers and others in the state system who identified themselves as key stakeholders in public services. The latter group became more important with time, not least as the nature of employ-ment altered. Thus, no longer using coal, trains had one-man operating crews (the driver), signalling was automated, and the rail system required far fewer employees. Proportionately, in addition, more of these rail workers were in service functions such as marketing, cater-ing and accounts, even more the case due to the relative decline of rail freight in the face of the greater opportunities provided by larger trucks, which transformed the economies of scale on the road system.

Transport fulfilled numerous roles. Bridges, for example, symbolized the desire to transform the environment in order to increase the 'connectedness' of human society. The impact of bridges was local, regional and national, the last most dramatically with the creation of successive links from Jutland on the European mainland, via the Danish islands, to Sweden. The engineering feats involved were frequently impressive, as also with the digging of the Channel Tunnel, which was opened in 1992. The desire for transformation seen in the Jutland–Sweden links remains strong at the planning level across Europe, for example with the scheme for a link between Sicily and mainland Italy, which is designed to replace the unpredictability of ferries and is part of the erosion of the differences of island Europe. Within Continental Europe bridges overcame earlier barriers in creating major links that symbolized and reflected the ability to plan and execute change, as with the viaduct across the deep Tarn valley in France, opened in 2004, a bridge that is higher than the Eiffel Tower. These bridges, however, often carried roads that were the subject of much eco-opposition.

ENVIRONMENTALISM

Moving from such achievements to more general progress on environmental matters exposed the difficulties of trying to make such progress, not least the contrasts between aspiration and reality. It was possible to make changes, for example with the dramatic cuts in the use of plastic bags, as in Ireland from 2002, when a tax was introduced. This policy was an aspect of the efforts in various European countries to separate and recycle waste, such as the German 'Green Dot' programme which started in 1990. However, the efficiency of such programmes is often questioned.

Energy issues, moreover, proved far more difficult. Thus in February 2007 the environment ministers of the EU could agree in principle to cut greenhouse-gas emissions by a fifth from 1990 levels by 2020, but the consequences, in terms of policies, politics and living standards, proved far more problematic. Indeed, in 2007, the challenge that proposed EU limits on car carbon emissions posed to German car manufacturers led to energetic lobbying by the German government. It is remarkable that Germany still has no speed limits on most of its *Autobahns* (motorways), despite the efforts of the Green Party and other environmentalists, and this certainly makes fuel consumption higher than it need be. Ironically, the government supports a cut in Germany's 1990 greenhouse-gas emissions by 40 per cent by 2020.

The issue of car carbon emissions brings government regulation, public concern about the environment, manufacturers' strategies, and consumer preference into focus, with clashes between each being important. Consumer preference, in turn, relates to social and cultural trends, ranging from the greater significance of female purchasers, most of whom, especially if not needing to transport lots of children, are ready to invest in small cars, to questions of masculinity, notably with reference to a commitment to quicker and larger cars, with more powerful engines. Preferences in car types were also linked to national car industries and national stereotypes. French and Italian manufacturers, such as Peugeot and Fiat respectively, were readier to produce less powerful cars than their German counterparts.

Discussion of environmental factors might seem needlessly modish, but they were more of a constant in this period than much of the politics that habitually engages attention. These factors also exposed the difficulties that governments experienced in giving force to their goals, as well as the problems of reconciling priorities. In particular, the argument, often but not invariably flawed, that there was a trade-off between environmental protection and economic activity, particularly growth, led frequently to a shelving of the former in favour of the latter, especially at the national level.

Allowing for this, there was, nevertheless, some progress in environmental policy. Ironically, the most important progress was the result of the fall of the Iron Curtain in 1989, as the Communist states had been especially ready to subordinate protection to growth and, indeed, had frequently castigated the former as a bourgeois affectation. The lignite-burning power plants and industries of East Germany and Poland had proved particularly noxious for air quality. The UN Earth

Summit in 1992, held in Rio de Janeiro, concluded that East Germany had the highest per capita carbon dioxide emissions in the world. River quality in Communist states was also poor. In East Germany, where in a far less favourable political environment Green consciousness was far less than in West Germany, the levels of toxic emissions were very high, and these levels led to poisoned rivers and groundwater: in Bitterfield, the pH level was 0.9, representing an acidity between battery acid and vinegar. The West German downriver stretches of rivers, especially the Elbe, were greatly affected by such pollution. After 1989 the spread of private car use, as an aspect of the newly potent post-Communist consumerism and individualism, created fresh problems, serving as a reminder of the multiple links between environment, society and politics.

Environmental issues achieved greater prominence across Europe from the late 1960s and 1970s, although the process was very patchy and, for example, it was not until the 1980s that protest brought a West German dam-building project to a close. Environmentalism involved not only the mobilization of group consciousness and action over hitherto neglected topics, but also issues of prioritization and even vocabulary. Thus, the word *environnement* only came into common usage in France in the 1980s. The Ministry for the Protection of Nature and the Environment had been established there in 1971. The following year, the Club of Rome produced its study on 'The Limits of Growth'. In part environmentalism drew on the counter-culture of 1968 and its critique of industrial capitalism, and in part on older ruralist currents. One product of the latter was a rural protectionism against development expressed in part by some of the support for the CAP, but more pointedly by the creation of national and regional parks, such as that in the Camargue in France in 1973. It proved more difficult, however, to define positive environmental images and policies that would work for the bulk of the urban population.

In most European states Green political parties had only a marginal impact, although from 1983 they were represented in the West German Bundestag and from 1988 in the Swedish Parliament. The Greens have participated in coalition government in Finland in 1995–2002 and since 2007. In 1995 this led to the first Green minister in a Western European national government. Green parties, however, had a limited impact in terms of electoral results in part because other parties had to embrace some of their ideas in order to be competitive; the same goes for the comparative loss of liberal influence since the nineteenth century. Environmental concerns were increasingly important to the currency of mainstream politics. The EU backed the Kyoto Protocol of 1997, under which the major industrialized states agreed to reduce, by 2008–12, their emission of the greenhouse gases held responsible for global warming to an average of about 5 per cent below their level in 1990. It proved difficult, however, to reach a consensus on how to enforce the agreement, although the EU created a carbon market to allow companies to trade their credits. The rejection of Kyoto, in 2001, by the USA, increased trans-Atlantic tension, and in 2005 Jürgen Trittin, the German environment minister, a Green, described the USA as 'climate-polluter headquarters'. Leaving aside the rhetoric, the far higher per capita consumption of energy in the USA, compared to Germany, and indeed Europe as a whole, had implications not only for the environment but also for energy availability and security in the world.

Economic difficulties in the mid 2000s led to a downplaying of environmental concerns in favour of those over growth, but they remain a factor greatly shaping the future of Europe's population. These concerns can be seen in hostility to genetically modified organisms, a hostility that leads to a more critical governmental stance toward genetically modified crops than in the USA, Latin America or Asia, despite the higher yields offered by such crops and their lesser need for pesticides. In conclusion, far from being marginal, environmental factors and change have great importance not only in themselves but also for other aspects of European history and life.

Chapter 3

Changing Peoples

The percentage of the world's population living in Europe fell substantially: from a peak of about 18 per cent in 1900 to 15.6 in 1950 and 9.4 in 1990, this percentage excluding the Soviet Union. The fall in percentage terms arose because, although the European population rose to an unprecedented height, from 395 million in 1950 to 498 million in 1990, again excluding the Soviet Union, its growth rate was considerably lower than that in many other areas. This contrast was not only true within the West, where North and, even more, Latin America enjoyed higher growth rates, and notably higher ones than the European 'Latin' countries, such as Italy and Spain. It was also true of Asia where the respective percentage figures for 1950, 1980 and 1996 were 55, 58.9 and 59.7.

The overall shift in Europe's position was the product not only of general trends but also of very varied situations between and within individual countries. Unlike in the USA, where there are high rates of movement – about 3 per cent of the population move state each year – there is considerable reluctance to move between European countries. This reluctance is particularly true of families, and even more so of poor families, for whom issues of linguistic flexibility and social welfare, the latter in particular relating to the availability of publicly rented housing, are significant. Nevertheless, the situation became more flexible in part because the legal bounds of mobility changed dramatically with the

63

expansion of the EU, especially from 1986, when Spain and Portugal joined. This flexibility interacted with the very different success of individual national economies, creating a geography of opportunities and problems, a geography that provided a key dynamic of perception, and thus a context for the decisions of individual migrants. Alongside the variation of national trends, the general trend of migration was from Eastern and southern to Western and northern Europe. In particular, the industrial centres of West Germany and the service sectors of Britain were beacons that offered employment.

To a certain extent this pattern was replicated by immigration from outside the EU and, indeed, Europe, with Germany being a particularly attractive destination. This pattern was complicated, however, by political issues, not least the availability of asylum within the EU. Refugees who qualified under asylum rules posed a different issue and challenge to those raised by economic migrants. Political issues drove migration within Europe, notably with the conflicts in the former Yugoslavia in the 1990s and the 'ethnic cleansing' this entailed. By 1995 there were nearly 350,000 Bosnian refugees in Germany, and this refugee flow increased political pressure for a settlement of the Balkan question. Defeated Serbs fled Croatia, Bosnia and Kosovo, ensuring that by 2000 Serbia had the largest refugee population in Europe. As Serbia was not a member of the EU it was unable to export this burden to other countries. The Balkan conflicts also led to significant numbers of refugees in other states including Croatia and Hungary.

Alongside immigration, there was also emigration, the rate and impact of which varied greatly. The character of Ireland's emigration, for example, was very different to that of the nineteenth century and the first half of the twentieth. It was not so much that there were no jobs in Ireland from the 1970s, as that emigrants from Ireland (and also Britain) were, largely, highly educated young people seeking professional-level opportunities abroad. By the 1990s, in contrast, economic growth in Ireland was such as to encourage the return of emigrants, both within the EU (particularly Britain) and from further afield, especially the USA. This return, moreover, was another aspect of the longstanding generational contrast between a willingness to work abroad when young and a reluctance to do so when having children or, even more, becoming elderly.

The impact of immigration was accentuated by contrasts within the European demographic regime. Thus, where native population growth was more limited, as in Italy, or there was native emigration, as in Britain, the relative impact of immigration from outside Europe was more striking. Overall population growth was relatively low, with European birth rates lower than in the USA, and, as a result, the median age was higher. By 2006 the median age in Germany and Italy was 42, in Ukraine 40, in Britain, France and Spain 39, and in Poland 38. Moreover, in Germany and Italy 26 per cent of the population were over 60, 22 per cent in Britain and France, and 21 per cent in Spain.

The consequences of such aggregate figures for notions of identity and practices of affection are far harder to probe despite their importance for social mores and expectations. As a result, it is all too easy to resort simply to statistics, whether or not provided in the form of charts, and to leave readers to consider what they mean for individual experience. The possibility of seeing grandchildren grow up has become more common than in the past but, conversely, many couples do not have children. The average person has fewer siblings, cousins, uncles, aunts, nephews and nieces than in the past, but knows family members across a greater age-range. Steep declines in infant mortality may also have discouraged the need for 'insurance' babies to cover possible deaths by other children, while the fall in the agricultural workforce ensured less of a need for male babies, as did changing social assumptions about family structure and inheritance. For example, the commitment to 'keeping the family name' declined across Europe. The falls in infant mortality were particularly steep in the 1970s, especially in Portugal, Greece, Italy and Spain.

The relationship between demographic and social trends is problematic, but the growing frequency of artificial contraception, and, indeed, of both abortion and artificial fertility techniques, has markedly increased the role of choice in demographic trends. This role also brings in public policy. Cultural trends, moreover, play a role, not least in terms of the relationship between nuclear and extended families, the extent to which family is defined in terms of one or the other, and the demographic consequences of these and other attitudes. For example, if childless adults identify with nieces and nephews does this reduce the sense of loss felt through not having children?

There are significant national differences in population figures, with the German birth rate being lower than that of France, Britain, Italy and Spain. There was a massive drop in the birth rate in East Germany immediately after the fall of the Berlin Wall; from 200,000 in 1989 to 115,000 in 1991, and this continued alarmingly in the 1990s. Moreover, while birth rates in France, Britain and Italy in 2006 were similar to their figures for 1997, and the rate for Spain has risen, that for Germany has fallen, in births per 1,000 inhabitants, from 9.9 to 8.2. France, whose government actively pursues pro-natalist policies, and has long regarded it as normal to do so, in contrast, has the highest figure of these countries, at over 13, although its success is in large part a product of the immigrant, particularly Algerian, birth rate, rather than of the 'native' French rate that is the political target. Similarly, although migration was not a factor, the fall in family size in the Soviet Union, which helped cause a decline in population growth, did not extend to the Muslims of Soviet Central Asia. As a result, the percentage of Muslims in the Soviet population rose, and this had notable consequences, for example in the mix of army recruits.

The range in overall birth rates between countries is considerable, although this range has to be put alongside major differences already in the early twentieth century. Indeed, the general pattern across Europe is for variations in the fertility rate (and in life expectancy) to decline at the national level. In part this reflects the fall in the average number of children per women, a fall to two by the 1980s from three in the 1960s. Contraception, abortion, the rise in the average age of marriage and normative assumptions about family size all played a role, with mechanistic means of limitation interacting with the role of cultural assumptions. This decline began across much of Europe in the 1880s and 1890s. At the same time the fall in birth rates was also episodic. In Austria, for example, there was a major fall in the 1900s and early 1910s, another in the 1920s and early 1930s, another in the late 1940s, and a last in the 1960s and early 1970s. Across Europe population density was not the key issue as the fall in birth rates was seen in areas with low density, both on the local and regional levels and at the national one, for example in Norway, Russia, Spain and Sweden, as well as in those with a higher density.

The population situation was particularly bleak in Eastern Europe. In 2000–5, the annual rate of population decline, in percentages, was 1.1 in Estonia, 0.9 in Bulgaria and Latvia, 0.8 in Ukraine, 0.6 in Lithuania and Russia, and 0.5 in Belarus and Hungary. Projections are tricky but this led to suggestions of a comparable annual rate in 2045–50 of 2.0 for Estonia, 1.5 for Latvia, 1.1 for Ukraine, 1.0 for Bulgaria, 0.9 for Russia, and 0.8 for Bosnia and Slovenia. The sole Western European state in this league was Italy with an 0.8 per cent per annum projected fall in 2045–50. The overall projected population decrease for 2000–50 was over 40 per cent for Estonia and Latvia, 30–40 per cent for Ukraine, Bulgaria and Russia, 20–30 per cent for Lithuania, Belarus, Hungary, Italy and Slovenia, 10–20 per cent for Croatia, Switzerland, Moldova, Czech Republic, Poland, Serbia, Bosnia and Greece, and 0–10 per cent for Portugal, Austria, Spain, Slovakia, Finland, Sweden and Denmark. High immigration – about 5 million in 1998–2007 – however, led to an upward revision of medium-term estimates for the Spanish population, from 45 million in 2008 to close to 50 million by 2015. This indicates the more general extent to which immigration could affect population figures.

As a result of its birth rate, despite immigration, the German population fell in 2003 by 5,000, and in 2006 by 130,000. The eleventh highest population in the world in 2000 was projected to be the 21st highest by 2050, with predictions that the population of what was West Germany would shrink by 14 per cent from 2006 to 2050, and that of the former East Germany by 31 per cent. In response, in 2007 the German government (a coalition which is headed by the right) launched a new policy increasing the payments for new parents if they stayed at home, and not making such payments income-dependent. Pro-natalist policies are particularly popular on the right in Germany, but they are sensitive due to their association with the Nazis' encouragement of population expansion.

The reasons for the contrast between Europe and the USA, where birth rates are higher, are controversial, but a lack of optimism in Europe appears to be a factor. The employment situation is very important to this lack of optimism. The labour market is stagnant in France, Greece, Italy, Portugal and even, despite the economy having until recently been more dynamic, Spain. For the average young person across much of Europe, the prospects are years of poorly paid temporary jobs, often in the grey economy. Meanwhile, child-rearing is ever more expensive, and so, logically, marriage and having children are put off. This trend is true even where unemployment is very low, as in much of northern Italy. The difficulties posed by relatively expensive and scarce housing are also significant, as they ensure that many young adults live at home, and this affects the age at which independent households are formed. This factor is particularly significant in Italy, which has a demographic crisis, with a particularly low fertility rate. Across Europe female work patterns are also important, with working women having fewer children than non-working counterparts. A cultural factor also contributes to the low birth rates. In Italy there is a demand for total security, with all the insurance and welfare guarantees that may be involved, before embarking on child-rearing, and this notwithstanding all the help that families give. The slightest hint of risk is enough to stop people from having children, which is the worst aspect of the blocked labour market, even if it is not as blocked as it used to be, but more than labour issues are involved.

Across Europe, there is no governmental anti-growth policy, though critics of abortion see its legalisation as hostile to natalist policies. In Europe there has been no equivalent to the demographic control attempted in India under Mrs Gandhi, let alone that in China, with its one-child policy, which has led to the killing of many female babies. Social welfare indeed can be regarded as a general support for child-bearing, as it removes some of the constraints for the poor. Conversely, house price inflation, and the fiscal policies that contribute to it, can be seen as a discouragement to large families for the socially mobile.

IMMIGRATION

Immigration figures are controversial because of the extent of illegal immigration. Nevertheless, by 1993, children born to legally resident aliens made up 14 per cent of births in Germany and 10.8 per cent in France, while OECD figures and estimates indicate that the percentage of the population that was foreign-born in 2005 was close to 25 in

Switzerland and over 10 in Germany, Sweden and Ireland. Having been only 4 per cent in Spain in 2000, it had risen to 12 per cent by 2007. In 1993–2003 about 200,000 Muslim immigrants entered Italy each year.

The German rate of foreign-born reflects both the low German birth rate and the extent to which those from abroad who came under the *Gastarbeiter* (guest worker) schemes that lasted until 1974 settled permanently, rather than temporarily as had been the intention. The offer of money in 1983 to migrants who returned home found few takers. By 2007 there were nearly 3 million Turks in Germany. As they increasingly claim citizenship and the right to vote, this population has become more politically significant. On the whole mainstream German culture has devoted scant attention to this migration. However, the politically committed filmmaker, Rainer Werner Fassbinder, produced *Ali: Fear Eats the Soul* (1974) about foreign workers.

Turkish immigration was from a country not in the EU and not then seen as part of Europe. It mirrored that to former imperial powers from their colonies, especially to Britain from the West Indies, Pakistan and India, to France from North and West Africa, to the Netherlands from Indonesia, to Italy from Libya, and to Portugal from Angola. As Germany had lost its colonies in the First World War this was not an issue there. At the same time, but generally attracting less attention in the receiving countries, there were important flows of migration in search of employment within Europe, especially from south to north. In this context, southern Europe meant Portugal, Spain, Italy, Greece and Yugoslavia. Thus, for example, large numbers of Portuguese travelled for work to France, settling there. In the 1980s the concierge in Parisian apartment blocks was often Portuguese. In the early 2000s about 50,000 Italians still emigrated annually.

The flow of the 1990s from Eastern to Western Europe was a new variant of this relationship of core to periphery in terms of migration. With numbers seen as a form of strength, not least, via conscription, for the military, and a large workforce required for construction and industrialization as well as agriculture, such a flow had not been permitted under the Communists. Indeed, there had been serious limits on internal migration. Thus in Albania those in collective farms generally were not permitted to leave the farms, which ended long-established migration patterns, not least seasonal migration. The impact of Communist policies in Albania was especially harsh in the extensive upland areas, as agriculture there was only able to support limited numbers of people. Under the Communists the end of the safety valve of migration led to an upland over-population that in some cases even had to be tackled by winter airlifts of food. Once Communist rule ended in 1991 there was significant emigration from these areas, both to Albania's cities and overseas.

Germany was a particularly important destination for migrants, especially because the 1949 constitution of West Germany allowed citizenship to all ethnic Germans who relocated there. This migration had ceased due to the establishment of the Iron Curtain, as indeed did other migrant flows within Europe. Numbers shot up anew in 1989–90: nearly 800,000 ethnic Germans from Eastern Europe migrated to West Germany. On top of that, economic opportunity led 538,000 East Germans to move into West Germany in 1989–90. Both flows continued thereafter, especially the latter, which was encouraged by the markedly contrasting economic fortunes of the two areas. Neither the inflationary and unrealistic valuation of the East German mark as equal to its West German counterpart nor massive government aid could prevent an outflow of people from East Germany, although, without these measures, it would have been far greater. This flow had an even greater impact if broken down by age, as it was particularly the young who left run-down parts of what had been East Germany, while pensioners were disproportionately ready to stay. Moreover, the movement to what had been West Germany was not uniform as migrants focused on areas with economic growth. The impact on former West Germany varied, but the newly arrived could create a marked sense of change. In Meersburg on Lake Constance in 1992 I was told that the town had been spoilt by an influx from former East Germany, a view that owed much to a snobbish disdain both for a new type of tourist and for an increase in tourism.

Migration in Germany therefore was not simply an issue of non-European migrants, but the extent of this migration of Germans increased tension about migrants from Africa and Asia (tension that had already led to a hostile response in the 1970s) by raising sensitivity to total numbers. An emphasis on an ethnic definition of nationhood left non-European migrants in a secondary legal and social position, as well as facing competition at the workplace from migrants from former East Germany. Similarly, in the 2000s, immigrants to Britain from South Asia and Africa found their position affected by the substantial inflow from Eastern Europe, and in 2008 the government announced pressure to limit that from South Asia and Africa: as this immigration was from outside the EU, the government had a legal competence and power it lacked with EU migrants.

At the same time the German government sought to rebut far-right agitation and to integrate the large immigrant community by aiding naturalization, while also limiting the constitutional right to asylum, which was a departure from the earlier situation in which the right of asylum had been the focus, and not a right to migration by ethnic non-Germans. In 1990 second- and third-generation residents were allowed to begin the process of naturalization and, in 1999, it was automatically granted to third-generation residents, while the children of foreign national parents resident in Germany for at least eight years received dual citizenship until, at 18, they were allowed to choose either German citizenship or that of their parents. This engagement with the substantial German community of non-German ethnic origins has not, however, yet greatly affected popular perceptions of Germanness, although the privileged position of foreign ethnic Germans in the nationalization process was also eroded in the 1990s, in what amounted to a major political reconceptualization of nationality, one pushed through by the SPD (Social Democrat)–Green coalition that came to power in 1998. A significant shift in migration flows occurred in the case of Greece, which moved from having net emigration in the 1960s and '70s to net immigration in the 1990s and 2000s. It is etimated that about 500,000 to one million foreigners live in Greece (many illegally) compared to a total Greek population of 10.5 million. Most are from Albania, but many come from Romania, Bulgaria, Ukraine, Russia and Georgia.

The shifting dynamics of core and periphery have been a central issue in European history over the last 40 years, although this should be understood in terms of a variety of cores and peripheries, with complex overlapping relations between them. In population terms the dynamic owed much to a decline of relatively unprofitable agricultural areas, not least as improved communications and freer trade in food accentuated this lack of profitability. Thus, alongside the movement from southern Europe, came emigration from rural Ireland and Russia to the cities, as well as from northern Norway, northern Sweden, and northern and eastern Finland. There was a substantial Finnish migration from the countryside, especially in eastern and northern Finland, to Sweden at the end of the 1960s and the beginning of the 1970s due to economic reasons. There was also a vertical dimension to migration, with a decline of mountain farming and a preference, instead, for lower and gentler slopes where the growing season was longer and it was easier to use machines. This trend was particularly apparent in the French and Italian Alps. Instead of agriculture, there was an emphasis on tourism, but this did not work for all areas, while there were also serious environmental consequences.

In turn the loss of people (human capital in the jargon) made these regions less attractive for non-state investment, and also reduced social opportunities. There was a particular age dimension, with emigration being concentrated amongst the young, many of whom did not find the terms of agricultural work attractive. Their change of employment was linked to change of location, with moves to the cities. In response to the deterioration of agricultural productivity and to the falling labour force, there was a reliance on what was termed 'structural reform', as well as on mechanization. Across much of the EU, especially in the Mediterranean, average farm sizes were too small to generate much profit, and this hit living standards and thus the domestic market for manufactured goods and services. As a key aspect of structural reform, attempts were made to encourage consolidation, both among individual holdings, which were often highly fragmented, and between them, but farm size remained a major problem, not least in Greece and southern Italy. This affects the potential for mechanization, by limiting local investment capital.

There was also a pronounced social dimension to agrarian policy, which was most apparent in Communist Europe, with collectivization and its reversal after the fall of Communism. Yet, what was presented as land reform was also significant in Western Europe after 1945, as it was in Japan. Particularly in Italy, Greece and Portugal, large estates were compulsorily divided up, or shorn of land, as part of a deliberate policy of creating owner-occupied individual farms, which matched longstanding aspirations for a form of agrarian democracy. The long-term viability of this social order was challenged by the pressures of global agricultural competitiveness, but it serves as a reminder of the political and social assumptions affecting agricultural policy, and of its potent location in contexts in which economic value was not the sole, or even key, criterion, which helped account for tensions over the CAP.

Agrarian policies, however, failed to prevent large-scale emigration from rural Europe, emigration which left traces on the landscapes including ruined buildings and farms, and abandoned terraces. Specific problems in particular regions reflected technological changes as well as global economic pressures. Thus the rural cork industry of southern Europe, particularly in Portugal and Provence, was hit by the manufacture of plastic-based corks, as well as by the scarcity of natural cork.

There was also an important age dimension, with migrants, whether from Eastern to Western Europe or from France to Britain in the 2000s, being overwhelmingly young. This was also true, that decade, of Germans seeking better-paid work in Switzerland, a migration that gave rise to hostile reactions there. Migration was widespread within countries, but this was not the focus of the debate. Instead, debate focused on international labour flows, and especially those from outside Europe. This debate was based on the false assumption that humans naturally live a settled life in static, self-sufficient societies, and that therefore migration, especially immigration, was an aberration by marginal individuals. Immigration, both legal and illegal, in fact helped to meet demands for labour, particularly in agriculture, meat processing, nursing and construction, although far less benefit was derived from the family reunification of immigrants. However, immigration also kept wages lower than would otherwise have been the case, especially for the less-skilled workers, and this encouraged the social differentiation among the workforce that posed a serious challenge to traditional left-wing collectivist policies, not least by putting pressure on native low-skilled workers.

Concern about the implications of immigration for public services was frequently raised. Indeed, the role of the state in education and health ensured that this was a governmental as much as political issue. Yet this concern varied greatly, both by country and within countries, as did the political use made of it. Concern was particularly conspicuous in Denmark, Norway, Switzerland, France, Belgium and the Netherlands, fuelling, for example, the rise of the Danish People's Party, the Swiss People's Party and the Vlaams Belang in Belgium. The Danish People's Party focuses on Muslims, arguing that their way of life and political attitudes are incompatible with Danish culture and politics. As a result the Party claims that integration is impossible and that conflicts and unrest will inevitably follow.

The Vlaams Belang was the party known as the Vlaams Blok until the heads of its non-profit organizations were convicted in 2004 in Ghent because of their racist ideology. One of their slogans was *eigen volk eerst*: own people first. The court in Ghent decided that the Vlaams Blok promoted the view of foreigners as criminals and as a threat to the Flemish people and their culture. This Flemish separatist party was created by Karel Dillen and Lode Claus in 1978 and the name referred to the coalition Vlaams Natinaal Blok under which the VNV, a Flemish party that would later collaborate with the German occupiers in the Second World War, went to the elections in 1936. The Vlaams Blok won support from older voters by exploiting their fear of crime, while younger voters proved more susceptible to its ethnic ideology. Highly successful in the Flemish elections, winning 742,000 votes in the 2003 Federal elections, and nearly a million in 2007 (when they were the largest Flemish party), the Vlaams Belang has been kept from government by the *cordon sanitaire*, an agreement between the mainstream democratic parties. Hostility to immigrants and those seen as immigrants was also important elsewhere. In Russia there is hostility to Moslems from the Caucasus and Central Asia, for example Azeris, while in what was East Germany xenophobia is still very strong. This is reflected in the strength of the far-right National Democratic Party.

Concern was less prominent in Spain, Greece, Ireland and Sweden, but still existed, for example in Sweden from the 1980s, and in Greece from the 1990s, especially toward Albanian immigrants. The 2007 elections led, for the first time, to a nationalist right-wing party, LAOS, which won nearly four per cent of the vote, gaining 10 seats in parliament. Historical factors played an important role in creating a particular culture toward immigrants. Economic growth and prosperity were also important. Concern about the implications of immigration has not been prominent in Finland, but discussion of the issue gradually increased in the mid-2000s.

The populist reaction against economic migrants led to restrictions on movement from the new states of the EU in Eastern Europe, but the situation varied greatly by state. Within countries, concern about immigration was strongest in areas where immigrants initially arrived, rather than where they subsequently settled. The apparent impact of immigration was accentuated by the concentration of immigrants in particular areas, generally those with low-cost housing and already established immigrant communities. The presence of mosques was also important, but it was not decisive because it was easy to transform premises into mosques. In the Netherlands the key indicators were the presence of inexpensive housing and the availability of jobs: the city must have industry, as with Amsterdam or Rotterdam, or have had industry, as in the case of Almelo and Ede, where textile factories were closed during the 1970s.

Economic difficulties also played a role in causing concern about immigration, but there was no simple correlation. Race was seen by populists as a signifier of identity, or, if this stance was not taken, the emphasis was on culture, which could be a cover for race. 'France for the French' was a slogan of the National Front which, under Jean Marie Le Pen, became more prominent from the 1980s. Across Europe immigrant labour was perceived as unacceptable by some populists, but greater saliency emerged from the question of the assimilation of immigrants, especially those who are Muslim.

Assimilation became a far more prominent issue after the Al-Qaeda-inspired attacks on Spain and Britain in 2004 and 2005 respectively, and the attempted attacks in Denmark and Germany in 2007. The question of national identity became one of 'who belongs' and this was made more charged by a sense of being under challenge from continual immigration. This perception inspired legislation in the mid 2000s, including a French law to limit immigration for family unification and an Italian decree easing the expulsion of EU citizens considered a danger to public security. The latter, a measure prompted by a murder by a Romanian worker, reflected the pressure of populist concerns on public policy.

At the same time, across Europe, some of the children and grand-children of migrants felt harshly treated and also disorientated by this perception. That many migrants were concentrated in unskilled and semi-skilled jobs increased their vulnerability to recessions, such as that in the mid-1970s. This vulnerability was due in part to discrimi-nation and in part to limited skills. Unemployment proved particularly high for young male second- or third-generation immigrants, and these could take boredom, discontent and despair into drug-taking, crime and rioting. Their sense of identity and meaning was often unclear, which contributed to a perception of society as under pressure both from them and from the response to them.

By 2006 the EU contained about 20 million Muslims, approximately 4 per cent of its population, but the Muslim population was scarcely homo-geneous. Its variety owed much to the different migrant streams that composed it. Much was due to colonial background, not least with Muslims from North Africa, especially Algeria, settling in France, and from South Asia, particularly Pakistan, in Britain. Yet other links were also important, as with the large Turkish population in Germany. In the mid-2000s France, with maybe 8–9 per cent of its population Muslim, has a higher percentage than the Netherlands (5.6 per cent), Germany (3.9) and Britain (2.8), although there is no section for religion on the French census form, and thus figures are approximate.

Nationality was readily acquired by immigrants. In France it is auto-matically obtained by children of foreign-born parents on reaching the age of majority, and the children of naturalized foreigners are also citi-zens. Alongside headline figures about aggregate numbers, which capture a sense of change and challenge, Muslims are not a united bloc, as the division between Shia and Sunni has made abundantly clear. There are religious, ethnic and political differences. For example, along-side fundamentalists are secularists like Naser Khader, who in 2007 founded the New Alliance political party in Denmark, which did very well in the recent general election there.

Although immigration engaged headline attention, an ageing population was at least as significant demographically. A fall in national death rates across Europe contributed to the overall shift in population figures. This fall was caused by improvements in health and the availability of adequate supplies of food and clear water. These affected death rates across the age range, although there were major geographical differences, due largely to differential prosperity and to varied public provision of health and social welfare. Improvements in medical knowledge were also important to falling death rates. Indeed, the ability to identify and treat disease changed exponentially. As this knowledge was readily spread, it was less significant than differential prosperity in explaining contrasting death rates within Europe.

A major increase in anaesthetic skills, due to greater knowledge and the introduction of increasingly sophisticated drugs, meant that complex surgical operations could be performed, while once-serious operations became routine and minor. There were also major advances in the treatment of the heart. Bypass and transplant surgery were developed as an aspect of the growth of specialized surgery. The transplantation of human organs was transformed from an experimental and often fatal procedure into a routine and highly successful operation. Open-heart surgery became possible, while major drugs for coronary heart disease were introduced. Medical technology developed in numerous directions, with artificial hip joints followed by knee joints. The pharmacological repertoire also expanded. From the 1980s anti-viral agents were used for the treatment of viral infections: antibiotics had been useless against them.

There was also a revolution in the knowledge and treatment of mental illness, which was found to affect an appreciable and growing proportion of the population, although the categorization of such illness differed greatly across Europe, as did the level of care. Institutional attention was particularly bleak in the Balkans. In part this was due to poverty, but a lack of concern about mental illness was also significant in Balkan public culture. The poor level of institutional support encouraged a reliance on family networks of support and thus a different social dynamic to the smaller role of the family across most of Europe. This contrast is more generally true of the response to ill-health and other adverse circumstances. With greater recognition of the importance of psychological and mental processes, diagnosis and treatment of mental illness both changed across much of Europe. The development of safe and effective drugs in the 1960s and 1970s helped with major psychoses and depression, dramatically improving the cure rate. Psycho-pharmacology expanded in parallel with psychotherapy.

Although developments in medical knowledge and practice had a major impact on individual and collective experience, and in decreasing anxiety, not all illnesses were, or are, in retreat. Illness rates are difficult to assess, partly because reporting issues may give a misleading impression of the prevalence of particular illnesses. Nevertheless, a more thorough collection of statistics during this period led to a more comprehensive coverage of health problems. This coverage fed into debates about the state of the people, which played a charged role in discussion about how far and how best to ensure health-care. The debates encompassed contentious issues of personal, corporate and governmental responsibility, as in the case in the 2000s of particular concern about obesity, a European-wide problem owing much to rising affluence and to a lack of self-control in the face of advertising and social norms. The issue of obesity was pushed particularly hard in Britain and France, but the contrast with the situation in some other European countries was a more general aspect of public policy-discussion across Europe. Public action against obesity focused on diet, although exercise was also a factor. The consumption of saturated fat and cholesterol helped ensure that the percentage of the population defined as over-weight or clinically obese rose, and this rise was linked to an increase in Type 2 diabetes. Obesity is also related to problems with mobility, fractures and bone and hip joint abnormalities and, indeed, to the need to change consumer products, such as hotel beds, bus seats and doorways, in order to accommodate larger average sizes. The most surprising groups were affected by the problem. By 2008 German soldiers, on average, were fatter and took less exercise than the population as a whole.

More generally, changes in lifestyle contributed to the spread of some diseases. In particular, lack of exercise stemming from sedentary lifestyles, in both work and leisure, and from an increase in food consumption, led to a marked rise in diabetes and heart disease. This rise was an aspect of the extent to which medicine was expected to cope with symptoms rather than the underlying causes of problems. The latter could be addressed only by public health measures and self-discipline, but both were made difficult by powerful social trends. For example, the popularity of television and video games has lessened the tendency to take part in sport. Indeed, for many, sport was increasingly a spectator practice, mediated through television, rather than a participatory activity. Exercise became a matter of searching for the television remote-control. The move from the countryside was also significant as agricultural work and rural lifestyles had led to much hard physical labour, while moving to the towns did not lead to an abandonment of the high-calorie diets necessary to support such labour, and the net effect was unhealthy.

Social distinctions also played a role in avoiding ill-health. The affluent were more able to afford the gym and golf, and also to buy organic and natural foods. Concern about diet, in turn, was responsible for fads and for a vast range of pharmaceutical and alternative medicines. Diets helped to dictate the success or failure of restaurants, and the popularity or otherwise of particular types of food and foodstuffs. A range of publications and television programmes also met this public interest in health, with news networks employing medical correspondents. The medical response to health issues was joined by lifestyle options, such as exercise and not smoking.

The resulting practices helped to divide individuals from each other, as well as to ensure common currencies of conversation, and also provided ways to identify personalities and to define sexual appeal. The first non-smoking law, that in Ireland in 2004, was rapidly followed elsewhere, including in England in 2007. In France, where there were 14 million smokers in 2007, café and restaurant culture, or at least habits, changed with the prohibition of smoking. France became one of the inside-out societies, with smokers leaving offices or restaurants in order to 'light up' outside in the public space of the pavement. Future archaeologists may well analyse the soil near the entrance to the remains of public buildings and conclude that humans in the 2000s burnt a substance in order to propitiate the spirits of these buildings. They can then debate whether the 'tobacco cult' crossed the Atlantic from west to east or east to west. The situation was very different in Eastern Europe, but the tolerance, until 2008, of smoking in the Netherlands, notably in the brown cafés, indicated that this was not a simple west–east contrast.

Pollution is another health issue. Increasing car-exhaust emissions and general pollution probably led to the rise in respiratory diseases, such as asthma, and to subsequent mortality. These diseases were combated by asthma drugs, clinics and nurses, but led to concern about the state of air quality. Uncertainty over the causes of asthma also fed into contention over health. Claims that pollution, and thus both manufacturing and consumerist lifestyles, was to blame were resisted. Asthma was an aspect of a major rise in the incidence and prevalence of increasingly diverse and dangerous allergic reactions. Allergies and food intolerances, for example to nuts, were more frequently reported and came to affect the food industry. Eye irritation became a response to particles in the air while, more seriously, the asbestos employed in insulation up to the 1970s caused cancer. The diversity of the environmental challenge to health was considerable. The massive increase in the movement, treatment and burial of hazardous waste led to concern about possible health implications. More generally, pollutants were linked to declining sperm-counts and to hormonal changes, specifically the acquisition of female characteristics by men. Global warming, a consequence of pollution, was also blamed for the spread of some illnesses.

Other problems were not related to pollution. Increased use of 'recreational' narcotic drugs led to considerable physical and psychological damage, much of which became apparent decades later. Narcotic drugs also resulted in many deaths. Differential legal policies complicated the situation. Thus in the Netherlands there was considerable tolerance in practice. This tolerance led to economic opportunity, with the growing of cannabis in nearby parts of Germany in order to supply the Dutch market markedly increasing. It is unlikely that this was the integration the proponents of the EU had in mind, although the permission given the Dutch police to stage raids in

Germany was certainly an aspect of it. Across Europe the irresponsible prescribing of tranquillizers and antidepressants was also a major problem.

Concern about the frequency of sexually transmitted diseases focused on the most potent, AIDS, which developed as a new killer in the 1980s. AIDS threw into sharp focus the extent to which the response to disease reflected social and cultural assumptions about personal conduct and the nature of society. AIDS also drew attention to the issue of human ability to understand disease. It punctured the confident belief and expectation that medical science can cure all ills, a belief that had developed with the antibiotic revolution. Food also gave rise to concern. Anxieties about the conditions in which animals were kept, and how the food chain operated, were related to worries about the impact on humans. There was particular anxiety about bovine spongiform encephalopathy (BSE), 'mad-cow disease', in 1996. The EU played a major role in coordinating the response, with Franz Fischler, the agricultural commissioner, doing a reasonably good job.

Previously unknown diseases recognized during the period covered by this book include Legionnaire's Disease, Lyme Disease and new hospital-acquired infections. These diseases reflected the impact of hitherto unknown bacteria and viruses that, for some, challenged confidence in human progress. The rise in global travel aided the spread of disease, and this became more insistent as the speed and frequency of travel increased. Not only humans travel. Thus in 2006 there was concern over the extensive spread across Europe of the H5N1 strain of bird flu, which can be lethal to humans. The virus also moved from wild birds to domestic poultry. Public anxiety led to a major fall in poultry sales, in part a sign of a lack of confidence in government assurances, because properly cooked poultry offers no risk.

LIFE EXPECTANCY

Although some human illnesses are rising, the overall picture remains one of an increase in average life expectancy. This increase was general across the continent although there were also important contrasts.

Leaving aside the persistently higher life expectancy at birth for women than for men (81 to 76 in Sweden in 1995 and 82 to 74 in France in 1995), there were marked contrasts, with Eastern Europe doing less well, although, as usual, this was not taken to include Finland where the figures for women and men in 2006 were 83 and 76. In 1995 the relevant male figures for Hungary and Bulgaria were 65 and 68, whereas those in the Netherlands and Ireland were 76 and 74. Such contrasts were persistent, being also pronounced earlier in the century. Greater average longevity meant precisely that, ensuring considerable numbers of widows and, to a lesser extent, widowers, and thus a rise in one-person households. This rise was particularly marked in Russia where there was a fall in male life expectancy, in part due to the serious problems with alcoholism that had led to legislation by Gorbachev in 1985. As an indication of the limited control of the Soviet state, and of the place of entrepreneurship (and corruption), in 1985 this led to a rapid rise in illicit distilling.

The rise in average life expectancy was linked to a change in the causes of death. Whereas infections were a major cause of death for the entire population in the first half of the twentieth century, by the 1990s they were far less significant. Instead, infections increasingly killed only those who were suffering from associated disorders and who were at the extremes of life. In their place, over the century as a whole, later-onset diseases, especially heart disease and cancers, became relatively far more important as causes of death. The decline in death rates from infectious diseases, such as tuberculosis, and their replacement by non-communicable diseases, such as cancer, bronchitis and circulatory disease, ensured a different relationship to the ill. There was no longer the need to isolate them, nor the tensions this created, both within families and in terms of the stereotyping of social and ethnic groups as alleged sources of infection. Overall figures for disease, however, concealed many variations, in which location, income, diet, lifestyle and gender played interacting roles.

Greater life expectancy and a modest birth rate ensured that the number of the elderly increased markedly, with 14 per cent of the European population being over 60 in 1997, compared to 5 per cent in Asia and Latin America. The workforce is increasingly over 50, which poses a problem for company finances in many countries, as those in this age group frequently earn far more than workers under 40, particularly in France and Germany. Indeed, an aspect of their labour rigidity is that seniority (and thus pay) is more commonly linked to age there than in less rigid labour markets such as Britain and the USA. Moreover, both countries have unfunded pension liabilities that are far greater than those in the USA or Britain. In Germany in 2007 the government decided to raise the retirement age to 67, but only slowly, which represented a caution that reflected the consensual tone of German government and society, and the constraints placed upon reform there. The retirement age was also raised in Italy.

SOCIAL SERVICES

Medical advances ensured that, across Europe, much of the elderly population was physically independent until close to death. Nevertheless, in terms of the percentage of the population not working, there was a marked rise in the dependency ratio. Retirement ages were a key factor: where low, as in Italy, the situation was exacerbated. A variant, not age-related, was provided by national differences over the hours worked, which became a serious political issue in France in the 2000s. Support for shorter working hours, which the French Socialist government capped at 35 hours per week in 2000–2, affected productivity and in his successful presidential campaign in 2007 Sarkozy campaigned against the limit.

Across Europe there was considerable pressure on health and social services budgets. Care for the elderly became a greatly expanded labour demand, not least because much of it was no longer handled within extended families. The resulting demand for support contributed greatly to the expansion of the service component of employment, especially because the increased amount of pension wealth and savings held by many (but by no means all) of the elderly helped to fund the process, particularly for nursing and home-help. Part of the low-wage demand was met from immigrant labour, without which the care industry would have found it difficult to operate. Care for the elderly was also a crucial aspect in the more general rise of health expenditure. Greater longevity put pressure on governmental and company finances, leading to governmental attempts to revise pension regulations: to cut benefits and/or increase contributions. Thus in France, where a full pension was provided to railway, gas and electricity workers after 37 years of contributions, the Sarkozy government's attempt to extend the period led to serious strike action in November 2007.

The lack of adequate funding for the future was matched by concerns about services in the present. The mental health of the elderly was a major area of inadequate provision, as greater life expectancy was matched by a significant rise in those suffering, and seen to be suffering, from senile dementia, Alzheimer's Disease and related problems. The cost of such care, combined with the institutional conservatism of public provision, and the desire of most insurance companies to restrict their liability to such long-term and incurable problems, led to a dire situation across much of Europe.

Health-care for all, not simply the elderly, proved particularly vulnerable to changes in governmental systems, notably where the changes were abrupt and the state hitherto had had a monopoly. This situation was an issue in particular for the ex-Communist societies, and there were serious health-care crises in the 1990s and 2000s, for example in Russia, although it would be highly misleading to suggest that health-care had always been first-class under the Communists. Instead, deficiencies were widespread, as was clear in the notorious case of Romanian orphanages, which were inadequate both under the Communists and subsequently. That the orphanages became the source for children for adoption in Western Europe provided another aspect of the core–periphery relationship already referred to.

Public care was very different in Scandinavia, where it was both a key aspect of national cohesion and identity, and a major source of employment. In Finland, for example, child-care provision is good, as is support for child-rearing at home. There is also good child-care provision in Denmark, Norway and Sweden. The Scandinavian welfare systems are characterized by universalism and by services provided by public authorities and financed by taxes, instead of individual insurance. This public provision is particularly true of the Danish system of 'flexicurity', which makes it attractive for employers to hire workers whenever there is need for more manpower as it is also easy to fire them again when a slump sets in. To compensate the labour force against such relative job insecurity, the unemployed can get unemployment benefits (provided by insurance associations financed by contributions from the workers themselves plus a significant amount of government grants to those associations) of around 90 per cent of their former wage and for a relatively long period. Furthermore, the publicly financed job centres provide compulsory counselling and job training etc. for the unemployed. The fact that it is easy for employers to hire and fire, and that unemployment and sick benefits are to a very large degree financed by the government and not by individual, compulsory insurances for employers and workers, promotes dynamism in the Danish labour market without losing the social security of the wage-earners.

The Danish system of 'flexicurity' has lately drawn attention from the governments of France, Germany and Italy as it seems to be a possible way of remedying the labour market problems within those countries, and the more so as unemployment in Denmark is extremely low. The pension systems of the Scandinavian countries are also notable: universalist, state-provided and state-financed pensions, which during the latest couple of decades had been increasingly supplemented by private pension arrangements. The right to receive an old age pension is a question of reaching a certain age and has nothing to do with the number of years one has been in the labour market. The negative consequences of the Scandinavian welfare-state models, however, include a very high level of taxation and other kinds of regulation of economic and social life which can be seen as leading to a lack of freedom as well as a restriction or inhibition of initiative and political protest.

CHANGING DEMOGRAPHICS AND DYNAMICS

The percentage of the world's population living in Europe, as the latter was generally understood to extend in 1970, is expected to continue to decline and also, as a related matter of cause and effect, to age. This trend is potentially complicated, however, by pressures for EU expansion, notably to include Turkey, whose population is growing rapidly. Moreover, as a separate issue, but one that is run together by some of those particularly concerned by the challenge posed by an increase in the Islamic population within Europe, the ability of Europe's population to sustain growth (and notably without the role of recent immigrant groups) is limited, which directs further attention to the impact of immigrants.

Yet again, therefore, it is impossible to consider a subject without bringing in a political dimension, while, as an integral part of the same process, politics cannot be understood without an assessment of these trends. There is a tendency on the part of some commentators to discuss political situations as if there were no fundamental social changes taking place that, in fact, inherently challenge both the classification and the analysis of the situation. There is also a habit of counterpointing change with some allegedly unchanging former condition or state of mind. These are not helpful views, because change is of the essence of the human and natural environment in recent decades, and, as a result, to propose some vision of continuity tells us most, not about conditions but, instead, about cultural unease and related political impulses.

The implications of immigration are easier for many to debate than the consequences of ageing, but both are aspects of a transformed demographic regime in, and indeed throughout, Europe. This transformation has to be borne in mind when assessing social structures. For example, ageing has increased the multi-generational nature of extant families, posing both opportunities for sustaining relationships of love and affection, and yet also difficulties not only in the support of the elderly, but also in familial roles. Public provision in health and social welfare has forced such issues onto the political and governmental agenda, but without any realistic public grasp of the resulting costs and problems. This problem became more acute as the gap between retirement and death rose, while unemployment peaks put pressure on the funds coming in to pay for the relevant health and social welfare systems. In some respects, the rate of female employment helped save them, as this meant a rise in the number of payers into social welfare systems as well as of workers in health-care and social services. Furthermore, the extension of direct taxation on income thanks to salary inflation, and of indirect taxation on goods and services, provided funds. These social welfare requirements crowded out other potential spheres of government expenditure, particularly the military and industrial investment. Collective solutions – NATO and EU anti-competition policies – made such investment appear less relevant (possibly highly unrealistically so), and thus helped in encouraging the focus on social welfare which became a defining characteristic of European states and one that accentuated their association with 'soft power', rather than the 'hard power' of military forces. The 'welfarism' or focus on social welfare, however, could not end concern about differential access to welfare, nor, indeed, the politics of envy that was an aspect of European social consciousness, both within and between what could be defined as social classes.

A demographic regime in flux thus emerges clearly from this chapter. Furthermore, the changes are interrelated but far from uniform across Europe. Large-scale change is not unprecedented, as any consideration of migration flows in the late nineteenth century will indicate, but the institutional context has altered considerably with the EU. The extent, however, to which attitudes about migration within Europe have been affected by its rate is unclear, although there is evidence of considerable opposition. Hostility toward the prospect of workers from Eastern Europe in France at the time of the 2005 referendum on the proposed European Constitution indicated the continued public understanding of Europe as an amalgam of national segments, each with different interests, rather than as a common European society.

How far an overall ageing of the European population has changed dynamics within families and social attitudes is also uncertain. The response to this ageing is affected by public policy, just as an ageing population has an impact on policy, notably over pensions and the retirement age. Social attitudes and public policy have also interacted over contraception, abortion and divorce, in each of which both individual choice and public acceptance play a role. Alongside the shift in the age-profile, arguments over the state–market balance in social welfare provision have become ever more intense, especially when economic growth is scarcely enough to keep things going without too much strain. Thus the centrality of economic growth as an issue returns.

Chapter 4

Social Developments

'What must people think when they see a tie displayed that costs more than the average weekly wage?'
Marco Carassi, 1983

What this chapter entails has changed considerably over the last four decades. At the outset it would have been all about social structures, in the shape of economic activity and opportunity understood in terms of class. More recently issues of identity have become more prominent, notably questions of gender, but also sexual orientation, race and consumerism. Class has been largely discarded, which has left a somewhat strange account of social developments; certainly a strange account when compared to those offered in the 1950s.

SOCIAL STRUCTURES

The ways in which Europeans are described and categorized have frequently become sources of contention, which is understandable as processes of identification, both of self and of others, affect the general sense of being, and are also at the root of political alignments and animosities. Such classification is also crucial to the market research and sales strategy of companies, and to political parties and governments, which, in this respect, act in a similar fashion. Indeed, the gathering of steadily more comprehensive statistics has provided greater opportunities for analysis.

At the same time, this situation leads to acute pressures for accurate classification, not least if rational decisions are to be taken, and these have become particularly important due to the spread of the welfare state, but also as a result of concern about its effectiveness and thus a pressure for more accurate information. With society joining the economy as the scope for governmental concern and action, so the need for more accurately informed policies has developed.

As a key aspect of classification it is worth asking what primarily motivates people: their nationality, economic position, parental background, personal assumptions or peer-group pressures? To what extent does any one of these flow from and into the others? Whatever its past social applicability and political resonance, does 'class' still mean much for the bulk of the European population and, if so, what? Do 'class' and related terms merely describe a situation (difficult as that is to do), or do they also explain it and, if the latter, what guide do they provide to the future?

The ambiguous nature of social categories, and the complexities of modern European societies, of social formation, interaction and self-perception, all complicate the situation. Furthermore, class-based analyses of society are seen by many as an unwelcome legacy of a divisive past, and of a past that is more divisive for having been fairly recent, notably in the case of Communist doctrines on social development.

A class is essentially a large group of people that shares a similar social and economic position. Much of the basis of class analysis is derived from Marxism and in Karl Marx's analysis class was linked to economic power, defined by the individual's relationship to the means of production, society being presented as an engine for the production of goods and for the distribution of tasks and benefits, an engine directed by the dominant class. Society, in the Marxist analysis, was divided between two self-conscious groups: the proletariat, or 'workers', who lived off the sale of their labour power, and the bourgeoisie, or property owners, who bought that labour power. These groups were assumed to be in conflict in order to benefit from, and control, the fruits of labour power, while society itself was the sphere for this conflict and was shaped by it.

Aspects of this analysis may indeed have been the case in the late nineteenth century, a period of rapid industrialization across much of

Europe, but the attempt to apply it after 1945, as the basis for understanding and moulding society, faced many problems. This was the case both in Eastern Europe, where Marxist analysis was an aspect of Communist rule, and in Western Europe, where Marxism had considerable influence in intellectual life and among left-wing politicians, and where *Marxisante* ideas influenced many others, more particularly as appreciating the nature of the social structure seemed the prime way to understand society.

In practice, however, the division between workers and owners was a less than accurate account of the nature of ownership. Moreover, although public ownership, which was dominant in Eastern Europe and common more generally, was presented as ownership by the workers, this did not capture the structure of society, although this presentation was used to justify the considerable sacrifices imposed on them in order to build up the system, notably in Eastern Europe. Unsafe working conditions, long hours of work and poor and crowded accommodation were particular issues. A Western European variant was the argument that limited individual consumption, flowing from heavy taxation, was necessary to permit public expenditure, which was presented as a matter of deferred and shared private benefit, although in practice the value of this public expenditure was frequently dubious.

Nevertheless, flaws in analysis and usage in support of questionable policies do not mean that economic analyses of society are without value. Whatever the formal system of compensation for labour, and despite redistribution via differential taxation and social welfare provisions that seek to reduce the effects of poverty, there were and are important social contrasts in income and assets, and these were further accentuated, in financial terms, by different attitudes towards savings.

Furthermore, there were important contrasts in social opportunity. The poor faced an impoverished institutional network, with fewer possibilities for good jobs, poorer schools, fewer banking facilities and other features of deliberate or, more commonly, non-deliberate, social differentiation, isolation and even discrimination. A lack of helpful connections was a common factor, whatever the formal nature of the political system, for without such connections it was generally impossible to circumvent bureaucratic regulations that operated as restrictions. Merit in the absence of connections meant little in Communist Romania or Christian Democratic Italy. Conversely, those who were regarded as well connected in the latter could get planning permission and did not have to bother with paying their gas bills, fines or taxes. More generally, across Europe, the poor had fewer opportunities to get into universities, let alone good ones, than their more affluent counterparts, at a time when educational attainment had become increasingly important for income and, therefore, social status and mobility.

Different opportunities were also the case with primary and secondary education. Here the key indicator of inequality was not the existence of private schools, although that could be important, but rather the differential role of social groups within the state education system. For example, West German *Gymnasium*, the better secondary schools, were disproportionately used by and for the middle class. The poor also had a worse diet and experienced worse health, with significant contrasts in most countries, although less so in Scandinavia.

Non-Marxist analyses of class were less led than their Marxist counterparts by the notion of conflict, and were readier to present social structures as more complex, and as dominated by income and status (in part, market position) differences between occupational groups. These analyses centred on a contrast between the 'middle class' – 'white-collar' (non-manual) workers – and the 'working class' – 'blue-collar' (manual) workers. Consumer analysts further refined these differences in order to understand possible markets. 'Blue-collar' workers were, in turn, in part defined by the extent to which they were affected by de-industrialization, which helped cause the fragmentation of working-class communities (although these were rarely as stable as sometimes suggested), with effects on politics, race relations and issues of gender. Governmental responses to such economic pressures, in part in the shape of subsidies, could increase a pronounced dependence on the state.

Whatever analytical approach was adopted, the competing interests and identities fractured the goals of social groups, and thus the categories of commentators. Competition ranged in scale and character, with the insistent blood feuds of Albanian villages being different to divisions in urban Europe. Contrasting national and regional interests were of importance, including in the Communist economies of Eastern Europe. The resonance of place as a political category was shown in the 1990s in the importance of the Northern League in Italy, and, more dangerously, in the paranoid nationalist ambition of Slobodan Milošević and many other Serbs. Each of these developments reflected a prior failure of national myths and sentiments, in these cases Italy and Yugoslavia and, instead, a preference for regional and ethnic senses of identity. Already, in 1981, as a sign of the latter senses of identity, there had been mass demonstrations by Albanians in the Kosovo region of Yugoslavia. More generally, across Europe there was a tension between democratic, national and international values and perspectives, each of which themselves was open to contention.

Returning to social classification, to classify in terms of jobs had weaknesses, not least in its focus on male occupations, while in some countries, such as Iceland, it was common for much of the workforce to do more than one job in order to support their living standards. In addition, classification in terms of jobs ignored the particular characteristics of the youth society that became more important. A stress on the distinctive lifestyles of youth, and particularly on youth independence, mobility and flexibility, underlines the more general fluidity of social life. Moreover, youth independence had political, social and cultural weight, most obviously in the widespread generational conflict of the 1960s as the post-war baby boom generations in Europe became adults. Thus in Germany there was a rejection of the conformism of the Adenauer years of the 1950s.

Furthermore, as another instance of the problems with standard classification, to be 'working' or 'middle' class meant very different things at various stages of life, while families also increasingly contained individuals who were in, or moved between, different social groups. All this challenged notions of class coherence, let alone unity. So also, in the Soviet bloc, did the reality of Communist government and ideology: a *nomenklatura* of privilege for the segregated Party élite, as well as a solid bloc of middle-ranking officials who defended their own interests, made a mockery of the idea that the common ownership supposedly characteristic of Communist societies had brought to an end conflicts of interest between competing social groups.

With a breakdown of confidence in public systems in the Soviet bloc, there was a reliance on the family, notably but not only in Poland. At the same time the family itself was challenged by the state's reliance on informers, as in East Germany, with the deliberate use of family members to spy on each other. The problems of Soviet society were bluntly outlined from a populist perspective in Boris Yeltsin's manifesto of March 1989 for the elections to the Congress of People's Deputies, in which he attacked the unjustified stratification of the population and the privileges of the *nomenklatura*. Yeltsin won nearly 90 per cent of the vote in Moscow. As another sign of the problems of Communist rule Yeltsin supported popular concern about environmental issues.

Social structure across Europe was not as rigid as much of the theoretical discussion might suggest. There was considerable fluidity in the concept of social status, while notions of social organization, hierarchy and dynamics all varied, and the cohesion of social groups involved and reflected much besides social status. All these aspects challenged class-consciousness and the discussion of society in terms of class, even suggesting that it was irrelevant.

One key area of variety was by employer, with the crucial contrast being between those in the state or public sector and those in the private sector. The former tended to have far more security and to be more unionized, and their pension provision was generally far better. In contrast, those in the private sector were less unionized, went on strike less often, and had less continuity in employment. The contrast was readily apparent in France where, in 2006, 5 million workers, about a quarter of the workforce, were in the public sector.

This difference in attitudes and conditions between public and private employment helped make the transition from Communism in Eastern Europe more complex and difficult. 'Socialist labour' had not been a welcome experience to those with initiative, but it did help form attitudes that became normative, not least those of dependence on the state, particularly for a job for life. In Western Europe there was a highly important political linkage to this contrast between the public and private sectors. The more heavily unionized public sector was more likely to be linked to the left, whereas private-sector workers were more commonly on the right.

SOCIAL CHANGE

Reference to the differences between public and private employees highlights the question of the extent of shared experience. Many of the pressures that helped define economic parameters and social issues were similar. Yet the opportunities offered individuals in their response to them were very different. This division, however, was not a simple matter of Communism versus the rest, because the corporatist nature of important parts of Western European economies and societies corresponded to Communism in proposing a situation in which the state apparently had the solution. Thus in both Western and Eastern European societies, as aspects of growth-oriented strategies that relied in part on raising consumption through equalizing income, there were attempts at social contracts or compacts. Examples included Czechoslovakia in the 1970s and 1980s and Britain under the Labour government of the late 1970s. These offered the population a welfare state and price controls in return for accepting stability in the shape of the dominance of the government and wage restraint. Such contracts and compacts made explicit the social theory of politics and the political theory of society that underlay much government regulation.

The statist nature of this model and its inability to provide individual incentives combined, however, to ensure that it could not ensure much economic growth in what was a very competitive environment. The resulting malaise led to pressures that challenged this system, both in Eastern Europe and further west. Yet, despite its limitations as an economic model, the idea of a social compact remained strong as governments sought to justify themselves and to find a social model that made their policies seem viable. Thus in 2006 the French government offered a new labour contract for the young.

Another similarity between Communist and non-Communist societies was provided by the emphasis on public housing, although the communal apartments normal in the Soviet Union were not the case in the West for other than marginal groups, such as immigrants renting in the private market. The type of housing that was built on both sides of the Iron Curtain contained many similarities: earlier housing was frequently replaced by estates of high-rise flats as well as by low-rise deck-access blocks. There was frequently an element of compulsion, notoriously in Romania in the 1980s, both in the towns and in the villages. Housing captured the social stratification of Western and Eastern European societies, as well as the habit of treating as a problem the poor, who were to receive support but whose views were of little interest to the planners.

Social stratification was an important constant in a Europe supposedly moving, through greater affluence and equal opportunity, into a classless society. This classlessness was emphasized by governments, which saw it as an attractive sign of progress and equality, and also was apparently demonstrated by a similarity in consumer tastes and habits. Yet the idea of a classless society concealed not only the problems of what was defined, in apparent contrast to this allegedly classless homogeneity, as the 'underclass', but also, more profoundly, the major differences that existed within the 'classless' societies.

IDENTITIES

Gender and race competed with class as a basis for social classification, identity and expectation. All were dynamic, but there was a widespread attention shift from class to gender and race. As far as gender was concerned the headlines were made by attacks on conventional assumptions. Nuclear families, the authoritarian role of men within households, and sexual ignorance and subservience were all criticized by feminists, although they varied greatly in their views. Men, moreover, were accused of expressing authoritarianism in their sexism.

The rise in divorce was important in challenging male assumptions as most divorces were initiated by women. This rise was an expression of a greater variety, indeed consumption, of lifestyles linked to a decline in religious ties, and was central to the growth of single parenting.

Divorce represented a repositioning of identity and family, with less of an emphasis placed on continuity and cohesion than hitherto, and was related to demands for the recognition of women's emotional and sexual interests. These included an assertion of women's rights to enjoy sex, to have it before marriage without incurring criticism, and to control contraception and thus their own fertility. There was also pressure for what would have been widely considered as more radical options, including an end to discrimination against lesbians, a firmer line against wife-beating, and the legalization of abortion. In many cases such options very much confronted established social assumptions.

Aside from demands for legal changes, feminism also led to pressure for changes in lifestyles and for social arrangements that put women's needs and expectations in a more central position. Jobs and lifestyle became more important as aspirations for women, complementing, rather than replacing, home and family. Indeed, women ceased to be seen largely in terms of family units – as daughters, spinsters, wives, mothers and widows – and instead many benefited greatly from a major increase in opportunities and rights, and from a widespread shift in social attitudes and expectations.

Religious divisions in the approach to women, however, remained. Unlike Protestant churches, the Catholic Church retained its firm opposition to the ordination of women as priests, while the sense of Turkey as different to Europe was amplified after 2002 when the Justice and Development Party came to power. Its proposed 'modernization' of the constitution included removing the clause decreeing equality between the sexes. Attitudes to women within Muslim communities challenged laws and conventions on human rights across much of Europe, with particular sensitivity about arranged marriages (notably in Britain), polygamy, female circumcision (especially in France) and honour killings. The 2004 French ban on prominent religious symbols in state schools was designed to stop the wearing of the Muslim headscarf and veil.

The limited role of ecclesiastical conventions was demonstrated in the political sphere where women rose to the top. From 1972 to 1976 Anemarie Renger served as the First Woman to the President (Speaker) of the West German Bundestag. Margaret Thatcher, Gro Harlem

Brundtland and Edith Cresson were the first female prime ministers of Britain (1979–90), Norway (1981, 1986–9 and 1990–96) and France (1991–2) respectively, while Vigdis Finnbogadóttir became President of Iceland in 1980, Mary Robinson was President of Ireland from 1990 to 1997 and Angela Merkel was Chancellor of Germany in 2005. Across much of Europe by the 1990s, when women were seen in terms of their relationship to men and to families, the emphasis was much more on their independence, and this was particularly true of role models. Thus, in 2007–8, the French president, Nicolas Sarkozy, was divorced as a result of his wife's initiative, and then began a relationship with a former model, Carla Bruni, noted for her free-living. The contrast with former presidents (especially with François Mitterrand), who had had longstanding adulterous relationships with women kept in the shadows, was very noticeable, and was commented on by Sarkozy who went on to marry Bruni in 2008. Some, however, view her as a trophy wife.

Variations in the public treatment of women were pushed to the fore with the growth of mass tourism and of related temporary (second homes) or permanent settlement. This process was especially the case in the Mediterranean as northern Europeans had very different conventions about the display of the female body to those of local societies, although the latter themselves varied. For example, Spain under Franco and strongly Catholic Malta were far less liberal than France or Communist Yugoslavia. The pressure of profit and numbers ultimately told in leading to liberalization, but so also did a relaxation of former constraints and inhibitions, notably in Spain. Social change was pushed further with the growth of even cheaper mass tourism from the late 1990s and British and Irish cut-price airlines developed networks elsewhere in Europe, moving yet more tourists toward the Mediterranean. This growth in foreign tourism contributed to a degree of homogenization in social behaviour or at least in customs, such as cuisine. Other factors are also in play across Europe in encouraging homogenization, notably the impact of urbanization, trade and advertising.

Another instance of similarity in diversity was provided by the rise in the female workforce across the Continent. Opportunity played a major role in this rise, not least with the growth in service jobs and light manufacturing. The strength of existing constraints – institutional, political, social and cultural – was also important. These factors over-lapped, although there were also important tensions and variations. Within the labour force the frequently restrictive attitude of trade unions to women workers was important: there was hostility to the idea of throwing open all form of work to fair competition and there was also a determination to retain higher pay for work seen as male. Moreover, political constraints were embedded in systems that were very much dominated by male assumptions, not that these were uniform. Alongside a reluctance to pass anti-discriminatory laws, and to establish good state child-care provision of the type that existed in Sweden and (at least in theory) in Communist states, there was also support for child-rearing at home, as with legislation passed by the conservative Kohl government in Germany in 1986.

Gender was an issue for men as well as women, although this was very much downplayed as part of the focus on female consciousness. The loss of empires and the end of conscription in most countries affected notions of masculinity and also gendered constructions of citizenship. That imperial loss was at the hands of non-Western forces added a racial dimension. Within Europe less emphasis was placed on what had been seen as masculine values, and some of these values, for example military service, were questioned, indeed mocked.

This questioning was part of a change in the image of masculinity. The decline of manual work, agricultural, industrial and mining, the growing importance, in numbers, prominence and seniority, of women workers, the feminization of a range of occupations, such as medicine, and the rise of feminism, all contributed to the same sense of changing, indeed in some contexts imperilled, masculinity. A sense of men as discontented because they were disempowered became an issue of social policy, because there was growing and widespread concern about anti-social behaviour among young men and about their readiness to neglect the obligations of parenthood.

Moreover, homosexuality became a more prominent issue in the discussion of masculinity, especially in religious denominations, and also an issue in identity. Homosexuality was legalized and the age of consent was equalized with that for heterosexuals, even in repressive East Germany in 1988. Such legalization increased the number of possible identities that people could adopt, or by which they could be categorized. Homosexuality was also increasingly a subject in the arts, for example in Fassbinder's film *The Bitter Tears of Petra von Kant* (1972).

These identities also opened up the potential for new lines of tension, as in the Netherlands in the early 2000s when a call by two imams for the death penalty for homosexuals led the openly homosexual politician Pim Fortuyn to campaign in Rotterdam on a policy directed against Muslim immigration. His Liveable Rotterdam movement did well in the Rotterdam council elections in 2002, although he was assassinated later that year. The movement then made an impact in the national elections, although Fortuyn's death meant that it lacked focus. However, Liveable Rotterdam reflected not only marked anxiety at local level, but also the extent to which this anxiety was not restricted to failed sections of the working class, as was frequently implied in discussion of racism. Fortuyn, indeed, was able to broaden the support for his anti-immigration party to the middle class, although his core success in Rotterdam was at the expense of the Socialists, who had held an absolute majority there for over 40 years. The anti-Islamism Fortuyn introduced in Dutch politics is still important, as can be seen in the subsequent ascent of Geert Wilders, and rejects the continuing impact of Islamic terrorism in the international arena, the admiration and support for it by a segment of the Dutch Islamic community, particularly the young, and the inability of a political culture, based on consensus and tolerance, to deal with this problem.

Changes in the position of women influenced social patterns, not least because of the tendency to have spouses and partners from a similar social background. Thus, greater opportunities for women in part entrenched social divisions. These opportunities owed much to social trends, but public policy was very important. Thus, a comparison of Austria with Communist Hungary indicates that a higher percentage of women in the latter gained success and recognition in employment, in part due to government policies. Conversely, discrimination against women in the workplace was stronger in Austria, as it also was in other Catholic countries. The Protestant percentage of the population was higher in Hungary than in Austria. At the same time, there was no equality of treatment for women in Hungary, and the same was true in other Communist states, such as Bulgaria, where, by 1987, 49.8 per cent of the labour force was female. Male suppositions remained dominant in these states, whatever the state of public rhetoric.

In Albania the pre-Communist subordination of women remained insistent despite the language of equality and an expansion in the education of women. One of the major exceptions, but again, like the vitality of kinship networks and village identification, indicative of the strength of pre-Communist practices, was that of 'sworn virgins', women who were allowed to retain a degree of independence and, crucially, to own property, because they swore to remain unmarried. As an indication of the subordination expected to flow from marriage and of the role of public symbolization, only these women were permitted to smoke in public.

The position of women in Eastern Europe in part changed with the fall of Communism, although anti-discrimination rhetoric remained central to the public sphere. This rhetoric was increasingly standardized across Europe and, at the same time, public policy in Western Europe became more uniform and less discriminatory, which affected in particular Catholic countries, so that in Austria in the 1990s the position of women in the job market notably improved. In contrast, in Croatia and Russia in the 1990s nationalists sought to use pro-natalist propaganda and policies in order to build up their 'people', although they did so in terms of traditional patriarchal themes. Whereas in post-1945 Yugoslavia the rhetoric had been egalitarian, in the 1990s, as part of the effort to create nationally homogeneous entities, women were pressed to adopt new symbolic roles. Nationalist-focused Croatia advocated a trinity of 'home, nation and God', with the female role in the family seen as a means to preserve traditional values and thus the national consciousness. Feminist organizations resisted, but a more potent resistance arose as a result of the need to work. The same was true of Russia but there, as in Croatia, the need for women to work was ignored by government.

Women were particularly hard hit by the successive economic crises that struck Yugoslavia after the death of its president, Marshal Tito, in 1980. They struggled with the purchasing problems created by high inflation and scarcities and, especially, when the economic crises eased, with the inadequate provision of day-care and other child-care services necessary if they were to enter the labour market. So also with anti-abortion policies and opposition to divorce: female views in favour of the options for abortion and divorce were ignored, but governmental effectiveness in limiting both was limited. Governmental family policies in these cases indicated the profoundly conservative nature of nationalism, not least because it is often a response to insecurity. As an indicator of the number of factors involved, the pro-natalist policies were less successful, particularly in Russia, than their interwar predecessors in Italy and Germany.

More generally, permissive measures across Europe were crucial in the developing role of women, especially in the shape of the spread of educational opportunity. Women benefited particularly greatly from the expansion of university education. Proscriptive legislation was also important. For example, in Norway a law passed in 2003 decreed that from 2008 at least 40 per cent of the directors of public companies had to be women, which led to an increase overall from 7 to 36 per cent, a percentage considerably higher than that in senior management positions. Similarly, in 2007 the Dutch decreed that all schools had to provide afternoon child-care, a measure seen as necessary in order to boost the percentage of women involved in full-time work, which indeed was low by British standards.

Throughout Europe equal pay legislation was important given the pay gap between the sexes in favour of men. This gap narrowed over the period, a narrowing that reflected not only legislation, but also the success of women in managerial grades and the major role of the public-sector employment in which such legislation was more scrupulously implemented. Yet the pay gap remained while opportunities for women were set within very varied economic circumstances. This can be seen, for example, with the position of women in former East Germany. Some benefited from the changes offered by unification, but others suffered from the weaknesses of family, work and neighbourhood support systems, weaknesses which owed much to large-scale migration to West Germany and to a different attitude on the part of post-Communist employers. Moreover, industrial transformation hit the economic prospects of many women who did not migrate, with numerous factories closing, although the service sector provided other opportunities.

As a reminder, however, of the variation of circumstances within Europe, the use of rape as a deliberate weapon was seen in the conflicts in former Yugoslavia in the 1990s, with possibly 50,000 Bosnian women subjected to sexual violence. The contrast with public policy across Europe was brutally stark. A more continuous form of violence against women was represented by the sexual trafficking that became more prominent after the end of the Iron Curtain, with Albanian crime syndicates particularly active in moving women from Eastern to Western Europe. This prostitution was linked to rape and to the deliberate encouragement of drug addiction in order to enforce control. Governments struggled with considerable difficulty to respond to this problem. Criminalizing prostitution made scant impact on the gangs, which encouraged some countries, particularly Sweden, to criminalize the purchasers of services. The widespread nature of prostitution, for example in provincial Russia today, is a stark comment on the nature of society and individual relations for many people, both men and women.

A different direction of concern about the intersection of crime and sexuality was provided by paedophile scandals that suggested both a high level of paedophilia and a degree of complicity by parts of the legal system, which was especially true of the Dutroux scandal in Belgium. Convicted of paedophilia before 1996, Dutroux, however, was released, and the sense of national shame led to the White March in April 1996 with 300,000 Belgians marching through the streets of Brussels. In 1998 Dutroux even managed to escape from a courtroom although he was recaptured later that day. Public anger with police and judicial incompetence (not to say a degree of complicity) led to the Octopus Accord in 1998 in which the Belgian government tried to reform both.

Accusations of and convictions for paedophilia, also seen in the Outreau affair in France, as well as in Britain and elsewhere, indicated the strength of uneasiness about the sexual portrayal of children, which had become more common due to the possibilities for pornographic distribution created by the Internet. Whether paedophilia was more common than in the past became an issue of controversy, but it was certainly perceived as more of a problem. In part this perception reflected the role of the media in creating an atmosphere of concern. This atmosphere was an aspect of the troubled culture of the period, for the portrayal and treatment of children captured unease about sexuality, consumerism, order and, indeed, the possibility of innocence itself.

The mentality of the witch-hunt was also at play, as in Toulouse in France in 2003 when, in the *Seconde Affaire Alègre*, there were accusations of sado-masochistic orgies linking magistrates and the police to pimps, prostitutes and drugs, with murder, rape, torture and corruption allegedly all part of the brew. Such paranoid fantasies are far from new but they also reflect a social uneasiness about sex and power that lends itself to personal antagonism and to media campaigns. That child abuse was particularly associated with (a few) Catholic clergy, and with related cover-ups, for example in Ireland in 1994, added both to the conspiracy theories that were important in public culture and to the difficulties of positioning sex and power in any account of European society and culture in this period.

EUROPE IN CRISIS

If consumerism was a driving force in society, the economy and politics, the terms by which it would have an impact were actively debated and a matter for political contention and governmental action. This context was more apparent than in the USA where consumerism, in contrast, was very much a matter of individualism, increasingly unshaped by professional structures, although it was heavily guided by corporate pressures, especially advertising and pricing. The American model, however, also pertained in Europe, although with a greater role for government. Thus major projects to build international-level golf courses in Scotland and Spain were supported by local government in 2007–8, the latter part of a regional scheme for a 'European Las Vegas' that was backed by the government of Aragón. Tension over competing types of consumerism was accentuated because technological change led to newly affordable products, such as the Internet, which helped ensure a dynamic character to the debate over how to respond to consumerism. Political and ideological legacies were also important to the debate, not least collectivist pressures, practices of governmental direction, and anti-capitalist discourses.

Understanding the social background of the period in terms of powerful consumerist pressures ensures that the dependence of politics on society is underlined, and in a different fashion to the Marxist and other structural accounts of society discussed earlier in the chapter. This focus on consumerism emphasizes the role of behaviour in social classification and expression. By spending, people identify: they assert their individuality but also their conformity to particular images. Within Europe the range of groups through which to identify, and with which it is possible to conform, increased, which has greatly contributed to a sense of fragmentation. This range of possible identification is at once an aspect of freedom but also the product of the insistence of a visual culture in which ideas and images of style are propagated more powerfully than ever before.

Ideas and images of style also change more rapidly than before. This rapidity can be attributed to the pressures of an economic system that needs the regular purchase of new ideas and products irrespective of questions of obsolescence and utilitarianism, but that approach is a needlessly mechanistic analysis of societies in which the consumer is not simply a ductile product of market forces, just as, despite suggestions to the contrary, libertarian tendencies have not been squeezed out by the surveillance capabilities of the regulatory state. Relations between systems of consumption and control and the people in practice are far more complex, not least because these systems work if their values are internalized by the public.

Alongside these top-down pressures, indeed, can be seen the higher aggregate and (over the long term) per capita wealth of the population and its greater access to education. Each contributes to an individualism and breaking down of old social bonds that pose great problems for business and, even more, for government. Most obviously, the state determination of need and benefit epitomized by Communism failed totally, but Socialist echoes have only succeeded in part and then principally with the more vulnerable in the community. In Britain the impotence of the Blair government, despite its parliamentary majority, in the face of public hostility to higher fuel prices was particularly instructive. The difficulties faced across Europe in pension reform are another demonstration of governmental weakness in the face of an articulate and independent society that does not regard the electoral mandate as conferring control. This weakness is given constitutional depth by the independent role of the law.

As far as business is concerned control is again challenged by individualism, which has become far more pronounced over the last decade as consumers have responded to the opportunities offered by different providers across the range of communications services. Moreover, national monopolies or *de facto* cartels have been far more effectively challenged by other EU providers than in the first four decades of its history. The conclusion is one of an interchange, with business and government trying to benefit from and structure the opportunities and problems created by societies in which many assert their autonomy through a determination to avoid fixing and dictation through classification.

This chapter can be combined with the material on demographic trends in Chapter 3 to ask, as is sometimes suggested, whether European society is in crisis, not least in a comparative context. There is the argument that American society, despite its many problems, is healthier, more dynamic, meritocratic, mobile and growing, than that of Europe, and that this contrast is important as a description and proof of European or, at least, Western European failure. If all or part of this analysis is adopted, there is also the question of whether this situation is the inevitable result of longer-term trends and a more profound European failure, or whether problems are more contingent and specific. The discussion in the next chapter throws some light on these issues.

Chapter 5

Ideology and Culture

Lenin Shipyard, Gdansk, Poland, August 1980. A picture of John Paul II, the Polish pope, is hung on the front gate.

The cultural trends of the 1960s, 1970s and 1980s appeared readily apparent and coherent to many contemporary commentators but, looking back, this clarity seems far less obvious from the perspective of today. The current lack of certainty is true in particular of secularism, which was a dominant trend as far as commentators were concerned and one that underlay the standard account of 1960s values. Unexpectedly, however, to the many outsiders who had failed to understand the nature of Eastern European societies under Communism, the fall of the Iron Curtain revealed and reflected the continual strength of Christianity in the most secularist of state systems. Perhaps in part this strength arose from the degree to which the Church offered a home to opposition movements, but that is too reductionist an account of religion. Whichever position is adopted, to begin an account of ideology and culture with a discussion of religion represents a very different approach to what would have been the norm.

At the same time the general trend across the continent as a whole in the late twentieth century and the 2000s continued to be one that posed serious problems for organized religion, and this was very important in itself, as well as for other aspects of thought and action. The established churches were challenged greatly by the expansion of state activities, by political measures, and by social trends, each of which is important, although there was also a considerable overlap between them. The expansion of state agencies in education, health and social welfare challenged the place of religious bodies in these spheres, and thus of churches as a whole, while the pace of social change, particularly of migration, put great pressure on the religious ministry and its ability to reach out successfully to the population. Moreover, aside from the current of secularism and skepticism, there was a marginalization of the role of churches among many who considered themselves religious.

Across Europe the churches were affected from the 1960s by general social currents, especially the decline of deference, of patriarchal authority, social paternalism, the nuclear family and respect for age. In part these social characteristics had also been challenged by the communitarian norms of Communist societies. However, the insecurity resulting from the arbitrary and harsh policies of these regimes, and their failure to fulfil promises of social security, ensured that in the Communist years there was a continued need for non-state systems of identity and support and thus a powerful social place for religion.

To a certain extent social trends across Europe interacted with intellectual fashions, as did government policy. The public role of religion, as a source of ideology and morality, was widely condemned by self-styled progressives. Moreover, as a private source of meaning, hope and faith, religion was treated in some circles as a delusion best clarified, like sexuality, by an understanding of anthropology, psychology and sociology. As such, religion was subject to the scrutiny of relativism, a powerful intellectual charge against established beliefs. More generally, the stress on the subconscious and, in particular, on repressed sexuality, in the psychoanalytical methods developed by Sigmund Freud (1856–1939) and in the psychological theories of the Swiss psychiatrist Carl Gustav Jung (1875–1961), increasingly entered the mainstream. These ideas challenged conventional ideas of human behaviour and also affected the arts, as writers, composers and others sought to explore psychological states.

Radical intellectual influences contributed to a sense of flux and also to established norms and values being seen as simply passing conventions. Structuralism, a movement that looked to the anthropologist Claude Lévi-Strauss (1908–) and the French literary critic Roland Barthes (1915–1980), treated language as a set of conventions that were themselves of limited value as guides to any underlying reality. Although links (like definitions) were far from clear cut, this looked towards the Postmodernism that became influential in intellectual and cultural circles in the 1980s and in some respects, with its stress on the difficulties of asserting meaning, was a culture of despair. Moreover, Existentialism, a post-1945 nihilistic philosophical movement closely associated with Martin Heidegger (1889–1976) and Jean-Paul Sartre (1905–1980), stressed the vulnerability of the individual in a hostile world. Heidegger presented choice as an empty possibility while Sartre, who backtracked on Existentialism by going along with Marxism, saw it as a necessary duty.

The impact of such ideas on those who devised policy is unclear, although Postmodernism tended to begin by denying right and wrong or purpose, but always ended by privileging Socialism. At any rate culture, philosophy in particular, has (and had) a far greater prominence in public life on the Continent than it does in Britain. For all their defects leaders such as François Mitterrand were highly cultured men. France was notable for this (although Nicolas Sarkozy is no intellectual or writer, unlike his one-time rival Dominique de Villepin), but Germany and Italy were little different, and this situation completely altered the texture of public debate and gave apparent legitimacy to positions, especially on the left, which are thought totally irrelevant elsewhere.

Not all the changes in policy directly related to the authority of the Church, as those on abortion and divorce did. For example, abolition of the death penalty, as in France after the Socialists gained power under Mitterrand in 1981, reflected a powerful liberal plank. It had already been abolished in West Germany in 1949; East Germany followed in 1987. Yet even if not all changes directly related to the authority of the Church, nevertheless, in many respects, permissive 'social legislation' flew in the face of religious teachings and left the churches confused and apparently lacking in relevance. This lack of relevance was particularly serious for an age that, on the whole, placed more of an emphasis on present-mindedness than on continuity with historical roots and teachings. As far as Christianity was concerned, belief lessened in orthodox Christian theology, especially in the nature of Jesus as the Son of God, and in the after-life, the Last Judgement and the existence of Hell. Moreover, the public perception of religion, as captured on television, in plays or in films such as *The Da Vinci Code*, was frequently critical. Furthermore, the churches found the laity willing to condemn, as well as to cease, religious observance.

Most prominently, the hold of the largest Christian Church in Europe, the Catholic Church, over many of its communicants was lessened by widespread hostility towards the ban on artificial methods of contraception in the 1968 papal encyclical *Humanae Vitae*, which was written by Paul VI (pope 1963–78) himself. Conservative influences in the Catholic Church were challenged and resisted by liberal theologians, most prominently Hans Küng, a Swiss Catholic priest, Professor of Theology at Tübingen and adviser to the ground-breaking Second Vatican Council, summoned by Pope John XXIII in 1962. Küng denied the teaching of papal infallibility in *Infallible? An Inquiry* (1971) and was eventually stripped of his right to teach as a Catholic theologian (1979). Thereafter he became a liberal Catholic, accusing Pope John Paul II (1978–2005) of turning the Church against the Second Vatican Council and toward extreme conservative doctrines. Küng eventually embraced the idea of married clergy. He, however, was a marginal figure compared to John Paul II, who was a towering presence during his years as pope, and who enjoyed huge prominence, not least by a very astute blending of old doctrines with an up-to-date use of the media.

Lacking the conservatism associated with Paul VI and, even more, John Paul II, for example in his account of Catholic moral teaching in the encyclical *Veritatis Splendor* (1993), change in the Protestant churches proved more insistent. There were common features with the Catholic Church including a clergy who placed less of an emphasis on formality and more on inner conviction. Nevertheless, the Protestant clergy proved more willing than their Catholic counterparts to adopt heterodox causes, to become openly politicized, to propound an alternative theology, and not to preach the Gospel.

A supporter of the veneration of saints, particularly the Virgin Mary, and a strong opponent of the idea of a married clergy, John Paul II proved especially keen on promoting conservative clerics and on canonizing more saints than any earlier Pope. His interventions, for example in beatifying clerics who had been killed by Republicans during the Spanish Civil War (1936–9), were very much on the conservative side. This position was continued under his protégé, theological enforcer and successor, Benedict XVI, leading to controversy in October 2007, with charges from the left that the papacy was ignoring the partisan role of the Church during the Civil War. Nearly 500 priests, nuns and monks killed by the Republicans in the 1930s were beatified. In contrast, clergy killed by the (Francoist) Nationalists were not beatified, which was justified by the Church on the grounds that they had been fighting for a political cause and were not killed due to their ecclesiastical position.

Benedict XVI also continued his predecessor's partisan support for conservative clerics. For example, the recently appointed members of the Bavarian episcopate are hardliners. The net effect was a more doctrinally conservative and centrally directed Catholic Church. Benedict XVI, the German-born Joseph Ratzinger, had become more conservative in his attitudes in part in opposition to the student activism of 1968, which he saw as a challenge to the Church. At that time he was a priest teaching theology at the University of Tübingen. In 1981 he was appointed by John Paul II to head the Congregation for the Defence of the Faith, the body charged with maintaining Catholic orthodoxy. In this role he was regarded as John Paul II's 'enforcer'.

Aside from tensions within churches there was also a long-established challenge to Christianity from cults. Both 'new age' religions, sometimes based on pre-Christian animist beliefs or, rather, what were held to be these beliefs, and, more fashionably, Buddhism appealed from the 1960s to many who would otherwise have been active Christians. These beliefs reflected a widespread crisis of confidence in the Western values of enlightenment, notably rationalism and science. For many, the cults proved better able than the churches to capture the enthusiasm of those who wished to believe amidst a material world where faith had become just another commodity. The popularity of cults was also a reflection of the atomization of societies that now placed a premium on individualism, self-expression and personal responses, rather than on long-established practices legitimated by a historically grounded and organized faith.

As far as Western Europe was concerned it is unclear whether an earlier decline of religious belief and practice had not itself permitted the development of a more individualistic society in the 1960s, or whether the society of the 1960s had caused that decline. The diversity of the 1960s and subsequent decades complicates the situation as far as both description and analysis are concerned. So also does our limited knowledge and understanding of popular religion and folk belief. It is unclear, for example, how best to understand the popularity of astrology and, in particular, how far this popularity should be seen as compatible with Christianity, or as an aspect of a magical or non-Christian religious worldview.

Christianity did not collapse in Western Europe but it certainly declined. By 2006 church attendance rates in Ireland, Italy and Spain, all formerly noted for Catholic devotion, had fallen to below 20 per cent, while in Lutheran Sweden, where there is a close connection of church and state, the percentage had fallen to 5 per cent. On the whole the decline was stronger in Protestant than in Catholic Europe, and notably so with the Church of Scotland and the Church of England. This contrast was also true of Eastern Europe, with Catholicism stronger in Poland and Lithuania than Lutheranism was in Estonia.

The indications of decline varied. The number of vocations for the priesthood fell, spectacularly so in Ireland, and this ensured that shared ministers became more common, which greatly challenged the relationship between cleric and parish. Many church buildings, moreover, were sold, as in Britain and the Netherlands. Fewer Catholics went to confession. Alongside changes in the fabric of religious life came a tendency on the part of political parties hitherto locating themselves as Christian to dissociate themselves from this tradition, as with Angela Merkel, the German Christian Democratic leader, in 2005. Nevertheless, in Germany the established churches continued to be supported by a national church tax.

Moreover, across Europe, there were still many committed Christians, as well as a large number of conforming non-believers. Thus in Spain, where about three-quarters of the population class themselves as Catholic, the Church supported large demonstrations against the legalization of gay marriage in 2005 and helped get over 150,000 followers onto the streets of Madrid in December 2007 for 'Christian Family Day', an attack on the social policies of the Socialist government. Tensions increased after the Socialists' re-election in March 2008, and Benedict xvi has identified Spain as a key battle-ground against secularism. The Opus Dei movement of committed Catholic laity, a movement encouraged by John Paul ii, has proved influential in Spain, linking Catholic activism with politics.

From his election in 2005 Benedict xvi has been very supportive of the constant commentary by Italian bishops on the politics of the Italian state. In the case of opposition to the left-of-centre Prodi govern-ment of 2006–8 the Church's attitude reflected rejection of state support for homosexual civil partnerships, but even more of the government's proposals for partially withdrawing support, particularly fiscal relief, to private schools. In Italy these are nearly all Catholic and their academic quality is generally poor. At the start of 2008 the politi-cal pressure that helped lead to the fall of the government owed much to Catholic activism.

Aside from political activism there was an upsurge in some reli-gious practices. For example, pilgrimages by Catholics became more common, notably to Lourdes in France and Jasna Góra in Poland, but also to other sites, including Santiago de Compostela in Spain, Fatima in Portugal, Knock in Ireland and, more recently, Medjugorje in Bosnia. Far from becoming redundant, pilgrimages benefited from the grow-ing availability of low-price air flights, an aspect of the degree to which (as it always has been) modernity was not without important possibil-ities for religion. In contrast other traditional aspects of Christian activity became less popular and more marginal, for example monasti-cism, which withered due to a lack of vocations. Thus lay activism was a central aspect of Catholic practice.

Some established Protestant churches also saw manifestations of traditionalist energy. Within the Finnish Lutheran Church there is the strong Laestadian religious movement. Conservative and fundamen-talist, this movement opposes abortion and still, in some cases, television and the theatre.

Moreover, at the same time as Christianity declined overall in its traditional manifestation of established churches, there were important signs of energy in some of the non-established churches. The impact of the USA was seen in the growth of Pentecostalism and, to a lesser extent, Mormonism and Scientology. The Church of Scientology, which has an imposing headquarters in Berlin, was the focus of much debate in Germany in the 2000s. There was also a major growth in non-established churches ministering to Christian immigrants, especially from Africa, such as the Nigerian-based Redeemed Christian Church of God and the Brazilian-based Universal Church of the Kingdom of God. Evangelicalism and charismatics were also of growing significance within the established churches, both Protestant and Catholic, but particularly the former.

The relationship with continued religious faith is far from clear, but there was also a strong, albeit often secret, commitment to less systemic aspects of providentialism. Ranging from wise women to horoscopes, this was not simply a residual feature that was a matter of frontier or rural areas, such as Petrich in Bulgaria, where in the 1960s and 1970s Baba Vanga, an elderly blind soothsayer, had a massive following, but also of urban life.

Yet, both for most Christian believers and for the less or non-religious, faith became less important, not only to the fabric of life but also to many of the turning points of individual lives, such as death, although the role of the churches in the rise of the hospice movement qualified this. Events such as marriage ceremonies and baptisms declined in significance as occasions for displays of family and social cohesion, and this also lessened the role of Christian symbolism in the socializing of children. This decline was due to the simple fact that more couples were choosing to live together (rather than marrying), and more parents were choosing not to have their children baptized. Such trends were particularly the case in urban areas.

This shift in the display of faith and in social cohesion through church-based activities was true of Christian societies that were formerly noted for their devotion and for the authority of the Church. Contraception, for example, became more common in Catholic societies such as Italy. In Ireland, there were legal and political battles over divorce (legalized in 1994), homosexuality, contraception and abortion (rejected in a 2002 referendum), as the authority of the Catholic Church was contested. The same was true of Spain, with firm opposition by the Church and its lay allies to abortion, gay marriage, divorce and the removal of the obligation to study religion at school.

Abortion is permitted in Ireland only if the mother's life is at risk, and the 'right to life' of the unborn baby is enshrined in the constitution. There are similar restrictions in Poland and Spain, whereas most of Europe has a more liberal position, particularly in much of Eastern Europe where over half of pregnancies lead to abortions in most countries, the rates being highest in Romania (about three-quarters) and Russia (about two-thirds). Abortion at these rates can be seen as becoming a form of contraception. Abortion was banned in Romania in 1966 but illegal abortions were widespread, although large numbers of women died as a result. The post-Communist regime rapidly legalized abortion, leading to a very significant rise in its frequency, with over 200,000 annual cases in the mid 2000s. Cristian Mungiu's *4 Months, 3 Weeks and 2 Days* (2007), which won the Palme d'Or at the Cannes film festival in 2007, addressed abortion during the Communist years, presenting it in terms of difficult personal choices. In Western Europe the abortion rate was, and is, considerably lower and contraception is very much seen as the prime form of birth control. More exceptionally, in the Netherlands euthanasia became an issue for discussion and then legislation.

Education proved a particular battleground over religion, as indeed it had since the late nineteenth century. Governments on both sides of the Iron Curtain sought to limit the role of the churches in education. In part this was due to a struggle for control, with the education of the young seen as the major sphere of indoctrination. There was also a related issue of the competence of the state as opposed to that of the voluntarist sector, with established churches, which had once been seen as integral to the state, now banished to this sector alongside other voluntary groups. In part this was an aspect of the decline of these churches. Once they lost their monopoly or dominant position, and became simply one 'provider' of religious 'services', then the alternative to state provision ceased to be clear cut. In response religious bodies argued the case for a special position and notably for their role in education. In France in 1984 there were major demonstrations against the Socialist government's attempt to cut subsidies to private Catholic schools, which was correctly seen as motivated by a desire for secularization. On 24 June 1984 a million people marched in Paris against the bill, leading Mitterrand to announce its withdrawal on television. Such demonstrations, however, tend to be ignored in a narrative of protest focused on politics. This narrative is anti-conservative in the West, with the key story being 1968, and anti-Communist in the East, with the key story being 1989. A demand for change is the common theme in this narrative. The extent to which, in contrast, demonstrators could also be motivated by conservative goals proved far less attractive as a story.

Sex education was a particularly contentious aspect of education, not least because the earlier practice of revealing little was held to cause repression, while in contrast critics of sex education argued that it was responsible for promiscuity. The debate reflected the politicized nature of moral issues, and also the attempt to challenge church and family as spheres for moral education and administration.

Aside from pressures on the churches there was also a major shift in the character of Christian worship, not least with a greater role for feminine ministry and an associated feminization of aspects of theology. These developments reflected the degree to which religious practice and belief variously recorded, refracted and resisted social and intellectual changes. The decline in the emphasis on theology in the Protestant churches made them particularly open to social trends.

As a reflection of political aspirations there was also, particularly within Christianity, a development of ecumenicalism that lessened earlier divisions. Ecumenicalism had more of an impact intellectually and socially than institutionally, not least because of Catholic opposition to female ordination, but it was still important, especially between Protestant churches, and between Protestant and Catholic and Protestant and Orthodox clerics. In contrast the Orthodox church was more wary of the claims of the papacy, which asserted primacy, but once the Catholic Church moved away from the idea of reunion based on papal authority, an ecumenical dialogue began.

The secularist position that could be seen in Western Europe, especially from the 1960s, and in Iberia from the 1970s, was not matched in Eastern Europe and Russia. There, Communism failed to engage the affection of most of the population, although Party membership was often considered a wise career move and the figures for membership reflected this. Instead, to a considerable although far from universal extent, religion in Eastern Europe provided a powerful sense of identity as well as spiritual meaning. This was true of countries trying to respond to Soviet hegemony, most particularly Poland and Lithuania, in each of which Catholicism was strong, but religion as a source of identity was also the case in Russia where the Orthodox Church retained the support of much of the population and revived rapidly as a public force from 1991. Under Communist regimes, however, religion could also be seen by the government as an important symbolic force for identity and a form of regime stabilization. In Bulgaria the Communist regime spent heavily on restoring churches in the late 1970s, as an aspect of the national heritage, while in East Germany the Protestant Church was given partial autonomy in the same period. Yet government uneasiness about the role of religion continued, and the Solidarity movement in Poland, in which Catholicism played a major role, was regarded as a warning by other Communist regimes. In East Germany the Ministry for State Security, *Stasi*, spied on and sought to infiltrate the Protestant Church, which, indeed, played a role in the early stages of the anti-Communist reform movement in late 1989.

The situation of the churches changed with the fall of Communism. The revival in the public position of the Orthodox Church in Russia from 1991 was seen in townscapes and public memorialization, with the building of new churches and also with religion more prominently linked to the presentation of the past. Thus in Leningrad the secular 1970s monument commemorating the city's successful resistance to German forces in the Second World War and the eventual relief by Soviet forces was joined, in the 1990s, in what was now renamed St Petersburg, by a church to the same end. In 1998, with the support of Vladimir Putin, the remains of those members of the Romanov dynasty slaughtered by the Communists during the Russian Revolution were buried in an Orthodox cathedral in St Petersburg. This reburial was an indication of a more general search for historical resonance as nationalism was pushed to the fore in the post-Communist years. The massive Cathedral of Christ the Saviour in Moscow, demolished by Stalin in 1931, was rebuilt from 1997 to 2000, when it was reconsecrated on the Feast of the Transfiguration. Boris Yeltsin was given a lying-in-state and funeral there, becoming the first Russian ruler since Tsar Alexander III died in 1894 to receive an Orthodox funeral. In 2007 Vladimir Putin attended the Easter Vigil in the Cathedral and praised the role of the Orthodox Church and, on Ascension Day, he attended a ceremony there marking the reunification of the domestic and exiled branches of the Church, thus associating the state with this act and with the legitimation it was seen to provide. Religious validation was also sought and displayed elsewhere. When in 2004 Mikhail Saakashvili became President of Georgia, he first went to a revered monastery, founded by Georgia's most famous monarch, in order to receive a blessing.

In Russia the Orthodox Church provided support to the Putin government and, in turn, benefited greatly from its protection. The even-handed position of the Russian government toward different faiths in the early 1990s under Yeltsin was swept aside, and Protestants suffered in particular, while there was a significant growth of anti-Semitism in Russia and in Eastern Europe in general. This is a reminder that religious tensions were not limited to hotspots such as Northern Ireland and, more seriously, Yugoslavia. There, religion combined with (and helped to define) ethnicity from 1991, with the effect of wrecking the unity of the country and causing a bloody and protracted series of conflicts. Catholic Croats, Orthodox Serbs and Muslim Bosnians and Albanians (in Kosovo) proved the major protagonists. These developments caused more of a surprise for commentators who had assumed that religion was in some fashion a redundant force, than for those aware of its central role in popular culture and in social structures.

There was also growing concern about the ability of Western European states to assimilate their Muslim minorities. In 2004 the European Court of Human Rights found reliance on *sharia*, Islamic law, incompatible with democratic practice in Europe, not least because of *sharia*'s murderous response to apostasy and its treatment of women, and because this law interferes in many aspects of private life. Alongside concern, there was division over the policy to follow toward Muslim minorities, with a continuum from compulsory integration, as in banning headscarves in French state schools and other public buildings in 2004, to multi-culturalism. The latter was intended by governments to secure integration by the acceptance of different cultural and social norms, but some (maybe many) Muslims did not see multi-culturalism as a two-way street, especially in so far as accepting both secular practices and the authority of the state was concerned. The large-scale French riots in 2005 made the question of assimilation more prominent, as did the decision by the Conseil d'Etat in 2008 that nationality should be rejected on the grounds of 'lack of assimilation'. Multi-culturalism is an issue for churches as well as states.

REGIONALISM AND NATIONALISM

The continued salience of religion indicated the multiplicity of identities that co-existed in Europe. An important identity which also grew in prominence during the period, was that of regionalism. This became more significant as a source for popular identity, especially across much of Western Europe, although it is not always clear that regionalism describes what were really attempts to secure separate identities within a federal state. The latter was certainly the case in Belgium. Regionalism was also pushed in Spain, where autonomy enjoyed majority support in the Basque Country and Catalonia in particular. As in Scotland this regionalism was, in source and aspiration, a proto-nationalism, and one of the key thrusts linking ideology and culture in this period was the strength of such nationalism. Its manifestations varied but a stress on ethnicity was a crucial element. This stress was also true, within France, in Corsica and Brittany.

The least attractive product of proto-nationalism was violence, as with ETA and the IRA, terrorist movements for Basque and Irish nationalism respectively, and an ethnic hatred seen most viciously in the former Yugoslavia in the 1990s. The brutal slaughter of civilians by the

Serbs (and, to a lesser extent, by their opponents) reflected the extent to which ethnic groups were regarded as the units of political strength and thus as targets. In 1995 the Bosnian Serbs murdered about 7,000 unarmed Muslim males in Srebrenica alone, although what was termed 'ethnic cleansing' – the expulsion of members of an ethnic group – was more common. It was generally associated with the Serbs but was also used by the Croats against the Serbs, for example in the Krajina region. Although this Croat policy did not excuse Serb actions, it helped explain the paranoia that characterized their policymakers.

Whether defined in terms of regionalism, proto-nationalism or nationalism, there was therefore an equivalence to the strength of religion, for each had been supposed to be less relevant as a source of identity in a continent defined in other terms: either of a tolerant, liberal European identity or of the imperatives of Communism. Few believed in the latter, which was why nationalism was so important as the sole available alternative in Eastern Europe.

As far as the idea of a tolerant, liberal European identity was concerned, the EU offered a cultural and ideological definition of identity, a definition intended to smooth the path to supranational solutions to problems. The EU has an explicit ideological and cultural agenda, even if its politics of bartering frequently concealed this. The Tindemans Report of 1975 (drawn up by the Belgian Christian Democrat Leo Tindemans) called for a stress on common cultural traditions. Subsequently there was much talk of supposed common characteristics and episodes of European culture, or what Jack Lang, the French Socialist minister of culture for most of the period 1981–93, called 'Europe's soul', such as toleration, the Renaissance and the Enlightenment. Charlemagne was presented as the 'Father of Europe' while Erasmus and Socrates were appropriated for the EU's higher-education exchange programmes, and the Bologna agreement sought to standardize degrees across the EU. The *Media* programme supported transnational film productions. However, the EU found it difficult to give itself a cultural identity let alone a unifying message or myth, and its cultural programmes remain modest.

Despite talk of the ready co-existence of a multiplicity of identities, the approach for definition at the European level was, in practice, challenged by the vitality of national traditions, as well as by the advocates for regional autonomy, if not a nationalist separatism. This process was seen, for example, in Scotland and Catalonia, while in Italy the Northern League pushed separatism hard in the 1990s and did well in the 2008 election with its call for an end to the subsidizing of southern Italy.

When control over education was transferred to the regional level, as in Belgium through the language law on education of 1963, such ideas were institutionalized. In 1993 Belgium became a federal state, but this has not worked well due to a mutual distrust that has complicated and limited the unifying role of the federal state. There are struggles over separatist rights, over boundaries and over funding. The French-speaking population presses for more money and for a corridor towards Brussels, while the Flemings feel oppressed by the French language and the high costs of supporting French-speaking Belgium and Brussels. Proportionately the costs involved are greater than those West Germans transfer to the former East Germany. In contrast, in England, regionalism is very weak, although the EU backs it because a Europe of regions rather than states suits it.

In many respects across Europe separatist accounts of identity were traditional ones that were based in the theories and practices of nineteenth-century nationalism: traditional, but eager to use new methods, as with the creation of regional television networks, for example in the Basque Country, Catalonia, Galicia and Wales. In contrast a more challenging separatism was mounted in the case of assertiveness by distinctive groups that were religious or ethnic, or both, but that lacked any such geographical focus to serve as the basis of separatism. This situation related in particular to Islam. The assertiveness of minorities was in part based on a rejection of the current national myths, not least their support for toleration. Thus the rejection of nationalism came from a number of directions: it was in part a reaction by other nationalisms, and in part a challenge to collective consciousness by those who pressed narratives of ethnic, religious, gender and other differences.

There was also a wider question of the value, indeed legitimacy, of nationalism. One approach was to assert its value in terms of the supposed challenge presented by globalization. The latter could be regarded as denying individuals much of a sense of value, other than as consumers, or of identity, except through membership in a global community that did not, in practice, fulfil their desire for community. Nationalism, both in Europe and elsewhere, in this light could be seen, indeed, in part as a defence mechanism that helped communities and individuals to respond to changes and problems, although the same point could be made about minority consciousness and assertion. Thus nationalism could be presented in democratic terms as well as, more negatively, in those of ethnocentrism. The two were not necessarily separate, for the ethnic dimension, understood in terms of a fixed identity and one linked to ownership of a particular territory, may provide much of the content of the democratic movement. For example, the programme of the Austrian right-wing Freedom Party endorsed at Linz in 1997 affirmed what it termed a national right to cultural and political 'self-determination'.

There were also important differences between defensive ethnic and triumphalist ethnic nationalism, as, for example, between Estonia and Serbia. Serbian nationalism drew much of its energy, in the 1980s, from a determination to entrench Serbian national claims to the autonomous region of Kosovo at the expense of its Albanian minority. This determination ensured, however, that within Yugoslavia the Serbs found it difficult to win support from non-Serbian politicians and intellectuals. The nationalist draft *Memorandum of the Serbian Academy of Science and Arts*, leaked to the press in 1986, demonstrated Serbian assertiveness. In turn, the *Contributions for a Slovenian National Programme* from Slovenian intellectuals argued the case for greater autonomy within Yugoslavia for Slovenia. This argument led to criticisms but the Slovenian leader, Milan Kučan, defended it. His Serbian counterpart, Slobodan Milošević, who had seized power in Serbia in 1987, having failed to become a new Tito wielding power across Yugoslovia, instead pressed the case for Serbia's ability to defend his construction of its nationalist interests and for their expression in a Greater Serbia. In March 1989 much of Kosovo's autonomy was removed by the Serbian government.

In some aspirational nations, such as Catalonia, there have been moves away from such ethnic nationalism, and it was never particularly strong in Scotland, where indeed, unlike Catalonia, the linguistic element to nationalism is not pushed. In contrast in Corsica and Flanders, where there was such ethnic nationalism it was associated, in particular, with hostility to immigrants. In Flanders this is directed against immigrants from outside Europe, but there is also strong hostility to the French-speaking Walloons. In Corsica and in many other areas a touchstone of tension was provided by the issue of housing, with incomers regarded as taking away houses and thus homes and opportunities. A hostility to immigrants was also seen in the Swiss national election in October 2007, with the Swiss People's Party (SVP) taking a stance that was very much focused on opposition to immigration. Critics accused the SVP and its leader of policies and attitudes similar to the Nazis (the practice of family liability for crimes) and the Italian Fascists (adulation of the leader).

Any contrast between ethnic nationalism, seen as atavistic and bad, and civic nationalism, presented as modern, modernizing, benign and good, however, is far too simple. It is rather the case that there is a continuum. As elsewhere, nationalism in Europe, like democracy and religion, can therefore be seen as a category containing contrasting drives. These include both a notion of essentialism (generally racial), with all the negative implications about others and outsiders that that implies, as well as a more liberal concept of nationalism.

Nationalism involved a stress on the vernacular and on distinctive features of national cultures in some states, as with the emphasis on the Welsh language in devolved Wales. French legislation of 1975 and 1994 banned the use of foreign words in official documents, advertising and packaging, if there were French alternatives. These bans were an indication of a mixture of hubris, stubbornness and lack of confidence. A resistance to the cultural aspects of trade liberalization was clear, with the French devoting much energy to subsidizing their cinema and to resisting American cuisine. It is unclear how far this resistance can be related to the xenophobia seen, for example, in restrictions on immigration, particularly the legislation and would-be legislation of Charles Pasqua, minister of the interior from 1986 to 1988 and again from 1993 to 1995. Although not generally pushed to the same extreme, similar policies of trying to maintain national cultures were also seen in other states, not least with the sponsorship of supposedly endangered vernaculars and of distinctive cultural forms.

At the same time a cosmopolitanism was seen in the ready use of international languages, particularly English, and global brands. In France, despite criticism of McDonalds, 'le Happy Meal' was very popular in the 2000s, as was pasta. There and elsewhere the strength of both cosmopolitanism and xenophobia contributed to the sense of flux over identity. Travel and tourism, which have grown markedly, have greatly contributed to at least a superficial knowledge of other European countries.

CULTURE AND POLITICS

The discussion hitherto may seem far removed from the classic understanding of culture, namely the world of poets and painters. The latter is indeed important and also displays autonomous tendencies, not least in stylistic terms. Yet at the same time cultural life and developments are not separate from political and social pressures, and therefore narratives. Indeed, cultural life and development can be seen as a classic site for the insistent and persistent struggle between state control and the marketplace, a struggle that has been so important to European history across the period. The salience of cultural elements within this struggle reflects their significance as expressions and moulders of identity, as well as a self-conscious intellectualism on the part of many advocates and practitioners of state control. Moreover, it would have been surprising, in a period in which government increasingly intervened in large areas of society, and taxation played a greater role than earlier, for the world of culture and leisure to have escaped intervention.

Additional reasons for state action varied by country, although there were common themes. An inherited concern with morality, or at least propriety, had left governments with powers of censorship and, more significantly, with a widespread expectation that censorship could, should and would be exercised in order to 'protect' society. Censorship was exercised in a number of ways, the most obvious being the suppression of works that were disapproved of. Laws about propriety, for example against blasphemy, could be applied. The Appeal to the Soviet People by the anti-liberal would-be coup leaders on 19 August 1991 called for action against 'the propaganda of sex and violence . . . glaring immorality'. Aside from government action, there was also self-censorship by authors or publishers, and their equivalents, in order to avoid the prospect of government action, as well as in support of a particular agenda, for example in discussions of immigration, gender or capital punishment. These types of self-censorship left far less evidence than government censorship but were more effective. On the other hand, much of this type of censorship was a matter of internalizing the rules of states, notably of authoritarian ones such as the Communist states.

Also significant were the pressures created by the institutional structure of particular industries, as well as the expectations about their goals and roles. These were accentuated by the state role in radio and television across Europe and in non-Communist as well as Communist countries. In many cases in Western Europe, the state's role was linked to clear political purpose, and the importance of television was indicated by the occasional use of violence to secure control of programming and transmission. Thus in 1991 Soviet troops seized the television station in the Lithuanian capital, Vilnius, and in 2007 in Georgia special forces closed down the Imedi television station because it was owned by an opposition leader. More generally there was an interweaving of political and business interests, with television and radio licences being key to the currency of power and influence, a currency that was applied from both directions.

This interweaving was true from the outset of the issue of such licences, as was also the case in the USA. Indeed, in Europe the interweaving of interests over television and radio licences was an aspect of a corporatism that spanned business and politics, and that requires mention in those chapters but also in this one. Such corporatism became more apparent as state media monopolies were challenged by the establishment of independent channels, for these were heavily regulated as an aspect of state control. For example, French television channels (unlike their American counterparts) were not allowed to earn money through product placement until (in 2007) it was made legal from 2010. Regulation became a major topic of political contention, not least when political leaders and groups owned channels as, most prominently, with Silvio Berlusconi, through his holding company Fininvest, in Italy in the 1990s and 2000s.

Even when permission was granted for independent channels their operating parameters were set by government. Broadcasters were expected to conform to an agenda that reflected the established culture of polite society as mediated by the state. Thus they were required not to broadcast material that was deemed obscene, cruel or blasphemous, nor to encourage people to break the law. In the widest sense the prime agency for cultural transmission became an adjunct of a certain view of society, although that reflected the range of activity within the purview of law and governance. This situation was a matter not only of proscriptive (what could not be broadcast) content, but also of prescribed content. Thus radio and television encouraged a sense that 'family values', as traditionally understood, were normal. Television, which was the predominant cultural technology from the 1960s, rapidly supplanting radio, first, in fashionability and then in popularity, set out to offer few challenges to dominant norms, and difficult work was marginalized. The values, however, were affected in many countries by a drive for the trivial and prurient in, particularly but not only, commercial television. Berlusconi's use of Italian commercial television was blamed, with reason, for helping take the latter down market, and the banalities of reality television contributed to the same result in Britain in the 2000s.

State intervention in culture, as in the media, was fairly apparent, but government was not so much a fixed agent on the proscriptive/prescriptive boundary, as a variably flexible body that reflected, in its flexibility, political, social and cultural pressures and trends. This reflection was a key dynamic in the cultural history of the period, and one that helped give character to particular episodes. Allowing for a degree of flexibility, government was most interventionist in culture in authoritarian societies. This intervention was particularly the case of Communist regimes, as they had an all-encompassing intellectual and cultural prospectus. The control of the state over Soviet education and culture was very tight, reflecting a strong belief in the importance of their ideological value. Indeed, political education was regarded as a goal of the system. As seen with the 1970s song 'My address is not a house or a street/ My address is the Soviet Union', the Soviet government was also concerned to develop a nationalism separate to that of its constituent republics, although its success was very limited not least because in the latter Soviet policies were frequently perceived as Russian in origin and goal.

The linkage of culture with politics was demonstrated in the Palace of the Republic opened in East Berlin in 1976. It housed the East German parliament, leisure facilities and works of art commissioned under the rubric 'Are Communists allowed to dream', notably Hans Vent's painting *People on the Beach*. In the event, the use of asbestos in the Palace led to it being condemned shortly before the fall of East Germany. Utilitarianism was important to Communist cultural supervisors, although not only to them. Functionality, for example, was a key goal in East Germany, as in the influential Office of Industrial Design, but, for Communists, this functionality could not be defined simply in terms of consumer appeal.

Alongside the support of Communist cultural agendas there was an attempt to repress anti-Communist accounts and, alternately, to suppress or to marginalize non-Communist ones. Alexander Solzhenitsyn, who won the Nobel Prize for Literature in 1970, was arrested and exiled in 1974 for his description of Stalinist terror in *The Gulag Archipelago* (1973–8), a work that had a considerable influence in Western Europe. Two years later East Germany expelled Wolf Biermann, a prominent satirical balladeer. Yet there was also a secret circulation of hostile literature that challenged Communist viewpoints. Critics in Eastern Europe engaged directly with Marxist notions of history. Thus Jan Patočka, a Czech philosopher of history, provided accounts that broke from the materialist nature and teleology of the latter. In his *Plato a Europa* (*Plato and Europe*, 1973), which began as private lectures, he emphasized the value of the unconstrained pursuit of knowledge, while, in *Heretical Essays in the Philosophy of History*, illegally published in 1975, Patočka also came to the unacceptable view that history lacked meaning, a radical break from the Communist approach. As a consequence, to Patočka history scarcely recorded the progress of the working class, which was the proclaimed goal of

Communist history and historiography. Patočka's political allegiance was underlined by his role as the author of the Charter 77 of Human Rights, a key critique of the reality of Communist governance delivered to the government in 1977, while the response of the authorities was demonstrated by the fact that his works were not published until after the Czech Communist Party fell from power in 1989.

Indeed, party orthodoxy continued to be propagated until the end of the Communist regimes, as did the by-now formulaic Socialist Realism in the arts. Thus in 1987 the Museum of Revolution was opened in the Maarjamäe Palace in Tallinn, Estonia. A mural, *Friendship of Nations, Depicting the Achievements of Peoples' Friendship and Socialism*, was painted by Evald Okas. Construction of the grotesque and vast 'House of the People' continued in Bucharest. In contrast Western official sponsorship of culture as part of the Cold War was far more subdued, especially by the 1970s, by when it was largely discredited. For example, *Der Monat*, an American-funded German magazine which published works by non-Communist intellectuals, ceased in 1971, was revived in 1978 and ended for good in 1986.

After the fall of Communism artistic life became much freer in Eastern Europe; and this contrast was clearly highlighted by the controls that continued to be exercised by those regimes that were still authoritarian. Thus in 2004 Uladzimier Mikhniuk was prevented from taking up the post of Director of the Institute of History of the Belarus Academy of Sciences because he clashed with the politicized control over academic affairs exercised by the Higher Attestation Commission, and he died suddenly soon after. The suppression of freedom of expression was central to Belarus policy. Elsewhere in Eastern Europe the situation was very different, not least as the symbolic world of Communism was dismantled. Thus the calendar was no longer dominated by Communist celebrations, most obviously of May Day. Earlier there had been cultural liberalization when conservative autocracies collapsed in Greece, Portugal and Spain, and this liberalization contributed greatly to a marked upsurge in Spanish cinema, as in the films of Pedro Almodóvar in the 1970s, as well as an explosion of pornography.

Across Europe one obvious sphere in which the role of states was important throughout the period was patronage. The state was not only the single most important patron of the arts, but also far more active than any other body. This activity reflected, in part, the extension, with public ownership, of the state's role in the economy, but also more generally the growth of government. Patronage was readily apparent not only in obvious aspects, such as the commissioning and running of museums, but also in wider spheres, such as architecture. Public bodies were the biggest commissioners of new construction, and this was true both of large individual works, such as hospitals, and of multiple units, especially public housing. Once constructed, moreover, buildings had to be decorated. The importance of public commissions encouraged the production of designs that were believed likely to appeal, and this moulded the architectural profession more widely than the actual commissioning process itself. Furthermore, the impact of approved techniques and styles was extended through the insistent planning system. New buildings required planning permission, if not public funds, and this provided opportunities for the propagation and enforcement of specific agendas. Design, in these, was a matter of social programming more than of aesthetics, as shown in London by the displays on the hitherto empty plinth in Trafalgar Square.

In architecture the roles of proscriptive and prescriptive public pressures were readily apparent, but they were also insistent in other fields thanks to the institutionalization of state patronage. This patronage was both an opportunity and a problem. It was an opportunity because it freed the arts from dependence on the marketplace, with the pressures that created, not least conformity with what was believed likely to appeal, but it was a problem because it created another marketplace, which was politicized, not so much in terms of public politics, although this could be very important, but rather in terms of less public but still bitter artistic politics. Stylistic fashions played a major role in this governmental marketplace but so also did notions of relevance, as well as pressure on behalf of particular cultural institutions and identities. Decisions about which exhibitions to mount provided an obvious instance of cultural politics, as did the appointment of gallery and museum directors. The holders of such positions often changed dramatically with new governments, as with the Socialist victory in Spain in 2004. Although his 'style' was very eclectic, under Mitterrand in France the very expensive 'grands projets', such as the 'People's Opera' at the Bastille, the new National Library and the Grande Arche at La Défense, were seen as a justification of the government and as an opportunity to advance its views. Containing an exhibition centre as well as a library, the Grande Arche, finished in 1989, was seen as a modern equivalent to the Arc de Triomphe, one focused on humanitarian ideals and not war.

Public patronage attracted much attention and considerable controversy. In one sense this was an aspect of a tripartite culture war between the criteria established, and ranking set, by government, those of the artistic establishment and the vernacular culture of popular taste. These divisions were central to the cultural politics of the period. They were also shifting divisions that were affected by a general loosening of the constraints within which the arts could operate. For example, *Uten en tråd* (*Without a Stitch*, 1966), a novel by the Norwegian Jens Bjørneboe, which centred on the need to overcome guilt-ridden attitudes to sexuality, led in 1967 to the author's conviction for writing pornography, but in 1988 the novel was republished and became generally available in Norway. The antics and intimacies of the contestants in the 'Big Brother' genre of 'reality' television, a genre that began in the Netherlands in 1999, would not have been acceptable on mainstream television twenty years earlier. Formats were copied across Europe and not only with 'Big Brother'. Thus *Fame Academy* became the popular Spanish show *Operación Triunfo*.

Popular taste was mediated through the marketplace, with consumers playing a role in determining the success of particular art forms and artists. This consumer pressure was usually in favour of Realist cultural tendencies as opposed to the experimental moulding of form seen with Modernism, which tended to attract the favour of the artistic establishment. Wary of popularity and therefore accessibility, Modernists reacted against positivism and representational culture but, in turn, were under pressure from Neoclassical revivals.

Alongside the rhythm of stylistic change there was a fissure between élite and popular cultural forms, a wide disjuncture between 'high' and 'low' brow works, although Americanization was a common element to both, while museums, exhibitions and festivals, the television and cinema, represented places and means for juxtaposing and, at times, reconciling the old and the new, the foreign and the local. Nevertheless, the overwhelming characteristic of popular 'low' brow works was a reluctance to experiment with form and style, which helped ensure that there were very differing understandings and experiences of culture and the arts. The difference was more than a matter of stylistic pluralism, as it also reflected the wider cultural politics of societies containing very varied levels of income, education and expectation.

Alongside class there were cultural differences very much linked to place, and, in particular, contrasting rural and urban models of national identity. Ruralist notions had been greatly pushed by the right in the interwar years, and urban ones by the left. This contrast continued to be a dominant post-war pattern, and can be linked to the EU's backing for the CAP. At the same time this ruralism presented problems for the right at a time of rapid urbanization and the expansion of a conservative urban middle class that had scant interest in ruralist notions. While this shift on the right created issues for the politics of identity, it was not a prime cultural fissure, for ruralism declined markedly as an artistic theme.

Yet the still powerful capacity of ruralism for offering both identity and heritage was indicated in the continued appeal of *Heimat* (Homeland) for Germans and, more mundanely, by the popularity in England of the National Trust and the Campaign for the Preservation of Rural England. More than 400 books with *Heimat* in their title were published between 1995 and 2001 and polls indicate that the word has very positive connotations for Germans. The *Heimat* film genre, which was popular there in the 1950s, offering a sense of security and restoration, revived from the 1980s, in some cases providing a linkage with *Problemfilm* on social problems. German reunification in 1989 strengthened the emphasis on *Heimat*, although, in film, this was directed in part to incorporate areas that Germany had lost as a result of the Second World War. It was unclear how far this should be seen as a depoliticized sense of loss and how far as a more significant declaration of irridentism, pressure for the return of lost territories. Leaving aside this sense of loss, Edgar Reitz produced three effective television series called *Heimat* about the sense of belonging, which were located in a discussion of German history from 1918 until 2005 from the perspective of a village community in the hills of the Hunsrück.

In Germany and elsewhere cities, particularly large and industrial ones, have tended to lack this quality of heritage, while national constructions of identity are generally not urban. That of Switzerland, for example, focuses on the Alps and supposed related values, and not on the cities in which the bulk of the Swiss population actually lives. Yet there was also in some countries an interest in the city as a long-standing cultural entity, as was seen in West Germany notably in the rebuilding of bombed cities, such as Nürnberg, on the basis of the old city. Whereas this stress on cultural entity had not been a theme for most bustling West German centres in the 1950s and 1960s, it became more important from the mid-1970s, encouraged by 1975 being chosen as the European Year of Historic Preservation. In the 1990s this theme of a longstanding urban cultural entity was conspicuously extended to former East Germany with the large-scale reconstruction of the former centre of Dresden.

National pride has revived considerably in Germany in recent years, with the football World Cup competition of 2006 being particularly important, with its scenes of large numbers clad in national colours and singing the national anthem in public places. The earlier post-war lack of any national rhetoric, or even thought, in public discourse, a consequence of the heritage of American re-education after the Nazi era, has been replaced by a growing re-evaluation of national pride, although not to the level of French or British nationalism. The starting point was German reunification and later the Schröder government of 1998–2005 with its public commitment to a 'German' foreign policy with renewed self-confidence. This re-emerging sense of nation, however, clashed with post-war conceptions of national identity, and problems were posed as a result. Thus over the NATO mission in Afghanistan Germans confronted the question of whether foreign policy entailed the commitment to pay and send a robust army into conflict with likely casualties.

In Russia there was also a rethinking of nationalism, which included Soil and Church nostalgia for pre-Soviet days. In 1990 Solzhenitsyn's citizenship was restored and he was awarded the Russian State Literature

Prize. Returning from exile in 1994 he increasingly offered a Slavophile/Russian nationalistic viewpoint, to which Orthodox Christianity contributed greatly, that propounded a critique of both Communism and the West, especially of atheism and consumerism respectively. The government's focus on Russian national identity also led to a celebration of writers judged appropriate, as with the lavish Pushkin commemoration in 1999. There was also a nostalgia focused on the Soviet Union. Soviet films and songs enjoyed a certain popularity and the television series *Staraia kvartira* (*The Old Apartment*) made the artefacts of Soviet life seem welcomingly familiar. In East Germany a degree of public nostalgia for the Communist past (*Ostalgie*), for example for its material culture, was accentuated by the extent to which German unification was seen in terms of conquest by West Germany but, nevertheless, it was limited. In Hungary there was nostalgia for the 'Goulash Socialism' of the Kádár era, as well as a marked rejection of it.

There was also, across most of the former Communist bloc, but least in Russia and Belarus, an active depiction of the oppression and brutality of Communist regimes, and a recovery of the history of the lost years. In Budapest in 2002 the Terror Háza Múzeum (House of Terror) opened in the very building where the secret police once did their worst. This preserves the cells and the torture and execution chambers. Riga now has Latvia's Museum of Occupation, 1940–91, while the townscape of Tallinn, the capital of Estonia, is a rejection of Communism. There is a Museum of Occupation, while the former KGB headquarters carries a plaque reading 'This building housed the headquarters of the organ of repression of the Soviet occupation power. Here began the road to suffering for thousands of Estonians'. In Freedom Square, which was used for military parades under the Soviets, the Freedom Clock was installed in 2003. It shows both the current time and the number of years since Estonia became independent. Across the former Communist bloc the new order was reflected in new names for streets, apartment blocks and much else.

The end of Communism also meant the end of censorship across the Communist world. In the Soviet Union this occurred in August 1990 and was followed by an openness to the outside world and by a massive expansion in the number of publishing firms and magazines.

Readers rushed to read genres hitherto unavailable, such as self-help books, religious literature and romances, for example novels by Barbara Cartland. The moralizing, uplifting works produced (and then only in limited editions) during the totally controlled Communist years were no longer of great significance. In turn, with the revival of assertiveness, now Russian not Soviet, under the presidency of Vladimir Putin from 2000 to 2008, there was an attack on Hollywood's role in Russia and the establishment of a quota system and funding from television channels encouraged by Putin that ensured a major revival in the Russian film industry: from 2 per cent of the national market in 2002 to 23 per cent in 2006.

The British are traditionally reluctant to see culture as political and politicizing, but an emphasis on artistic content and style underplays the profound sense across much of Europe of culture as an expression of much more than artistic endeavour. The wide dimensions of this were captured in the Danish cartoon crisis in 2006. Cartoons considered blasphemous by Muslims were published in a Danish newspaper, leading to huge demonstrations, the torching of Danish embassies and the boycotting of Danish products. The issues of freedom of expression and the relationship between collective rights and communal pressures were widely aired, and the subject was reprised in 2008 with Dutch criticism of Islam. Cultural questions seemed very political. In these and other issues, the extent to which cultural questions were very political was amply demonstrated.

Chapter 6

Economic Worlds

The key developments of post-war Europe were continued from the 1970s. These developments included the emphasis on innovation (notably in applied science) in raising growth, as well as the move from agriculture and the land, the growing role of the service industries, and the pressures of international competition.

In addition to this competition, and also in part as a consequence of it, European countries were greatly affected by pressures also seen elsewhere. The most significant are those described as globalization. This gathered pace in the late twentieth century, as money, credit and debt became more mobile and plentiful, and because investment in new production processes was more significant. Established plant, processes and markets, in contrast, were less valuable in the context of rapidly altering demands and technologies. The relative decline of metal-bashing manufacturing industries and the marked rise of electronics were important to this process. Steel works were hit by foreign competition, as were shipyards. Competition from Japan and South Korea was particularly acute for the latter. British shipyards were very hard hit. State support played a role in competition between shipyards and was particularly important in Communist countries, for example with shipyards in Gdansk (Poland), the site of the Solidarity action in 1981, and Rostock (East Germany) being heavily backed as sites for economic growth and the creation of strong worker-communities. The end of Communism exposed such shipyards to the hard scrutiny of the EU's competition laws, with their opposition to subsidies.

More generally, transitions in industry hit much more harshly than bland remarks about transformation might suggest, and were also politically and culturally significant. Heavy industry was the bedrock of trade unionism and its decline created issues for left-wing political parties, as well as transforming the nature of the left politically. Moreover, working-class ideas of appropriate masculine behaviour as based on hard manual labour were challenged, as were the collective bonds of trade unionism. The impact of economic change was felt more harshly because heavy industry was concentrated in particular locations, especially on coalfields.

Despite state assistance, new jobs that lasted did not tend to be located in the areas of traditional heavy industry. Instead they were characteristic of regions not hitherto noted for industrialization, such as Baden-Württemberg, the Thames Valley, and the Rhône Alps region of France. At the same time this industrialization was very varied in character, not least in its environmental impact and in its beneficial consequences for other industrial sectors. Thus petrochemicals on part of the Mediterranean coast of France had a very different 'print' or impact to electronics near Grenoble and to the mobile phone industry in Finland: by the mid 2000s, Nokia, the flagship of the latter, had 40 per cent of the world market.

CORPORATISM AND THE STATE

Economies that responded best to changes were those that were culturally and institutionally attuned to flexibility and market mechanisms. Neither was a factor in the Communist world, but there was also a problem in Western Europe, where both from the left and from the right there was a longstanding preference for regulation and corporatism, a suspicion of profit and a concern with the social cohesion offered by full employment. This concern encouraged investment in manufacturing that frequently turned out to be uneconomic and/or requiring a large subsidy, such as that in southern Italy. Such subsidies were only obtained by taxing more productive sectors of the economy and thus reducing their competitiveness. Uneconomic plant led to overcapacity, which hit other producers, as with shipbuilding and petrochemicals.

An emphasis in economic history on government regulation and planning has its limitations, because this top-down approach puts a stress on the governmental context rather than on wider economic tendencies. These tendencies, of course, cannot be separated from the context, not least because the actions of governments affected them, but it is inappropriate to ignore the extent to which economic tendencies and pressures were not readily disciplined by the dictates of politicians. Despite this weakness, not to say failure, there was a widespread conviction on the part of politicians and political commentators of the value of government direction and planning. Partly as a consequence, struggles over corporatism or, at least, over its operation were a key element in the politics of the EU, not least in terms of tensions between interests at the EU and national levels. The development, transformation and, in some cases, dismantling of the resulting institutionalization of control was a crucial aspect of the history of this period. At times, as with the bonfire of regulations in Britain in the Thatcher years (1979–90), the process was readily noticeable and highly controversial, which was especially true of commentators considering their own country.

Frequently, however, commentators were less mindful of similar shifts elsewhere. Thus the British underrated the extent to which there was an important shift of policy as part of the austerity associated with Raymond Barre, the French prime minister from 1976 to 1981. He removed most price controls, enabling public services, such as the railways, to raise their prices and thus cost the state less, and also cut down on the industrial aid designed to maintain employment. These policies were part of the opening up of the French economy to outside influences, which brought benefits in terms of growth, but also led to problems.

Indeed, Barre's fate indicated the difficulty of this shift away from state control and direction. Reducing industrial assistance was more controversial than removing price controls (although the two were linked through encouraging competitiveness), because the former had immediate implications for employment. These implications were seen in France in 1979 with the crisis in the steel industry that was central to the traditional economy in Lorraine. Barre pressed for a reduction in capacity that entailed the laying-off of 20,000 workers, but this led to mass-agitation there, and he had to back down and provide more state money. Moreover, Barre's *rigeur* made him very unpopular, helping the Socialists to win the 1981 elections. This unpopularity confirmed the latter in their determination to use state subsidies to maintain employment, which was very much the initial policy of the Mitterrand government.

Ironically, the threat to Lorraine's steel jobs, in this case from the new, foreign-owned employer, led Nicolas Sarkozy, President of France, to fly to Lorraine in January 2008 in order to pledge his support for the workers there. They were not part of the traditional constituency of support for the French right, but a national steel industry was widely seen as a key aspect of economic strength. In contrast jobs in the service sector were underrated.

Deregulation, in France and elsewhere, was not always as pronounced and controversial as during the Barre ministry, but was often a strong pressure on established practices. Popular attitudes to economic activity and its social context proved more resistant to government policy, and this resistance was shown in the widespread commitment to getting someone else to pay the bill, including subsidizing one's job. Yet there were significant changes. One obvious measure of deregulation was the privatization of nationalized companies, as in 2005 when *Electricité de France* was partly floated (privatized), with over 5 million of the French population happy to become shareholders. There had been earlier tranches of privatization in France in the late 1980s and mid 1990s and also elsewhere, for example, from different political backgrounds, in Britain and Spain in the 1980s and in Eastern Europe in the 1990s.

Deregulation was not simply one process. There were important variations, just as there was in what is termed 'corporatism'. For example, Barre sought to control inflation by reducing liquidity, and did so by imposing higher taxes and monetary and credit controls, as well as spending cuts. For Margaret Thatcher, the Conservative prime minister of Britain from 1979 to 1990, in contrast, such controls and policies were unacceptable. Although she did not always cut taxes, especially in the early stages of her administration, she desperately wanted to reduce them in order to set consumers free, and was far less concerned about both the stability of the currency and the trade balance than was Barre. His conservatism was, in the French fashion, more *dirigiste* and top-down, whereas hers was liberal and free trade.

Across Europe public policy could only achieve so much in the face of competitive pressures. This weakness could be readily seen in the agricultural sector, where much farming was uncompetitive despite the determination to preserve rural life, not only for political and social reasons but also to sustain ruralist notions of national identity. These notions have dwindled, for example in Britain and Italy. The move of labour from the land was in large part a product of rising agricultural productivity, both in Europe and more generally. Thanks to the 'Green Revolution', especially the widespread use of chemical fertilizers and pesticides, mechanization and increased use of irrigation water, the average amount of grain available per person around the world rose from 135 kilos in 1961 to 161 kilos in 1989. As a result of greater world production, particularly in North America where producers looked unkindly on European protectionism, there were fewer prospects for inefficient European producers, although there was a sustained attempt to use protectionism to preserve their position. Indeed, that was a key element in the CAP of the EEC (see pages 24–5, 45–6). The marked increase in world food prices in 2008 made agricultural economics even more sensitive.

Protectionism and indeed corporatism as a whole were encouraged by but also under strain from competitive pressures. In the 1990s and, even more, 2000s these pressures were generally seen in terms of manufactured imports from East Asia, but this was not the sole factor. In the 1970s there was the recession stemming from the oil price crisis, although other factors played a role. These included the problems produced by the earlier boom of the 1950s and 1960s, particularly cost-issues linked to the availability of raw materials, as well as an over-investment in manufacturing plant, competition from non-Western manufacturing, and the development of institutional rigidities, especially vested interests. In turn the oil price crisis put a serious fiscal burden on governments, not least by hitting their tax-raising ability at the same time as the balance of payments. As a result interventionist planning suffered a major crisis between goals and means. For example, the popular image Belgians have of this crisis in the 1970s is that of boys playing football on main roads.

The recession of the 1970s contributed to an abandonment of 1960s optimism and pressure for change, although this abandonment also owed much to the fracturing, indeed atomization, of this pulse and to the resilience of conservative tendencies. The overall consequence was a decline of the emotional drive for a new political order in economics, an order, reflecting 1960s optimism, that was to be focused on economic justice, collective ownership, environmental concerns and happiness, if not hedonism. In practice attempts to turn these aspirations into legislation, action and a new economics had been limited, but they contributed to the corporatist reliance on state ownership as a panacea, remedy or at least sticking plaster, at the time of the 1970s recession. The waning of 1960s aspirations in economics helped ensure that business (like the trade unions) could return to seeking to mould corporatism to its interests.

Moreover, the crisis between goals and means in interventionist planning and public discussion was sustained into the 1980s. In part this crisis led to a rejection of interventionism, explicitly so with the Thatcher government in Britain. It was more common, however, to see a limitation of interventionism, as the economic sectors and geographical areas designated for help were greatly reduced. This limitation, however, accentuated the regional disparities already arising from the decline in economic opportunity.

At the same time as there were serious problems in long-established activities it proved possible for economies that had hitherto been largely agrarian to make major advances in industrial and service sectors. This growth was a process eased by EU assistance and the availability of investment and also reflecting the range of opportunities for catching up provided by existing industrial and service models. This process was particularly true of Ireland and Spain. Their economies changed radically from the 1980s, with both countries attracting new industries and becoming important centres for financial services.

The Communist economies liked to present themselves as different to those of the capitalist West and as removed from their problems, notably unemployment. Protectionism from global competition was certainly one of their defining characteristics or, at least, aspirations. These economies constituted a bloc, with the Soviet Union the main customer and supplier for the other Communist states. This bloc took part in comparatively limited external trade, and then mostly in the form of the export of raw materials or of trade linked to political preference, such as the export of Soviet hydro-electric power turbines to Egypt to work the Aswan Dam. Within the Communist bloc, moreover, there was scant reliance on an economic market of value. Instead, the stress was on production and quotas of production drove the system.

A lack in pricing of any real understanding of value ensured that barter, which of course still offers a sense of value, played a major role in trade within the system. So also did an element of coercion, with the Soviet Union using the terms of trade in order to draw benefit from Eastern Europe, although at the same time the latter was provided with oil and natural gas by the Soviet Union at below world prices. Moreover, some of the goods from Eastern Europe were, like Soviet goods, of a quality that could not be sold on world markets. Yet there were also important qualitative changes in the Communist economies, not least a decline in agricultural processing (food processing, textiles, furniture) and an increase in more complex manufacturing processes. In so far as the statistics can be credited, machinery production as a percentage of Bulgarian industrial production rose to 14.2 by 1983 while food processing fell to 26.9; the 1939 percentages were 2.4 and 51.2 respectively.

Despite their claims of self-sufficiency and superiority, the Communist economies were also hit by the economic downturns of the mid-1970s, and the Soviet government of Leonid Brezhnev lacked an effective response. These downturns interacted with already pronounced systemic faults. Heavy investment in armaments was distorting for these economies while, more generally, they suffered from the role of state planning, particularly by *Gosplan*, the Soviet State

Planning Commission, which drew up the five-year plans, and from the failure to develop the consumer spending that was so important in the USA and Western Europe. This failure had a serious long-term consequence for the stability of the Soviet system, for a lack of popularity, particularly in Eastern Europe, made it difficult for the governments to view change and reform with much confidence. Assessing the Soviet economy is difficult due to the unreliability of the production figures, but it has been argued that the economy's decline began earlier than in the 1970s, and that the high-point was actually in the 1950s.

There were other serious problems for the Soviet bloc economies, in particular a failure to ensure adequate mechanisms for incentive. These reflected the lack of a culture of incentive, entrepreneurship and capitalism. Indeed, with bright people unable to follow the Western pattern of raising money for investment and, moreover, generally excluded from state monopolies governed by timeserving and unimaginative bureaucrats, it was not surprising that the Soviet system could not engage adequately with change. This inability to engage with change was seen dramatically in the failure to produce sufficient computers, which was indicative of an unwillingness to put an accurate cost on the use of human time, as well as an unhappiness about departing from paper mechanisms of recording and deploying information. This unwillingness was a symptom of a more systemic management incompetence and planning failure that helped ensure that effort did not yield qualitative improvements in the economic system. The focus solely on output, or rather on claims of output, proved greatly misconceived. There was scant concern with the market, and this led to numerous instances of the supply of only part of a process: shaving cream without shavers, for example.

Traditional forms of economic activity were also suffering serious problems in the Soviet Union. A failure to fulfil the goal of agricultural self-sufficiency ensured that grain had to be imported. Much of this was from the USA, creating, under an agreement of 1975, an unexpected constituency of interest in continued good relations, one that included such Republican states as Kansas. In large part the Soviet failure was due to the inability of collective forms of management to realize the potential of Soviet agriculture, a problem repeated across Eastern

Europe. Managerial quality and peasant motivation were lacking in the collective farms, while some of the biggest planning disasters occurred in Soviet agriculture. These problems were a major issue for Mikhail Gorbachev who, in the early 1980s, was the Politburo member responsible for agriculture.

Given these problems with agricultural production it is not surprising that both life expectancy and infant mortality were unsatisfactory in the Soviet Union. This, in turn, fed through into economic problems, for a decline in population growth hit the increase in the labour force in the 1970s and even more in the 1980s. Soviet labour needs had, in part, been met by high employment rates among women, but now there was less female labour that could be added to the workforce.

Economic and other statistics from the Soviet era are unreliable, and notoriously so with Uzbek cotton production, which was greatly exaggerated in order to obtain billions of roubles from *Gosplan*. Azerbaijan was also a major source of fraudulent returns. Nevertheless, there is little doubt that measures of economic improvements show a fall in the Brezhnev era (1964–82), with earlier rates of increase in national income, production, productivity and return on investment not being sustained. This fall also represented a failure in the planning set out under the five-year plans, and these failures were presented publicly in information published during the Gorbachev years (1985–91) in order to demonstrate the need for change. When these aggregate failures were combined with a lack of economic transformation toward innovation and new product ranges, then the situation was indeed serious. The command economy, with its micromanagement in planning and execution from the centre, was failing. Limited growth, moreover, intensified competition for resources, and the state lacked an adequate mechanism to cope. The nostrums of Marxist-Leninism offered no help and decreasingly little inspiration.

In Eastern Europe there was a degree of greater flexibility, which was most the case in Yugoslavia, which, from 1949, was outside the Soviet system and as a result found it easiest to trade with the West and, more significantly, to borrow money there. Within the Soviet bloc this flexibility was especially seen in Hungary, where the availability of consumer goods was regarded as part of a silent bargain to secure popular compliance with the Communist dictatorship. Consumerism and leisure were also emphasized in East Germany from 1958, and especially by the 1970s, in place of the earlier focus on work and production. In particular consumer goods were more widely available in Eastern Europe than in the Soviet Union, although shopping in East Berlin and Dresden while doing my research in East Germany in 1980 revealed this to be a very limited achievement. Choice was certainly very limited, again in part due to the focus on output.

There was also a small degree of openness to capitalist companies that were seeking market opportunities. Toyota started operations in Poland in 1980, the year of the Gdansk strike (see page 189). The Communist command economies, however, were in serious difficulty by the mid-1980s. Hamstrung by ideological mismanagement, earlier attempts to reform them had proved flawed. The 1970s *détente* had led to substantial Western loans, particularly, but not only, as a result of West German *Ostpolitik*. There was a willingness on the part of Western European governments to provide export guarantees and credits. However, due to the indiscriminate distribution of loan money through the 'watering can principle', these loans had not been translated into effective investment and economic take-off and had, instead, enabled a postponement of necessary economic reforms while increasing indebtedness. These substantial debts reduced the options for Eastern European governments.

The debts thus created a shared dependency on *détente*, at the same time as they exposed the weaknesses of the Eastern European economies. Economic limitations and financial problems made it difficult to import Western technology, and this difficulty accentuated the political pressure to turn to low-efficiency Soviet products. Moreover, economic problems, notably low productivity and massive underemployment, combined with the high rate of military expenditure, which was true across the Communist bloc, not least to support large conscript armies, limited the funds available for social investment and consumer spending. This limitation increasingly compromised popular support for the system, especially because television made the public aware of better times elsewhere, particularly in East Germany due to the heavy exposure to West German television.

In East Germany the government pushed 'Socialist social policies' as it sought to reconcile economic with social policies and to use social welfarism to enhance productivity. Instead, this welfarism proved a potent drain on the economy, while failing to satisfy rising popular expectations and, indeed, undermining the incentive to work. The East German economy was anyway hit by a lack of natural resources. Like most of Eastern Europe it was dependent on Soviet assistance, not least in the form of cheap oil. The provision of this assistance helped ensure an ability to cope with structural weaknesses but in the 1970s Soviet assistance to Eastern European states declined. This decline led in Eastern Europe to the build up of very large external debts, as well as big internal deficits. Such debts and deficits did not permit the capital accumulation necessary for the industrial modernization that was required in the 1980s if the Communist economies were to compete, if only to service their debt.

More than financial factors were at stake, however. Economic rationality was not possible due to the political structure and ideology of Communist states. This lack of rationality was particularly true of the ideological commitment to heavy industry, especially steel. Nor was it possible to provide productivity increases that could sustain the relatively high wages that workers received, nor indeed produce the goods for them to buy. One clear sign of failure in East Germany was that workers had a high saving ratio, as they could not find sufficient things to buy.

The second oil price hike, that of 1979 due to the overthrow of the Shah in Iran, had helped precipitate a global economic shock that posed a major problem for the weaker economies. This was particularly true of the Eastern European states but, due to their political system and ideology, their inability to service their debts did not lead to the economic transformation necessary for them to modernize.

Falling life expectancy was a clear symptom of the social failure of the Communist economies and challenged their legitimacy, which Communist governments based on social progress. Moreover, political failure was seen in the prominence of corruption, not only for personal profit but simply in order to get economic processes to work. Unreported and illegal production and trades were necessary for the economy to function, not least through the barter system. They also led to the development of a parallel world of personal gain regulated by bribery, both of which made a mockery of Communism.

EASTERN EUROPE FROM 1990

The collapse of Communism was not followed by rapid economic growth across the whole of the ex-Communist bloc. For example, the successor parts of the Soviet Union were to prove less than the sum of the former whole. In particular it proved difficult in the former Soviet Union to establish effective, transparent and incorrupt monetary and fiscal mechanisms, and indeed a state monopoly over the means of exchange: barter, instead of money, remained important. Moreover, turning to Western ideas on economic and financial policies, in particular free market economics with a minimum of regulation, within a context of a general devolution of power and governance, contributed to a more general crisis in Russian self-confidence. Western loans were necessary in order to prevent a total collapse of Russia in the 1990s, but Russian debt payments caused a severe crisis in 1998, leading to a default and devaluation that helped lay the basis for a degree of recovery, as well as sustaining strong suspicion of the West.

Both there and in Eastern Europe there was no smooth transition to capitalism and democracy. Instead the bankruptcy of large parts of the former Communist command economies, much of which had been uncompetitive, and the dismantling of unaffordable social welfare, led to a major rise in unemployment, poverty and social polarization. Large-scale underemployment was a key aspect of the Communist economic system and, under the pressure of competition, much of this was transformed into unemployment, although high levels of underemployment also continued to be part of the Communist legacy. Public culture was affected by disillusionment and government corruption, the symptom of both a wider concern about and disinclination for reform, as the now-privatized economies displayed a new vulnerability to international trends. Corruption was very conspicuous, most so in Romania, but with Bulgaria and Serbia close competitors. The 'pyramid selling' schemes in Albania and Romania were very destabilizing. Public anger at corruption, however, had no impact on governmental conduct there or elsewhere. Indeed the process of law was put under great pressure in a culture of compliance with power.

The fusion of politics and business was more prominent in Eastern than Western Europe. The break up of Yugoslavia and subsequent conflict there posed particular economic and fiscal burdens, which were exacerbated by the rampant corruption and related mismanagement of the Serb leadership. In December 1993 Serbia had the highest European post-1945 inflation rate.

By 2000 Poland, Slovenia and Hungary had recovered to surpass their GDP of 1990 (Poland was the first to succeed), while the Czech Republic only managed to equalize this, and in Romania, Bulgaria and Russia there had been a decline. However, the extent of post-Communist decline assumes accurate GDP figures during the Communist period, which is problematic, not least because they included a large amount of fairly useless production.

There has also been a significant change in incentive structures. Under the Communist system the incentives were all for producers, whatever the situation from the perspective of the consumer, to claim quality and quantity in production that they had not in fact achieved. An aspect of the 'campaign' or propaganda economics that took precedence over any rational assessment of means and ends, this contributed to an exaggeration of productivity not only by the Communist governments but also by foreign commentators, West Germans being particularly prone to exaggerate that of East Germany. Now, with taxation, the incentives are precisely the opposite. The result is that the extent of decline has been systematically overstated.

As a consequence it is more useful to note trends over the last decade. These show very different rates of growth. For example, in the last quarter of 2007 the annual rate of growth in the Czech Republic was 6.9 per cent and in Poland 6.1 per cent, but in Hungary only 0.7 per cent. The former East Germany benefited from major investment from what had been West Germany, notably in micro-electronics (which East Germany had long sought to develop), and biotechnology and car-making. East Germany was reconstucted economically, a unique example of the transformation of Communist economy by it being directly fused with an existing free market economy.

There has also been a massive EU operation to rebuild the economies of Eastern Europe, while the effect of the fall of trade barriers has been generally positive. Changes in the direction of trade have contributed to a new geopolitics. For example, non-Communist Finland had traded heavily with the Soviet Union, and the collapse of the latter was responsible for serious economic problems in Finland in the early 1990s, including unemployment at over 15 per cent. In turn, integration into the EU boosted Finland's economy as its trade links changed. Western capital helped the process of such integration with, for example, the *Deutsche Bahn* seeking in the late 2000s to develop trade corridors for rail and road into the Balkans.

Whatever the extent of changes in production, the opening up of Eastern Europe to consumer goods ensured that the world of things across Europe became more uniform. This uniformity was a matter of imports not only from Western Europe, but also from the rest of the world. In Poland, where Honda was established as a distributor in 1989, it took 4.8 per cent of the market in car sales in 2006; Toyota, its Japanese rival, took 14 per cent.

WESTERN EUROPE SINCE 1990

The increase in imports from outside Europe was a symptom of the extent to which in the 1990s and 2000s the EU countries steadily and rapidly became less competitive. The expansion in the world economy in the late 1980s and early 1990s, like that in the early 2000s, helped Europe, but growth did not match that in East Asia, in part because of the contrast between diminishing returns in the already developed Western European economy and growth from a low base in East Asia. Western Europe was also affected by higher labour costs and by expensive social welfare systems, while the fiscal consequences of the terms of the reunification of Germany in 1990 seriously hit the West German economy and public finances. As a clear sign of a fall in the EU's global competitiveness the percentage of trade between the member states of the EU as a percentage of their total trade rose markedly. Between 1985 and 1991 exports between its member states grew by 40 per cent, while those to other states fell by 3 per cent.

This process continued in the 1990s, helping drive the currency union that led to the adoption of the euro. Furthermore, investment in Western Europe in the 1990s rose far less than in the USA, in part because of lower productivity in Europe, although not in all aspects of the European economy, and lower investment inhibited further productivity gains. Concern about the economic fundamentals, not least labour inflexibility and costs, instead encouraged European companies to invest in the USA and East Asia, each of which, particularly the latter, proved more successful in serving global demand. In 1996 by value Germany was the world's second largest exporter, France the fifth, Britain the sixth and Italy the seventh, but growth rates in East Asia rose more rapidly over the following decades. A different index of economic activity and success was provided by multinationals, which had a particularly prominent stake in Western Europe, especially in Britain, France, Germany, Spain and the Netherlands.

Partly as a result of limited growth and of the lack of flexibility in the labour market, unemployment levels in France and Germany were far higher than in the USA: for example, 10.0, 10.6 and 5.5 per cent respectively for the second quarter of 2005. Having risen from 2.8 per cent in 1999 to 3.5 per cent in 2000, economic growth in the Eurozone fell to 1.5 per cent in 2001 and 0.8 per cent in 2002. The position was more serious in France than in Germany, because the latter has a greater public commitment to entrepreneurship and to the enterprise culture. This contrast helped lead in France to a major rise in government debt, which acted as a drag on the economy, although in January 2008 the fall of sterling against the euro ensured that France replaced Britain as the world's fifth largest economy, behind the USA, Japan, Germany and China. By the first quarter of 2008 economic growth in the Eurozone (a zone not identical with that of 2002) was at 2.1 per cent per annum, with the Netherlands (43.3 per cent) and Spain (2.7 per cent) doing better than France (2.2 per cent), and Italy (0.3 per cent in the third quarter). Despite the different growth rates the German economy (with a rate of 2.6 per cent) remains the biggest in Europe and has had a major impact in Eastern Europe. Germany is a key exporter on the world stage and is pulling along other European economies, such as Italy, independently of their membership in the EU.

Variety is, and was, a major theme amongst the European economies, as it also is and was in East Asia: Thailand is not competitive with China. Germany (but not Britain, France and Italy) can match Japan, but not China. European variety was abundantly clear in the case of Ireland, which broke free from its historical dependence on agriculture and the British market. The high rate of Irish growth was not so much due to EU 'transfers', the instructive double-speak for subsidies such as investment in infrastructure (although, as in Spain, they were important), as to the emerging dynamic of Irish entrepreneurship combined with positive government strategies. Despite ranking as only the 38th largest economy in the world, Ireland was ranked the 22nd largest exporter in absolute terms in 2000: no amount of aid can create or sustain that dynamic, and the prime minister from 1997, Bertie Ahern, was rewarded by being re-elected in 2002 and 2007, before having to resign in May 2008 due to a corruption scandal, a besetting problem in recent Irish politics.

The national level, however, is not always the best for studying economic trends, a point abundantly made by a consideration of Italy. There north and south operate as different economies and are seen as doing so, not least by the government. To a lesser extent the same is true in Britain, with a reliance on the state being particularly pronounced in the economies of Scotland, Wales and northern England, but not of southern England, which subsidizes them through the tax system. At the same time the regional dimension can be seen as supranational, with a concern with core–periphery relationships within Europe as a whole drawing attention to the position of less developed areas such as southern Italy. Although the use of the core–periphery idea is fruitful, many of these less developed areas are not on the geographical periphery: this is particularly true of former coalmining regions and areas of heavy industry, such as the Nord, Pas-de-Calais and Lorraine in France. Less prosperous areas are defined not simply by lower productivity, incomes and participation in the European economy, but also by cultural, social and political indicators of difference. The extent of the EU ensures that there are also frontiers of economic opportunity within it. These provide possibilities for investment and growth that create hotspots of expansion. In turn such expansion can create misleading impressions at the aggregate national level.

Moreover, it is important to scrutinize the causes of economic growth with care. Thus in the early and mid 2000s high rates of expansion in Spain were misleading. This expansion, like that of Iceland (which is not in the EU), was driven by ready credit based in part on capital inflows and on loose fiscal policy. In Spain there was also the impact of a shift in values, with investment in housing helping to cause construction and economic growth. Moreover, greater employment opportunities were met by large-scale immigration, which, in turn, led to demand for more housing. Although growth faltered it was still sufficiently high to help the Socialist government win re-election in March 2008. Thereafter, there was a marked economic crisis.

Investment in housing was a product of a change from a heavy emphasis on rent to an interest, instead, in home-ownership, a change also seen elsewhere, for example in France, Ireland and Italy. This is also a factor in former Communist states and is a reminder of the importance of shifts in consumer values. A desire for space also played a role as home-ownership more frequently meant house-ownership.

The freedom of movement and investment within the EU was significant, with high rates of northern Europe investment in housing near the Mediterranean, especially from Britain and the Netherlands in Spain and France. This investment helped make control over permission to build a murky issue, bringing together politics, business, law and crime. Xenophobia also played a part, not least in Greece and Spain, in each of which foreign homeowners were accused of taking land and breaching planning regulations. The related movement of people led to appreciable shifts of pension income to the Mediterranean as many of those who moved there were retired. The development of communities of foreign retirees was a significant aspect of social specialization and one that revealed the extent to which land and housing were commodities in a European market.

Any account of European economic development has to take note of the wider context, not least relations with East Asia and the USA. These relationships were very different in character, that with the USA having a greater impact on European culture. Consumer aspirations and practices were moulded by the USA, especially through television, which made them seem normative and desirable. Europeans, whether in France or in Poland, consume American fast food, not least McDonalds, while the USA is one of Europe's biggest markets.

East Asia was far less important as a source of aspirations but provided a growing percentage of Europe's goods. Indeed, in the 2000s, trade integration in the EU declined in the face of Chinese imports. In Italy, itself a major car manufacturer, Japanese car distributors were present from the start of the 1990s and by 2006 Toyota had over 5 per cent of the market share and Honda had 1.2 per cent. The Toyota share in Finland was 15 per cent. Earlier, Japanese manufacturers had encouraged in European industry the spread of new manufacturing practices, such as just-in-time inventories.

At the same time the EU has not found it as easy to adapt to the opportunities provided by the global economy. Its advocates emphasized Europe's role as the largest exporter, of both goods and investment, and the leading market, and proclaimed the adaptiveness of the EU. At the Lisbon Summit of 2000 the EU agreed that by 2010 it would be the most competitive, dynamic and knowledge-based economy in the world, as if that declaration would ensure these results. So far, indeed, the evidence is of declining competitiveness, certainly compared to East Asia.

Far from Europe coming to the front in international economic competitiveness, European companies and investors have found it easier to invest in foreign companies and/or to 'outsource' and/or 'offshore' activities. The same is true of European consumers, as the import of East Asian goods and services, especially Chinese manufactured products, enabled them to afford what was less easy to obtain within Europe at comparable prices. By late 2006, the EU trade deficit with China was an average 15 million euros an hour. In some respects this made Europe more competitive by reducing inflationary pressures, not least because the Chinese rembidi depreciated 40 per cent against the euro in 2000–7, which ensured that imports became cheaper, but imports from China also created serious rivalry for European industries. The resulting tension between consumer and producer interests in Europe was seen in struggles over restrictions and tariffs on imports of clothes and footwear from China and Vietnam. These struggles, which were bitter in the mid-2000s, opposed producer interests, particularly in Italy, to consumer interests, both convinced of the value of free trade and mindful of the concerns of consumers. Britain and the Netherlands were conspicuous on that side of the debate.

Such debates pushed the role of the European Commission to the fore and also underlined the political dimension of its regulatory activities. This dimension owed much to longstanding differences in national culture as attitudes to the desirability of government regulation varied greatly. This variation was noted in reviews such as the Fraser Institute's Economic Freedom Index: for 2005, Britain tied for 5th place and Germany tied for 18th, but Spain tied for 44th and France and Italy for 52nd. The violent anti-globalization protesters at the international summit held at Genoa in Italy in 2001 were beaten back by the police, but some of their ideas were closer to mainstream attitudes than this might have suggested. Of the major economies in Western Europe France and Italy have the highest share of state ownership. They also have a commitment to corporatism that is inimical to liberal economic measures, as can be seen, for example, in their opposition to the liberalization of energy markets and supply systems. In 2008 France made clear its hostility to any foreign takeover of the poorly managed bank Société Générale. The previous year a foreign takeover of Gaz de France was blocked. The net impact of such protectionism was to reduce choice to consumers and to keep prices artificially high. Whereas Britain, Italy and Spain split power production and distribution, France and Germany resisted doing so. In this and other matters national differences appear more crucial than the EU. Returning to performance indicators, on most of them it is the Scandinavians who come out on top, whether or not they are in the EU. Indeed, if the EU is so baleful and heavy handed, it may be asked why there are such differences in national outcomes after all these years.

The chase for lower costs opened up tensions within Europe, as offshoring meant the shift of manufacturing to Eastern Europe, where labour costs are lower. Thus Renault builds its successful Laguna car in Romania while Nokia has closed down its production plant in Bochum, Germany, and moved manufacturing to Romania. Minimum wages in Poland and the Czech Republic in 2007 were less than half those in Ireland, the Netherlands and France. This process puts pressure on wages in Western Europe especially, but not only, for less skilled jobs, leading to serious agitation in France in 2008. However, the non-liberal nature of EU regulations works to restrict the chase for lower costs.

It has proved far harder to trade services than goods in the EU because of the persistence of barriers between European countries. This persistence reflects regulatory restrictions and consumer preference, which are expressed in legal and cultural differences between national markets. Market harmonization, a goal of the EU, has not worked well at this level and, as the role of services has increased, so this emphasis on the national has proportionately become more significant. In 2005 Jacques Chirac, the French president, forced the European Commission to back down over its plan to open the EU's market in services. This Services Directive had been central to the five-year 'jobs and growth' strategy for his Commission set out in February 2005 by José Manuel Barroso, its president from 2004.

CRIME, BUSINESS AND POLITICS

The thwarting of the Services Directive of course did not extend to any limits on the circumventing of regulations by criminal networks, which themselves run major business empires, and not simply in markets that are noted for criminality. Indeed, one of the most successful European sectors was that least affected by regulation: crime. Criminal syndicates based in Europe developed links with the wider world, especially in illegal trade in drugs, prostitution, migrants and arms. Like much of the (more) legal economy, these syndicates found it easiest to make money fostering imports into Europe, especially of drugs and illegal migrants. The Italian syndicates, notably the Mafia of Sicily, the Camorra of Campania, the 'Ndrangheta of Calabria and the Sacra Corona Unita of Puglia, proved particularly successful. Their varied fortunes helped provide an important context for trends in politics and business (and vice versa), contexts that tend to attract insufficient attention. Thus in Italy state action against the Mafia in the 1990s, stemming from the decline of the Christian Democratic Party that had long protected it, provided opportunities in the drug trade for the Camorra.

A focus on Italian syndicates leads to an underplaying of other criminal networks. Here, a key development was the opportunity provided for Eastern European networks by the end of the Cold War and the consequent opening up of the 'European space'. Moreover, the failed state character of some Balkan countries, as well as the linked close relationship between business and politics mediated by corruption, a relationship that opened the path for organized crime, proved a perfect base for criminality. Thus alongside the Kosovar, Serbian and Albanian networks associated with failed states came the equivalents from countries where business, corruption and politics were closely linked, such as Bulgaria and Romania. After the Communist élite the criminals were usually the best organized, and once Communism collapsed the criminals merely filled the vacuum, although in Russia they had to compete with the secret police, who had earlier been restrained by the position of the Communist Party within the government. Under Putin (2000–8) the secret police won.

Organized crime can be seen as a cost to business and society, a negative externality, rather like war, and this is the response in much of Europe. Crime becomes an unwanted protection cost, literally so in the case of extortion, which is, for example, a major source of Mafia revenues, and a variant on the official insurance market. Yet as a key element of recent European history it is also pertinent to present such crime as integral to business and society, a form of alternative authority and power that interacts with the formal mechanisms. This is a point that could be made in the politics and society chapters, but it is particularly appropriate for the business one, as criminal networks and illegal practices provide a way not only to satisfy greed but also for businesses to circumvent regulations or to gain commercial benefits.

The extent to which those at the highest level were involved in dubious practices considered corrupt was seen in 2004 when Alain Juppé, a former French prime minister, was convicted of political corruption over embezzlement between 1977 and 1995 when his patron, Jacques Chirac, later president, was mayor of Paris. In 2007 Chirac himself was charged with embezzlement as he was no longer covered by presidential immunity. Chirac's last prime minister, Dominique de Villepin, had already been charged in 2007 with falsely claiming, in the 'Clearstream affair', that his then ministerial rival, later president, Nicolas Sarkozy, had profited from an arms deal.

Such scandals, however, diverted attention from more systemic links, such as those between the French government, the oil giant Elf-Aquitaine, and the oil-producing states in which it operated, particularly Angola and Gabon. These links provided an opportunity for France to secure oil supplies and to avoid dependence on non-French (i.e. American and British) oil companies, but the web of corruption involved not only corrupted government in the oil states, but also secret funds that washed round French politics and business. Banks played a major role in recycling the substantial wages of corruption, while the French right proved particularly eager to accept the money on offer, both from the oil states and from Elf. Indeed, in 2002 this money funded an unsuccessful attempt by Charles Pasqua to seek the presidency.

The strength of the connection between government, Elf and the oil states was such that when the Socialists under Mitterrand gained power in 1981 they found it expedient to maintain it, while Mitterrand's son took a prominent role in the politics of patronage in francophone Africa. Moreover, Elf was party to the Mitterrand–Kohl slush fund scandal that was revealed in the 1990s. As part of French acceptance of German unification Kohl promised Mitterrand that French companies would be allowed to acquire East German state-owned companies in the rapid privatization that was pushed through, not least in order to limit German government commitments in the local economy. Elf bought an oil refinery and, in return, paid about 256 million French francs to various lobbyists, including 'provisions' for Kohl and other Christian Democrat politicians. The former head of Elf admitted this, but the German investigation was cut short and all files relating to the matter were destroyed when Kohl left office in 1998. The funding scandal nevertheless implicated Wolfgang Schaüble, the CDU chairman, and Kohl was eventually stripped of his title of honorary chairman of the CDU.

As a reminder of the difference between national political cultures, the awarding by Britain, the Netherlands and Norway of licences to drill for oil and natural gas in the North Sea was not characterized by anywhere near the same level of corruption. Moreover, though bribery played a role in gaining some foreign contracts, for example with BAE's success in Saudi Arabia, the profits did not water the springs of British politics.

Oil was not the sole bonanza on offer. The massive transfers of assets involved in privatizations after the fall of Communist regimes attracted the attention of profiteers who, depending on one's perspective, can be seen as criminals, businessmen and/or politicians. The same was true of state subsidies in the West, at every level of government, from the EU to the local council. Agricultural subsidies and regional development funds were the EU programmes most susceptible to corruption. The court of auditors, the EU's financial watchdog, has qualified the EU's accounts for over a decade. The court reported that 12 per cent of the 32 billion euro regional fund budget was paid out in error in 2006, with receiving states unable to provide adequate explanations for how they have spent the money they received. Four-fifths of the EU's budget (which totalled 107 billion euro in 2006) is spent nationally. Planning agreements were another major sphere for corruption, as in Ireland, notably with the prime minister in 1979–82 and 1987–92, Charles Haughey, who had a justifiably dubious reputation.

Banking proved another key instance of corruption, with soft loans from banks being used to reward political allies and to finance the purchase of assets, and this was seen in particular in the privatization of state assets after the fall of Communist regimes. These soft loans frequently became non-performing (could not yield interest), which put pressure on the banking system, for example in Slovakia by 1998.

Regulation of what was often fraudulent involved political favours, while the entire process, which was obviously not transparent, shut out foreign investment.

In Russia the richest European state as far as natural resources are concerned, rival security services played an additional role, and competing interests ensured that the overlaps between crime, business and politics that Putin sought to control still remained inherently unstable and even destabilizing. These overlaps made the nature of Russian politics particularly opaque, and rendered most political reporting of it of limited value.

This process can be seen as limited to Eastern Europe but that would be inaccurate, as soft loans, political connections (and financing) and an absence of appropriate regulation were also seen in Western Europe, notably in France and Italy. This situation helped explain the opposition of their governments to foreign takeovers, as well as their resistance in the EU to the liberalization of services.

If this appears somewhat alarmist to anglophone readers who are not used to seeing so much emphasis placed on corruption, it is worth considering both Italy and post-Communist Eastern Europe, and to do so without imagining that these issues are restricted to them, as any consideration of Mitterrand's circle would indicate. In Italy the miasma of corruption encompassing crime, business and politics included, and drew on, the secret services and focused for a while on P2, the Masonic Lodge Propaganda 2, whose extensive membership included leading members of the military, the secret services, the judiciary and the business and political communities. The Lodge, a 1970s phenomenon mostly neutralized by the end of the 1980s, sought to spread its power within Italy deliberately in order to increase its political influence.

Related networks played a prominent role in the Vatican, and the death of Roberto Calvi encouraged fresh speculation. The head of the Banco Ambrosiano, he was convicted in 1981 for financial offences and released pending an appeal. In 1982 his bank was saved from collapse by the Vatican's bank, with which he had been involved in questionable deals. Later that year Calvi was found dead in London. Initially presented as a suicide, there were many reports, especially in Italy, of

Mafia involvement in his murder at the behest of the Vatican. The suicide of another banker, Michele Sindona, was also seen as a murder.

Moreover, the linkage of P2 with the secret services and, through them, the CIA, provides an instructive way to consider the anti-Communist struggle in Italy and more widely in Europe. The CIA played a major role in anti-Communist activities in Italy, for example in the Gladio system. Designed to organize resistance in the event of Soviet occupation, this proved a basis for secret political action. The links between this alignment and the Vatican, which, under John Paul II, was particularly vigorous in its hostility to Communism, are unclear. The business aspects of covert political links varied: arms manufacture, for example, tended to be particularly linked into the networks already discussed. Yet other businesses were also important, not least as means to channel funds. If Italy was exceptional in Western Europe, aspects of the situation there could also be found elsewhere, notably in France.

Unlike in Italy, in post-Communist Eastern Europe the secret services were seen as a throw-back to the Communist era. They provided, according to critics, for example in Poland and, even more clearly, Putin's Russia, a shadow-establishment in which political and business interests were both involved. This shadow-establishment was a carry-on of the structure of the Communist state which, alongside the Marxist rhetoric, entailed a coalition of interests shaping policy and dividing privilege, in secret and sometimes with intimidation and (occasionally brutal) trade-offs. Secrecy and the absence of democratic politics provided a helpful context for Communist-era corruption, while public anger enabled some politicians, such as Boris Yeltsin, when first secretary of the Moscow City Communist Party Committee from 1985 to 1987, to curry popularity by prominently attacking corruption. The Communist states also took an active role in foreign trade that involved trade-offs with the West, as well as more nefarious activities. Bodies such as the East German KoKo specialized in smuggling, industrial espionage and secret trade. In turn West German companies offered benefits to obtain economic links with East Germany.

The share-out of power between coalitions of interests seen in Communist states could also be observed in non-Communist systems.

This share-out was particularly the case where, as in Austria, these interests (in the form of political parties) were able to benefit from their control of particular parts of a federal system. Thus Socialists could expect to benefit from government in Vienna, and conservatives in Graz and Innsbruck, and so on. This system was known as *Proporz* (Proportionality) and was associated in particular with the period from 1970 to 1983 when Bruno Kreisky was chancellor. Anger against this system helped the far-right Liberals to gain popularity in the 1990s, and in 2000–6 they were part of the governing coalition.

The (varied) degree to which, across Europe, political and criminal forces were not extraneous to the world of business can be taken further by considering the political pressures involved in media regulation (see previous chapter) and in banking supervision. A focus on crony capitalism (or corrupt governance) in Europe, as in other areas such as Japan, challenges the discussion of economics in terms of quantitative models based on the free flow of resources, but such liberal tendencies are not hardwired into the political economy and political culture of Europe. That, however, does not mean that these tendencies do not play an important role, and this role has been expanded both due to the demands of the global market and as a result of the liberalization that was a requirement for accessions to the EU.

As so often with the EU and more widely, judgement depends on the point of comparison. What may appear an absence of liberalization from the perspective of Britain can seem very different from the perspectives of Greece or Bulgaria in 1970. Indeed, the 'catching-up' by formerly peripheral areas has been a key element of the period of this book, one that resumes a major theme of the pre-1914 expansion of the European economy. The significance of this 'catching-up' encourages an emphasis on the results of the collapse of authoritarianism in Greece, Portugal and Spain in the early 1970s and of Communist rule in Eastern Europe in the late 1980s. More generally, the political context and consequences of this 'catching-up' are a theme of the next chapter.

Chapter 7

Politics to 1991

Europe was transformed politically from the early 1970s to the early 1990s. The fall of Communism in 1989–91 dominates attention and I am struck by how many people see it as the key development of the period covered by this study. Indeed, the collapse of European Communism and the Soviet zone was highly significant in European and world terms. The early 1970s, however, were also very important, both in one particular part of Europe and more generally. They ushered in what was a terrible decade, a time of profound rupture with the entire post-war era of economic growth, expanding welfare and social cohesion. Instead, the oil shocks, double-digit inflation, unemployment and strike waves of all sorts made it the worst decade since the war. Alongside terrorism, democracy was strained to the limits in some places while, more generally, there were the battles of producer groups against the rest.

THE 1970S CRISIS

The problems of the late 1960s led into the crisis of the 1970s, notably fiscal and economic difficulties in the USA. Very slack American monetary and fiscal policies were a particular problem. More generally the different levels of inflation in particular economies in the late 1960s made it very difficult to manage the international economy and exchange rates established in 1944. Instead, in August 1971 President Richard Nixon suspended the convertibility of the dollar into gold, allowing the dollar to fall.

Difficulties were turned into crisis when the major producers in the Middle East grouped in the Organization of Petroleum Exporting Countries (OPEC) pushed up the price of oil from $3 a barrel in 1972 to $12 at the close of 1974. This increase hit oil importers and fuelled inflation, damaging economic confidence. The crisis of the 1970s did not match that of the 1930s but much of Europe matched the USA in suffering from stagflation, a combination of stagnation and inflation, which led to a sense of uncertainty and malaise. In Western Europe the crisis encouraged both the extreme left and the extreme right, providing a new stage for some of the tensions expressed in the late 1960s.

The EEC was unable to cope with the oil crisis and consequent upheavals but it tried. Indeed currency stabilization in the European Monetary System (EMS) was an attempt to shelter European currencies from the instability of the dollar. In doing so the Europeans sought to rely on the economic growth and strength of West Germany and on the stability of its fiscal system. The EMS and the Snake (by which exchange rates were only allowed to fluctuate within limits) in effect replaced the dollar by the West German Deutschmark as the European benchmark, and this was crucial to the eventual development of the euro. However, this development was not so much the result of a clearly conceived policy as the product of the problems posed by the outside world.

These problems included a geopolitical shift in which Western weakness seemed apparent. American political and fiscal difficulties, generally summarized by two words, Vietnam and Watergate, but, in fact, involving far more, were made ominous by signs of Soviet activity. After its Arab protégés were defeated by Israel in the Six Days War in 1967, the Soviet Union rearmed Egypt and Syria and they put Israel under considerable pressure, culminating with the nearly successful attack in the Yom Kippur War of 1973, which was linked to the oil price hike. The latter was seen as a way to put pressure on the West. Meanwhile the Soviets had deployed a substantial naval force in the

Mediterranean, challenging NATO's earlier hegemony there, and there was also Soviet action in Africa, particularly in Angola and Mozambique. The American ability to respond to these and other moves was gravely lessened by the focus on military resources on the Vietnam War in Southeast Asia. In turn American caution about making the war more total there, for example by invading North Vietnam, was in part related to an awareness of NATO's vulnerability in Europe to Soviet attack.

THE TRANSFORMATION OF SOUTHERN EUROPE

It was also in the early 1970s that dramatic changes occurred in southern Europe, a category in the shaping of Europe that tends to be forgotten when the emphasis, as is usually the case, is on Western and Eastern Europe. In 1974 the military dictatorship in Greece that had begun in 1967 came to an end. So also did the authoritarian regime that had headed Portugal since the 1920s. Moreover, in 1975 Francisco Franco, dictator of Spain since 1939, died. Developments in these three countries followed their own autonomous trajectories but were also related to and, more, perceived within the international context of the Cold War.

PORTUGAL

It was unclear that Portugal, Spain and Greece would make a transition to stable democratic government, and this increased international interest in them. António Salazar, dictator of Portugal from 1932, had died in 1970, but his authoritarian government had retained control, and change appeared unlikely. In the event a coup in Portugal on 25 April 1974 by the Armed Forces Movement was followed by a period of instability that lasted until 1976. As a reminder of the range of measures represented by political change, and of the degree of variety in the Europe of the 1970s, the coup led to the release of political prisoners, the legalization of a free press and of the Socialist and Communist parties, and the abolition of the secret police. The new government became increasingly radical, nationalizing much of the economy and collectivizing the land. Social tension increased, with the Communists active in land reform and using direct action to achieve their goals. Land reform proved particularly unpopular in northern and central Portugal, where much of the land was run by small family farms (unlike the estates of the south), and where a strongly entrenched and popular Catholic Church found itself the target of Communist agitation. As a result the Communists only won an eighth of the vote in the April 1975 elections for the Constituent Assembly. The Socialists did more than three times as well, which led to Communist talk of gaining power through a coup. It seemed possible that Portugal would become not only a left-wing, one-party state, challenging NATO, of which it was a member, from within Western Europe, but also a Communist one.

In fact the Portuguese Communists lacked sufficient support within the army and this led to the failure of an attempted coup in November 1975. Instead, in February 1976 the army handed over power to civilian politicians and in that April's elections the Socialists were again the leading party. This was not the end of the crisis, but it was the beginning of the end. In part thanks to serious economic strains, not least due to the transition to a post-imperial economy, the Communist vote increased to 19 per cent in 1979, but the Socialists remained both dominant and moderate. The Agrarian Reform Law of 1977 provided an acceptable limit to collectivization, essentially accepting it only for big estates in the south. The democratic system was sufficiently grounded to enable the replacement of the Socialist government by a right-of-centre one in 1980 that pushed through privatization measures.

These shifts were also of great importance in terms of Europe's position in the world. In 1974 Portugal was Europe's leading overseas colonial power (the Soviet Union can be seen as the leading colonial power, at least if Russia's position is considered), with colonies in Angola, Mozambique and Portuguese Guinea. Spain ruled a section of the Sahara, the Spanish Sahara. Both powers had been resisting independence demands and this ensured that Europe's colonial role was not simply a matter of the past. In Angola 70,000-strong Portuguese forces, supported by secret police, paramilitary forces, settler vigilantes and African informers, effectively restricted guerrilla operations there and, more generally, protected the 350,000 white settlers in the colony, albeit at great cost and with heavy casualties. Although the strains of inflation stemming from the oil crisis running ahead of public sector wages played a role, the coup in Portugal in 1974 owed much to military dissatisfaction with the longstanding counter-insurgency war in its African colonies and to popular hostility to military service. It was followed by the granting of independence to the colonies the following year. Similarly, the death of Franco in 1975 was followed by withdrawal from the Spanish Sahara the following year.

The legacy of these developments was important not only in the former colonies, but also in the imperial metropoles. This was particularly the case in Portugal as three-quarters of a million people from the large settler populations returned there with few possessions and with a potent sense of grievance. Many remained for years in hastily erected housing on the edge of Portuguese cities and this brought a degree of edginess to both politics and society. With time, however, the tension was eroded, in large part due to the benefits of economic growth that became particularly apparent after Portugal joined the EEC. Portugal had applied to join in 1977 as a key aspect of a political normalization and international acceptance that had already been seen when it was admitted to the Council of Europe the previous year. It was not to join, however, until 1986 because its entry was linked to that of Spain. The latter faced several problems, not least French concerns about agricultural competition: the French were worried about sharing subsidies and markets. However, the process of joining and wishing to be seen as acceptable was important in encouraging moderation in Portuguese politics. There was no equivalent to the attempted Spanish coup of 1981.

GREECE

Portugal was not alone in having a political history that owed much to the interaction of national with international developments. To a certain extent, the fall of right-wing regimes in Greece and Spain can also be placed in this context. The Greek junta sought in 1974 to strengthen its wavering domestic popularity by backing the long-standing demand for enosis, union with Cyprus, an independent state with a Greek-speaking Christian majority but where the Turkish Muslim minority were protected by the Turkish Cypriot role in the governing 'partnership' arrangement. In July 1974, with Greek backing, this government was overthrown and replaced by another that was designed to implement enosis. Moreover, the 'ethnic cleansing' of Turks was begun by the Greeks.

However, a rapid military response by Turkey – an invasion of much of the island which was accepted by the USA – led to the humiliation of the far weaker Greek junta. Its authority gone, the junta handed over power to Constantine Karamanlis, a conservative who had been prime minister from 1956 to 1963. His New Democracy Party won the elections in November 1974 and a new constitution was introduced in 1975. A political pattern similar to that of Western Europe was established, while Cyprus remained divided and about 165,000 Greek Cypriots were driven from the Turkish zone.

SPAIN

In Spain there was also a transition to democracy. Franco was implacably against democratic change and made Juan Carlos, grandson of the last king, swear an oath that he would uphold the values of the Francoist National Movement. Franco claimed that he had left everything 'all tied down, well tied down', but the struggle to keep him alive suggested how ill prepared Spain was for a successor. Moreover, Franco did not reckon with significant members of the political and economic élites who saw that the structures of Francoism were in decay. Yet the transition to democracy was by no means inevitable and there were a number of forces, especially the army, the left and the Basque terrorist movement ETA, which could have thrown a spanner in the works. Once a democratic succession was determined and took effect after his death it was uncertain whether former Francoists would co-operate with it. The prospect of another coup like that in which Franco had seized power in 1936 was a concern, however improbable that might seem today.

Power continued for a while to be held by Francoists, while the monarchy was reintroduced under Juan Carlos. The relatively orderly transition to a democracy in which there was a considerable amount of continuity was very much a shift encouraged by the USA, which wanted to ensure that Spain did not experience the instability seen in Portugal. Juan Carlos, crowned two days after Franco died, proved important to the shift. He took an active role, helping to encourage Francoists and the military, which looked to his leadership, to accept the new order. Under Franco there were no independent political parties and no free press and, outside the small group that ran the state, there was scant political life at a national level and no capacity for organized change. As a consequence it was the new king and the small group of Francoists that played the key role in what Spaniards term 'the Transition'. Franco's prime minister, Carlos Arias Navarro, was kept in office until 1976 when the king replaced him. This was because Arias had sought to keep the old system in place by arresting the heads of the newly constituted Democratic Coordination of banned parties of the left. Although the Transition was relatively orderly, political killings were rife in the late 1970s. For example, in January 1977 five Communist labour lawyers were murdered by right-wing assassins.

Juan Carlos replaced Arias with Adolfo Suárez González, a member of the Francoist system but one willing to see through change, rather like some of the ex-Communists who held power in Eastern Europe in the 1990s. Suárez created a political party, the Centre Democratic Union (Unión de Centro Democrático, UCD), and secured a national referendum for universal suffrage for a bicameral parliament, a measure overwhelmingly passed on 15 December 1976. The following spring Suárez legalized the Spanish Socialist Party, trade unions, the right to strike and the Spanish Communist Party, while the Francoist National Movement, once headed by Suárez, was disbanded.

The elections held in June 1977, the first in Spain since 1936, gave Suárez's moderate party just under half the seats, and the new Assembly drafted a Constitution which was confirmed in December 1978. This constitution added social and cultural reform to the institutionalization of a parliamentary monarchy: the death penalty was abolished, the voting age was reduced to eighteen and there was to be no state religion. Proportional representation and bicameralism were seen as ways to promote a moderation lacking in the pre-Francoist Second Republic. The abandonment of radical Marxism by the Socialist Party, which did well in the 1977 election, was also significant to the success of the Transition.

In a major break with the centralizing practices of the Francoist state, the Constitution recognized regional autonomy and, under the Statutes of Autonomy, such autonomy indeed followed for all of Spain, although the central government reserved key powers including foreign policy. Suárez won re-election in 1979 but tension increased with new-found rights for strike action and regional autonomy, creating unease and tension. As a result in January 1981 Suárez was forced out by his party.

Paranoid anxieties on the right, or, looked at differently, a response, drawing on a genuine hatred of democracy and on nostalgia for old ways, to the destruction of the old order, led to an attempted coup on 23 February 1981. Colonel Tejero of the Civil Guard took over the Cortes (parliament), while General Milans del Bosch, the head of the Valencia military region, called a state of emergency and pressed Juan Carlos to establish a military government. This coup was very much a make-or-break moment for democratic Spain, and led to many fears that there would be a return to a Francoist past, or at least instability. Juan Carlos, however, acted promptly and clearly, using television to broadcast his affirmation of the Constitution and democratic rule. His stance ensured that most of the army did not support the coup, which then collapsed. Juan Carlos was also significant in that he did not seek power for himself. Instead, he proved a successful constitutional monarch in a country with no tradition of such a monarchy, which serves as a reminder of the diversity of types of government in late twentieth-century Europe. In contrast the monarchy did not return when military rule ended in Greece, and there was no prospect of its return in Portugal.

The failure of the 1981 coup helped further to break the logjam of the past. The divided army was now weaker and the military budget was reduced. The army also became increasingly professionalized, and membership of NATO meant that officers' horizons shifted hugely, so that combating 'the enemy within' no longer became its primary purpose. This development was a key aspect of a more long-term departure from the alignments and issues of the 1930s, a departure that, to a considerable extent, had been carried out under Franco. In part this was due to the strength of his position and success of his policies, with anarcho-syndicalism and violent anti-clericalism both ceasing to play a role in Spanish politics. Neither revived in the 1970s. More significant was the social and economic transformation centred on the rapid move from the land. In addition, affected by the Second Vatican Council, the Catholic Church by the 1970s was more willing to consider change, while its new-found democratic credentials ensured that it was not the target for action.

As a consequence of the 1981 coup more social change could be pushed through, in the shape, in particular, of the legalization of divorce. As another sign of change, Spanish politics could more closely approximate those of other Western European countries. Turning away from dreams of Francoist return, the right consolidated itself within the democratic political system, backing the Popular Alliance, a new party. This backing reduced the range of manoeuvre for the UCD, not least because the uneasiness with change that had caused tension in the run-up to the coup remained strong on the right. Added difficulties arose from economic problems. The Francoist regime had not been best placed to respond to the economic shocks of the early 1970s and instead had exacerbated the situation by trying, like Eastern European governments or, for that matter, Britain's Labour government, to manipulate the situation in order to win popularity. This, however, had led to high inflation, fiscal problems and a major rise in unemployment, which produced doubts about the future of Spain, doubts strengthened by the problems stemming from the oil price shock of 1979.

The response was a corporatist one: the Moncola Pacts of 1977 and their successors down to 1984. In these, government brought employers and trade unions together to agree on measures to contain fiscal problems and reform the economy. There was a parallel with developments in much of Europe, including Britain's experiment with a social compact. In Denmark the two leading political parties, the Venstre and the Social Democrats, formed a coalition government in 1978 in order to implement an incomes policy to help deal with serious economic problems. However, it proved impossible to secure such a policy and the government collapsed.

Despite the Pacts tensions in Spain continued because economic problems remained serious. These tensions strained the social and political fabric with strikes, and with the Communist Party unhappy that the Pacts did not ease hardship. In October 1982 there was a political transformation, rather like that in France the previous year. The Socialist Party won an absolute majority in parliament, while the Communists were routed. There were also changes on the right, with the UCD destroyed electorally, while the Popular Alliance won just over half of the vote.

As with Mitterrand's Socialists in France in 1981 the Socialist Party under Felipe González won in part by exploiting populist hunger for change and widespread concern about the consequences of capitalism and, as in France from 1982, there was in practice to be a more prudential and pragmatic governance. Relatively deflationary policies intended to ensure fiscal stability were continued under González who remained prime minister until he lost the 1996 election. Moreover, as an aspect of the crucial international contexts, Spain anchored itself more widely, in 1986 joining the EEC and backing NATO membership in a referendum held later that year. Unlike Portugal and Greece, which had been longstanding members of NATO, Spain only joined in 1982, and membership of NATO and the EEC prefigured the same route that was to be taken by most of the states of Communist Europe. However, the domestic political situation was different because the left was more politically powerful and popular in Spain in the 1980s than in much of Eastern Europe after the fall of the Communist regimes. Indeed, in 1982 the Spanish Socialists had campaigned on a plank of leaving NATO, while there was also a strong Marxist plank to the party. González's breach with this was important to the more general transition of the Spanish left, and also to the developing character of the EEC at this juncture. He won absolute majorities in the elections of 1982, 1986 and 1990 although from 1994 he had to rely on Basque and Catalan nationalists.

The transition experienced by Greece, Portugal and Spain was considerable. It may appear not to have matched that of the former Communist states, but a comparison of Spanish society and politics in 2007 with that of 40 years earlier might suggest otherwise. The common note was of a liberalization that was not solely political, and this was also to be the case with Eastern Europe. Economic liberalization was also a challenge as free trade within the EEC threatened the viability of uncompetitive sectors of the economy, which had serious social consequences. The most important example was the challenge to traditional agriculture, especially to peasant producers.

Spain, Portugal and Greece also witnessed large-scale social and cultural liberalization, which was politically prominent because the earlier conservative dictatorships in each country had closely identified themselves with opposition to such liberalization, an opposition seen as affirming moral worth. The subsequent liberalization can be seen in terms of the crucial importance of governmental change but it can also be argued that this analysis exaggerates the importance of governmental action and that in practice there was already a major transformation, not least because the young were responding to trends elsewhere in Europe. This was particularly true of Spain, where the Francoist regime became less rigid in its last years.

WESTERN EUROPE IN THE 1970S

The EEC that Greece, Portugal and Spain all joined was itself changing structurally. In 1974 the heads of government decided to meet thrice annually as a European Council and that the European Parliament should be directly elected every five years, rather than having its members nominated by national parliaments. The first elections as a result were held in 1979. Moreover, as a sign of the greater significance of the European Parliament, transnational party co-operation developed there. The European Court of Justice also extended its activity. These structural changes were both a progressive working-through of the implications and possibilities of the EEC, a working-through newly possible as De Gaulle's legacy was discarded in France, and at the same time an attempt to create a stronger Europe in order to respond to the challenges of the 1970s economic downturn.

The volatility the latter threatened also encouraged interest in monetary union. Both trade within the EEC and the economics of the CAP were affected by changing exchange rates, and the problems of a number of the EEC currencies seemed particularly serious. Initially there was an attempt at fixing the limits within which currencies could vary, which was known as the Snake, and its creation was followed by an attempt to link the Snake to the American dollar. The system failed in 1974 but interest revived and, in 1978, a new EMS was agreed by the Council of Ministers. As part of the Snake this added the European Currency Unit (ECU), a unit based on a 'basket' of currencies dominated by the West German mark. The ECU was seen as the basis for a European currency while the Snake, which was to be controlled by the Exchange Rate Mechanism (ERM), established in 1979, was designed to facilitate fiscal stability and to squeeze out inflation. France and Germany dominated the system, which Britain did not join until 1990.

These were major changes within Western Europe but, meanwhile, the relationship between Western Europe and the wider world was changing. Here, with the exception of Portugal and Spain, it was not so much, as in the 1960s, a case of the end of European imperialism but, rather, a case of new policies toward the Communist bloc. Western Europe remained part of NATO but the American alliance became less influential as a result of America's involvement in the Vietnam War and the crisis of American power that accompanied and followed the fall of President Nixon (he resigned on 9 August 1974) and the economic and political travails of the early and mid-1970s. Moreover, American stagflation did not seem a good model while, indeed, Nixon's attempts at wage and price controls suggested that the Americans were seeking to follow European-style remedies.

OSTPOLITIK AND DÉTENTE

The major change, instead, was a shift in relations with the Eastern bloc, a shift that suggested the possibility of new developments within

Europe. Both Britain and, even more, France had seen themselves as able to negotiate with the Soviet Union, but the key impetus was provided by West Germany. Willy Brandt, the Social Democratic Party (SDP) leader, who became chancellor in 1969 when a Christian Democrat–Social Democratic coalition was replaced by a Social Democrat–Free Democrat coalition, wished to transform the inherited West German governmental hostility to East Germany and Eastern Europe into a more benign relationship that would bring stability and also enable West Germany to take a more central role in Europe. The SDP was not politically linked to the refugees from Eastern Europe, as its CDU rival was, and was readier to renounce what it saw as outdated and unhelpful policies. This was '60s politics in action. Brandt's *Ostpolitik* (eastern policy) sought to address the tensions of the Cold War, not least West Germany's refusal to recognize East Germany and to accept the latter's border with Poland, a border that represented massive losses of German territory as a result of the Second World War.

Under the Christian Democratic Party-dominated governments, there had been a refusal to consider *détente* with the East until the division of Germany and frontier disputes with Poland had been addressed, but this policy had failed to deliver results. Moreover, the understandably passive NATO response to the Soviet invasion of Czechoslovakia in 1968 confirmed that it was prudent to reach settlement in Central Europe and necessary to do so by negotiating with the East. *Ostpolitik* also reflected a degree of assertion based on West German economic recovery and political stability, as well as a rejection of the nostrums of a previous generation, and, furthermore, was a key instance of the recurring European search for political alternatives to the military logic of the arms race, a search which took different forms at particular times. Helsinki and *détente* were to confirm the worth of this strategy, as did the final stages of the Cold War, when the Americans took the strategy over.

Brandt wanted a German solution for a German problem and was influenced by De Gaulle's conviction that Europe should settle its issues itself. Yet American attitudes were also very important. Concerned about East Asia and forced by its weakened circumstances to accept change, the American government was unwilling to focus on the former goal of German reunification, a measure unwelcome to East Germany. Moreover, Nixon was willing to accept *Ostpolitik* as a means for stabilization, while the West German government took pains to ensure that the American support was retained during the negotiations. There were attempts by some West German commentators to suggest that the latter offered West Germany an opportunity to shift alignments and rediscover an 'Eastern vocation', but these got nowhere. West Germany was not to be neutralized like Austria and Finland. In 1970 West Germany signed treaties with the Soviet Union and Poland recognizing the existing borders.

The Soviet Union sought the acceptance of its dominant position in Eastern Europe as well as a stronger position from which to confront China. The prospect of cutting defence costs was significant to the Soviet leadership and there was also interest in the benefit of expanded trade, not least importing Western technology, which itself was an admission of the failings of the Communist economic system. *Détente* therefore appealed to different constituencies in the Soviet Union. Soviet interest in stability was shown in 1971 in Brezhnev's speech to the 24th Congress of the Communist Party of the Soviet Union in which he called for international security and devoted scant space to the international cause of 'national liberation'.

In France, less comfortable than Nixon with the strategic possibilities of *Ostpolitik* and its implications for power relationships within Western Europe, Pompidou abandoned De Gaulle's hostility to British entry into the EEC. Helped greatly by British willingness under Edward Heath to abandon longstanding national interests, accession agreements were finalized in July 1971, signed in January 1972 and took effect a year later. These brought Britain, Ireland and Denmark into the EEC, but Norway rejected membership in a referendum held in September 1972 (53.5 per cent voted no on a 79 per cent turnout). Pompidou's fears were assuaged by continued West German support for the EEC, while British membership was confirmed by a referendum in 1975, held to settle differences over membership within the Labour Party, which had won power in 1974.

The 1970 treaties were followed by the acceptance of East Germany as an independent state, thus ending the West German claim under the Hallstein Doctrine of 1955 to represent all Germans, which was a challenge to the legitimacy of East Germany. Under that Doctrine, which had been essentially abandoned by 1965, diplomatic relations were to be broken off with states that established them with East Germany. A special relationship had also been allowed in the EEC Treaty, which provided for a privileged economic relationship between the two Germanys.

In contrast to the Hallstein Doctrine, there was, as a result of the 1970 treaties, to be one German nation and two German states, a development enshrined in the Basic Treaty with East Germany signed on 8 November 1972 and ratified by the West German Parliament in 1973. Brandt's victory in the 1972 elections made this certain. The first inter-German governmental talks were held in March 1970. This 'normalization' meant, however, recognizing the legality of a totalitarian state that treated its citizens harshly, as any visit today to a *Stasi* prison will indicate, but that was part of the burden of 'normalization', indeed it meant acceptance of a regime that now put more of an effort into the *Stasi*. Another unpleasant aspect of the process were secret payments by the West German government in return for people being allowed to leave East Germany, many for family reunification. Although it was common knowledge that such payments were made, it would have been counterproductive and provocative to give them a great deal of publicity. The criteria adopted by the East Germans in judging who to allow out provide an instructive variant on the usual ways in which social structures are discussed. The killing of refugees by East German border guards continued.

Had Brandt not taken the lead other powers would probably have done so, but at the same time West German governmental and public complicity in the East German regime increased alongside engagement with it. This complicity was displayed both by Brandt's SPD successor, Helmut Schmidt, and by the latter's Christian Democratic replacement from 1982, Helmut Kohl. Complicity is a harsh term, however, as it can be argued that little would have been achieved by upholding the Hallstein Doctrine and continuing to refuse to enter into dialogue with East Germany. The change in policy brought real relief in the form of visiting rights and family reunifications, not to mention buying 'regime opponents' out of jail. The era of Schmidt, chancellor from 1974 to 1982, and of his East German counterpart Erich Honecker, led to a sober, measured rapprochement and a resolution of relations between the two states. The 1970s were seen as a period of a German–German community of responsibility against the background of a reduction of international tension.

As part of this community, concern within West Germany about the plight of East Germans, let alone about reunification, markedly declined. There was no real West German support for the citizens' rights movements in East Germany. Instead, stabilization was more significant as a goal. The easing of relations thus entailed an acceptance of the governing system in Eastern Europe: for example of the suppression of the Czech Spring in 1968. East Germany, recognized for the first time as a state by much of the world in 1973, was admitted to the United Nations and other international bodies. There was to be no 'roll-back' of Communism, no equivalent to the changes that were to occur in Greece, Portugal and Spain, although there was also the assumption that the Soviet Union and its allies would not seek to 'roll forward' by destabilizing these countries.

The easing of relations was also an aspect of a growing conservatism in the Soviet bloc, which owed something to the rejection of the adventurism associated with Nikita Khrushchev, who had fallen from power in the Soviet Union in 1964, and his replacement by the more complacent Leonid Brezhnev, and something to the gerontocratic character of government there and elsewhere in the Soviet bloc. In Eastern Europe the Communist Party declared 'peaceful co-existence' with the West to be 'a form of class struggle', which was certainly squaring the circle. It also ensured a reduction in anti-Western propaganda. The West German ambition of 'change by closer relations' was to prove more successful but only in the long term. Moreover, in the short term the Western aid, financial and economic, provided as an aspect of *Ostpolitik*, stabilized the Communist regimes without bringing much liberalization. Meanwhile, across Eastern Europe, anger about the Soviet presence, and individual and family memories of Soviet brutality in 1945, continued to play a role in the active oral culture that the totalitarian character of the state made important.

The Helsinki Accords of August 1975 were a European-wide process of stabilization, although, as proof of the necessity to use NATO in order to act as a counterweight to the Soviet Union, both the USA and Canada were also represented. Indeed, while flowing from the settlement of the German question, Helsinki owed much to an American policy of *détente* also seen in Nixon's visit to China in 1972. This opening made it less serious strategically for the USA to abandon South Vietnam, which the Vietnam peace settlement of 1973 facilitated, and Helsinki, a step agreed upon by NATO ministers in December 1971, was part of the same strategy. *Détente* in Europe was more than a product of American weakness and European stabilization. The American–Chinese *rapprochement* had rapidly altered the geopolitics of the Communist world, by making strategic use of the earlier Chinese–Soviet split. The Soviets felt it necessary to devote more forces to their frontier with a no-longer-isolated China, and the American sense that Southeast Asia would follow Vietnam ebbed. The war between China and the Soviet protégé Vietnam in 1978–9 might seem distant from the affairs of Europe, and was scarcely followed by its public, but it was linked to the revival of America's position and the gathering problems of that of the Soviet Union, both of which were to be important to the politics of the 1980s.

The Helsinki Accords accepted existing borders (Principle III) and non-intervention in the internal affairs of other states (Principle VI), thus meeting Soviet objectives. Although linked, in Principle VII, to remarks about human rights and fundamental liberties, the Soviet Union was sufficiently adept in preaching rights while practicing autocracy for this to appear to pose no problem. These glosses on Principle VII reflected the differing meanings of *détente*, in which the sense of Europe as a common space was underlined by agreements to co-operate in trade, industry, science, the environment and cultural and educational matters. That these became normative in an international treaty covering all of Europe was important, and can be seen as looking toward the aspirations of the EU, although the latter excludes Russia.

Furthermore, the combination of stabilization, rights and a European common space did provide a window of opportunity for dissidents in Eastern Europe who cited the Helsinki agreements as a cover for their activities. This window, however, owed more to the

changing nature of government in Eastern Europe, not least the abandonment of Stalinist repression. In Czechoslovakia the 'normalization'
regime of Gustàv Husàk sought to renew the Communist Party in
order to thwart the 'dissidents', such as Václav Havel, and their human
rights organization, Charter 77.

EUROPE FROM THE 1970S TO THE 1980S

In 1979 when the Soviet Union invaded Afghanistan, initially with
considerable success, it seemed at the peak of its power, not least because
it was in secure control of Eastern Europe. Yet those Communist supporters in Western Europe who felt able to claim that the Soviet Union
represented a more successful model than Western liberalism, for example the secretary-general of the French Communists, Georges Marchais,
had been hit by the invasion of Czechoslovakia in 1968 as well as by
exiles and dissidents reporting on what life was really like in the Soviet
Union. Even in Italy Communist strength was declining by 1979, while
the Italian Communist Party (PCI) contained plenty of space for members
who did not think of the Soviet Union. Euro-Communism was in practice a criticism of the Soviet Union.

Moreover, although global pressures helped give rise to xenopho-
bic, right-wing parties the West adjusted to the economic challenges of
the last four decades of the century with far less difficulty than did the
Communist states, and shaped the resulting opportunities far more
successfully. In the 1930s the crisis of the capitalist model had helped
produce a new authoritarianism in the shape of Nazi Germany and
other states characterized by populism, corporatism and autarky. In
contrast, in the 1970s, early 1980s, and early 1990s widespread fiscal
problems and unemployment linked to globalist pressures led either
to the panacea of social welfare or to democratic conservative governments. The latter sought to 'roll back the state' and pursued liberal
economic policies, opening their markets and freeing currency movements and credit from most restrictions.

Economic problems were accompanied by a major shift in industry,
away from the heavy manufacturing sectors that had been dominant

from the nineteenth century and toward both lighter industry and services. This shift had consequences for localities and regions and led to highly differentiated patterns in opportunity and unemployment. These differences fed through into the local weave of politics. Economic problems posed difficulties across the political spectrum as politicians struggled with how best to respond. On the left the declining position of heavy industries was a challenge to the trade unions that were central to left-wing political parties. Indeed, some of these parties were really an expression of the unions, funded by them, reliant on them for their local organization and seeing themselves as intended to fulfil the goals of the working class as represented in the unions. Left-wing parties were also challenged by their association with the Soviet Union.

The shift on the left was particularly pronounced among Socialist parties. Many broke from a model in which they resembled Communist counterparts while appealing to different trade unions. This was particularly seen in France. There the Parti Socialiste, having done very badly in the 1968 elections, collapsed, providing an opportunity for François Mitterrand, an opportunist originally from the far-right and more recently the centre-left, to launch a new Socialist Party which became his personal vehicle. It did so shorn of the ideological legacy of recent decades and, in particular, of the dominance of the Communists, with whom Mitterrand, in 1972, had initially formed an electoral coalition. Mitterrand was out of power in the 1970s but, within the Socialist International, there was the so-called Socialist Triangle of Willy Brandt, Olof Palme, Swedish prime minister from 1969 to 1976 and 1982 to 1986, and Bruno Kreisky, Austrian chancellor from 1970 to 1983. The last won three elections with an absolute majority: in 1971, 1975 and 1979. This 'triangle' contrasted with the conservative one of Adenaeur, De Gasperi and Schuman in the 1950s, and, as Social Democrats, to the Communists and those willing to ally with them.

On the right across Europe there was also a commitment to an often traditional and paternalistic conception of the working class, but also an understanding that the global economy was in flux and that this required a response. Both sides of the political spectrum sought to respond to changing circumstances but found themselves uneasy about aspects of liberal economics, especially free trade. In Britain the Conservatives under Margaret Thatcher won power in 1979. In comparison with recent eras in British politics Thatcherism was radical. The shift there to a post-industrial economy was deliberate and led from above. Yet nowhere else saw such a decisive experiment, not even the USA, which did so much to inspire it. Nevertheless, although instinctively protectionist under the pressure of economic crisis, Continental governments were deprived of some of the classic protectionist responses by the dictates of international trade laws and the EEC.

The politics of the late 1970s and early 1980s were complex and different trends can be discerned. In the late 1970s, Valery Giscard d'Estaing, the French president from 1974 to 1981, and Helmut Schmidt, German chancellor from 1974 to 1982, combined to act as a very strong stabilizing force within Western Europe and to relaunch the EEC project. At the same time, alongside the response to international developments, not least those in the USA, where the election of Ronald Reagan as president in 1980 initially served to strengthen the left in Europe, there was a need to react to powerful economic pressures.

FRANCE

This need to react was obviously intertwined with politics in France where the attempt to deny market constraints failed. During the presidency of Giscard d'Estaing the conservative Barre government (1976–81) had pursued an economic liberalization, cutting the government's role and emphasizing market forces, not least in putting control of inflation above unemployment. These policies were dramatically reversed in 1981 after the Socialist candidate, François Mitterrand, won the presidential election, which appeared a major break with the old order of sub-Gaullist conservative governments that had prevailed since 1969. Opponents covered the eyes of Giscard d'Estaing on his electoral posters with cut-out paper diamonds, representing the real diamonds he had received from 'Emperor' Jean Bokassa, the brutal dictator of the Central African Republic from 1966 to 1979, and also the sense of corruption associated with both the president and the old order. The story going round Paris, where I was doing research at the time, was of Giscard attempting to show his popularity by taking the Metro, only for it to be revealed before the attendant journalists that he did not know how to buy a ticket.

In the event Giscard d'Estaing and Jacques Chirac, his rival on the right, who had relaunched the Gaullist movement as the Rassemblement pour la République in 1976, together won more votes in the first round than Mitterrand and the unreconstructed Communist Georges Marchais. Nevertheless, in the run-off between the two leading candidates Mitterrand benefited from a consolidation of support on the left that was lacking on the right, where many of Chirac's supporters were unwilling to back Giscard: indeed, about a sixth of those who had voted for Chirac now voted for Mitterrand. This result underlines the folly of underplaying divisions within what might otherwise appear clear political alignments, in this case the right, and the hazard of assuming a degree of social determinism for these alignments. Instead, these complex alignments and divisions reveal the play of personality and policy and the extent to which social factors are generally far more complex than might appear to a superficial glance. Moreover, left, right and centre, which seem monoliths to many outsiders, each dissolve under scrutiny into a more complex reality.

The Mitterrand victory was greeted as the *grand soir* that would usher in a new political age. Large numbers of Mitterrand supporters flocked to public places to celebrate. Mitterrand's success as a directly elected Socialist head of state suggested to many that the failure of the left in 1968 had now been overcome. This was taken further when Mitterrand called legislative elections in which the Socialists won a majority in the National Assembly: there was no need for an alliance with the Communists, while the right was clearly defeated. Euphoria, however, led to a wave of unrealistic hopes about radical transformation through state-driven change. More soberly, the Fifth Republic had displayed a sophistication and stability capable of accepting an alteration between right and left.

In many respects the policies subsequently followed in France in 1981–3 linked the traditional nostrums of the left and of state control and intervention with the aspirations for regulation and social management that underlay aspects of the European integrationist movement. Reflation in France focused less on modernization than on support for historic constituencies (coal, steel and shipbuilding in the early 1980s, agriculture today), while a determined effort was made to control manufacturing and the financial system. There were large-scale nationalizations in 1982, as well as exchange controls in a futile attempt to prevent capital flight and to protect the franc. Taxation in France was directed towards redistribution, with a wealth tax matched by an increase in the minimum wage, a cut in the working week and a reduction in the retirement age.

This policy rested in part on a refusal to accept the disciplines posed by international economic competition – indeed, on their rejection as alien Anglo-American concepts. Mitterrand's ambitious policies, implemented by his prime minister, Pierre Mauroy, however, were rapidly thwarted by economic realities, part of a more general crisis of ambitious welfare state policies. In particular the disciplines of the EEC, not least the single market and the European Monetary System, posed a key constraint. A one-country siege economy was not possible for France, not least because it was unacceptable to West Germany. There Helmut Kohl's Christian Democrats gained power in 1982 because the Free Democrats switched to them. Thus there was to be no united move to the left across Western Europe. Indeed, in 1983 Margaret Thatcher was re-elected in Britain with a substantially increased majority, a victory that reflected hostility to Labour Party policies as much as the bonus brought by her robust leadership in the successful war with Argentina over the Falkland Islands the previous year. Thatcher was a resolute opponent of the Soviet Union and, if he was more cautious, Kohl's election led to the implementation of the NATO Double-Track Decision on missile deployment.

Alongside the isolation of France within an EEC that was not interested in one-country autarky, nor in Socialism for all, there were signs of serious tensions within France itself. Strikes and demonstrations were accompanied by a business crisis, by pressure on the franc within the EMS and by a large-scale movement of currency abroad, and this encouraged Mitterrand to decide on a reversal of policy from June 1982 although he only committed himself after the Socialists did badly in the municipal elections in March 1983. Elements of the Barre policy were reintroduced, not least a struggle against the inflation which hit business confidence and challenged the value of money, and thus the established social order. Public spending, which had risen greatly in 1981, was cut. A distinctive French path to Socialism was no longer the goal or rhetoric of policy, and instead Mitterrand broke with the left and pressed for a 'mixed' economy. Mauroy, now very unpopular, resigned as prime minister in June 1984, and was replaced by the technocrat Laurent Fabius, a self-conscious modernizer who sought to help private businesses.

Although he had to make this major adjustment, Mitterrand encouraged across Western Europe the non-Communist left which did not wish to go down the neo-liberal route followed by Thatcher. German developments confirmed this rejection of the latter: although Kohl was more conservative than Mitterrand, he would never be a Thatcher.

TERRORISM AND INTERNATIONAL CRISIS

In Western Europe economic pressures, therefore, did not lead to authoritarian regimes nor to governmental direction of national resources. There was little 'rolling back' of capitalism, a process that would have required stringent credit controls and the suppression of commercial advertising. In contrast there were large-scale privatizations of publicly owned economic assets. These privatizations very much restricted one-country corporatism, although partial state ownership remained commonplace, not least in France.

Economic difficulties did encourage the rise of far-right political parties, for example in Austria (the Freedom Party), France (the National Front, founded in 1972), Italy (Alleanza Nationale) and West Germany. However, neither they nor the radical left were able to gain power, nor even to exercise much influence on political or economic policies in West Germany and France. In Italy the far-right did not come into any government coalition in the 1970s as they (in a less extreme form) were to do in the 2000s, but there were, nevertheless, three far-right coup attempts and extreme-left street terrorism. The key group in the latter, the *Brigate Rosse* (Red Brigades), active from 1970, drew on a degree of support from the fractured left that owed much to the illusions of former students. Attacks on industrialists did not create the way for the worker-democracy of which revolutionaries dreamed, but were followed by assassinations of politicians that became an important factor in the political system.

The moderate left in Italy attempted to go for what was termed the 'historic compromise' between Communism and the established Christian Democrat-dominated political system. A pact was negotiated in 1976, with the Communist Party agreeing not to try to overthrow the Christian Democratic government. In 1978 this brought the kidnapping and death of one of the most prominent Italian politicians, Aldo Moro. Prime minister in 1963–8 and 1974–6, and leader of the Christian Democrats from 1976, he had played a key role in constructing this compromise but, to the *Brigate Rosse*, this was an aspect of control by the *Stato Imperiale delle Multinazionali* (Imperial State of Multinationals) and by the USA. Moro was subject to 'trial by the people', a process far harsher than that to which terrorists were exposed, and his body was symbolically abandoned halfway between the offices of the Communist and Christian Democrat parties in Rome. The *Brigate Rosse* hoped that by exposing the conspiracy that Moro allegedly represented they would inspire popular anger, paving the way for a proletarian revolution, an unrealistic aspiration.

In the event it was other alleged conspiracies that excited interest. Relations between aspects of the government establishment, criminal networks and political extremists, in this and other cases, were unclear, but led to widespread suspicions that sapped confidence in the entire system. Although claims by the *Brigate Rosse* provided no evidence, it was alleged that the Moro case was linked to the USA, the P2 Masonic lodge and the ambitions of Giulio Andreotti, the prime minister in 1972–3, 1976–9 and 1989–92 and a rival of Moro within the Christian Democrat Party. This was a crisis accentuated by concern about Italy's stability in the event of the Cold War flaring up. What is sometimes called the Second Cold War had gathered pace in the late 1970s with American concerns about Soviet developments in nuclear weaponry and about the Soviet role in the advance of radical movements in Latin America and the Islamic world. The USA, in response, greatly increased its military expenditure and moved closer to China. The Soviet invasion of Afghanistan in 1979 had led to a ratcheting up of fears and responses.

Tensions rose to a peak in 1983 with the Soviets fearing attack during a NATO exercise, the shooting down, over Soviet airspace, of a Korean airliner suspected of espionage, and the deployment of Cruise and Pershing missiles in Western Europe. The deployment of NATO missiles was particularly controversial in West Germany as, alongside left-wing criticism of nuclear weaponry and NATO, there was a sense that locating short-range missiles there would make it the prime target for Soviet nuclear attack. With the KGB providing inaccurate reports of US plans for a surprise nuclear first strike, the Soviets also deployed more weaponry. The cranking up of the Cold War by both sides, if in different ways, was very scary and helped make 1983 a terrible year.

The possibility that international and internal discontent would coincide and indeed interact, and that Italian radicals would be strongly encouraged by the Soviet Union (as opposed simply to receiving the secret service funds that were provided), was lessened by the hostility between radicals and both the Soviet Union and its Communist allies in Western Europe. The disruption that radicals could cause to NATO powers was apparently useful to the Soviet Union and ensured the provision of Soviet funds to radical movements in Germany, Belgium, Italy, France and Britain, but the radicals were not seeking a goal that accorded with Communist objectives, and these funds were far smaller than Soviet payments to the Communist parties.

As a result the Italian Communist Party, the most powerful one in Western Europe, not only dissociated itself from the *Brigate Rosse*, but also pressed for action against them. The Communist commitment under the new and able party secretary, Enrico Berlinguer, to the existing democratic system in 1973 reflected a sense not only of democracy as under challenge but also of society as jointly assailed by the extreme-left and the extreme-right. The latter was responsible for the most bloody episode of the period in Italy, the bombing of the railway station in the Communist stronghold of Bologna in 1980: 85 people were slaughtered in an atrocity that was even more troubling because of suspicions of complicity between the far-right and anti-democratic elements in the establishment. There was certainly co-operation between the two. With the Communists scoring 34.4 per cent of the votes at their peak, in the elections of 1976, there was unease on the right and in the USA that they might be able to gain a role in government.

The level of violence seen in Italy between 1977 and 1982 was not matched elsewhere in Western Europe at the centres of power, although the attempted Spanish coup in 1981 was, in the shorter term, a more serious crisis. The Provisional IRA was a major problem for the British government but no more threatened the overthrow of the political process than the Basque terrorist group ETA in Spain, nor the left-wing terrorist movements in Germany (*Rote Armee Fraktion*/Baader-Meinhof Gang), France (*Action Directe*), and Greece (November 17). In each case the ability to stage terrorist attacks, which in Britain included an attempt to blow up the Conservative Party Conference in 1986, in which Margaret Thatcher, the Prime Minister, was nearly killed, did not have a comparable ability to suggest a political breakdown similar to that which appeared possible in Italy.

In West Germany the Baader-Meinhof Gang's murders of such leading personalities as Hans-Martin Schleyer, the President of the Employers' Association, Siegfried Buback, the federal chief prosecutor, and the bankers Jürgen Ponto and Alfred Herrhausen, as well as the gang's connections to Palestinian terrorists, indicated their destructive power over a number of years. Yet the political system was not threatened with overthrow, and the Gang's imprisoned key leaders committed suicide in 1976–7.

In Belgium the *Cellules Communistes Combattantes*, which operated in 1984–5, was even weaker. Its goals were predominantly international. Its fourteen bombings attacked enemies of Communism, specifically NATO, American business firms, the Federation of Belgian Entreprises and the Christian Democratic party's headquarters. Ironically, when their leader and founder, Pierre Carette, was arrested in December 1985, it was in an American-styled, 'capitalist' burger restaurant.

Governments devoted quite an effort to countering terrorist movements, although they were not presented in the existential terms used to describe the Islamic suicide bombers of the 2000s. Nor was there any systematic campaign against ideas held conducive to terrorism, and certainly nothing to match the Soviet campaign against dissidents.

WESTERN EUROPE IN THE 1980S

Political violence across Europe encouraged a reaction in favour of order. The social polarization expected by radicals had not material-ized, and instead most politicians rallied round to defend the existing order. This defence was not the politics of optimism, and that itself was a cause of pessimism, if not anxiety. Instead, there was a stress on stability and a practice of muddling through. Membership in the ERM, for example, helped lead to a degree of fiscal stability in Italy.

Helped greatly by a more widespread recovery, economic growth resumed in Western Europe and there was a boom for much of the 1980s. This boom was accompanied by an electoral decline of the left in much of Western Europe. The Socialists won in France but the Communists collapsed there, while Labour's leftward urge made it unelectable in Britain and it lost heavily in the 1983 and 1987 elections. The Spanish Communists declined and, even though their Italian counterparts remained strong, they were not able to match, still less improve on, their 1976 results. These failures across Western Europe were largely a consequence of the decline in the electoral base of tradi-tional male trade unions in heavy industry, although the recovery in the European economies (but not of heavy industry) in the 1980s was also important in rallying support for the established system.

The policies of the left appeared of scant relevance. The failure of Communist parties to recruit the support of new, young electors was important. Moreover, Euro-Communism, a term coined in 1975 by Western European Communist leaders keen to demonstrate their democratic credentials, meant little to the electors as a whole and indeed angered some traditionalists, for example in France. Conventional Communist ideology was underlined in 1977 with the new constitution of the Soviet Union, which essentially confirmed that of 1936 produced under Stalin, and asserted without hesitation the role of the Party. It was declared both the leading and guiding force of Soviet society and the force that determined the course of Soviet domestic and foreign policy. It was not only that links to the Soviet Union created a problem for the Communists of Western Europe, not least when the Cold War hotted up after the invasion of Afghanistan in 1979, but also that Communism appeared less plausible and attractive an answer to political questions than the apparent panaceas of Social Democracy.

THE CRISIS OF THE SOVIET BLOC

With time the sham character of Communist progress became more apparent: to the peoples of the Soviet Union and Eastern Europe and to foreign commentators, although, in a serious failure of knowledge, analysis and assumptions, Western intelligence agencies were to be surprised by the speed of the eventual collapse. The Brezhnev regime (1964–82) was increasingly characterized by incompetence, corruption and sloth, and Brezhnev, who failed to see the need for change, neglected warnings of problems and proved particularly negligent in economic management.

Nevertheless, despite serious economic problems, the Brezhnev regime retained control, in large part because of the strength of the Soviet dictatorship. This strength was not simply a matter of coercion, although that was important. Much activity was devoted to spying on dissidents and persecuting them by methods such as imprisonment, internal exile and consigning sane people to psychiatric hospitals in order to drive them mad. In East Germany in the 1980s the *Stasi* read 90,000 letters and 2,810 telegrams daily, and also tapped telephones on a large scale. It was not enough to act against those judged dissidents, the entire population was under surveillance. Inertia, however, was more potent in maintaining Communist control than coercion. There was a sense that there was no alternative, while the government's ability to seem to offer some improvement was useful with particular constituencies of support. Enthusiasm, however, was limited and across the bloc the Communist Party, which did not succeed in inspiring, was pushed to the back by state bureaucracies that did not seek to inspire.

Alongside a rise in political opposition to the Communist regimes, especially the Solidarity movement in Poland, there was a widespread privatization of commitment on the individual and household level, a focus on getting by, on the shifts and expedients of life under Communism. This situation did not mean active opposition, but left government and the Communist Party in a vacuum, with Party members largely cut off from the working class they were supposed to represent. This helped ensure that political opposition, where it existed, could hope to win a measure of public acceptance, possibly support, even if it was denied the means of political expression employed in the West.

POLAND AND SOLIDARITY

Poland proved a lightning rod. This was not so much due to the failure of its economic system to deliver low-priced food, a failure alleviated for a while by borrowing money from the West and the Soviet Union. Instead, a key element was the power of the Catholic Church in the hands of the determined and charismatic Karol Wojtyla, Cardinal-Archbishop of Cracow, who became Pope John Paul II in 1978; the first non-Italian to be elected Pope since 1523. Unlike his predecessor John Paul I, a potential reformer, who was pope for only 33 days, and Paul VI, pope from 1963 to 1978, a cautious reformer who lacked charisma and was more willing to attune himself to power, John Paul II was once theologically highly conservative and determined to challenge Communism as an unwelcome excrescence, particularly in his native Poland. While a cardinal he had met opposition leaders in 1976, and his stance was important in a major shift from the earlier position of the Catholic Church hierarchy in Poland. In the 1960s this hierarchy had sought better relations with the regime but under the new pope there was to be no compromise with Marxism and, instead, a public affirmation of the authority of the Church. This was seen from 1979 when he staged a 'pilgrimage' to Poland. The religious component of John Paul II's visit was important and the popular response testified to the strength of popular religiosity, but this was also an intensely political event.

Later that year there was a resurgence in Poland in activity by 'free', in other words non-state and thus illegal, trade unions, pressing for workers' rights, but this was small-scale until a crisis was precipitated in July 1980 with an increase in the price of meat. Similarly, in 1976, price rises that reflected government concern about the extent of state debt had led to disturbances. In 1980 large-scale strikes were particularly prominent in the Lenin shipyard of Gdansk. The workers there went on strike on 14 August and Solidarity, an unofficial trade union, was established under the leadership of an electrician, Lech Walesa. After intimidation and negotiations had failed, the government backed down, and the right to free unions was accepted on 31 August 1980, as was a major reduction in censorship. Solidarity was a nationwide trade union with about 10 million members, and a key part of a newly organized civic society outside the structure of the Communist state. Solidarity became the expression of the largest opposition movement in the world, with about half the adult population involved in 1980–81.

Caution on the part of Solidarity's leaders prevented a breakdown in their uneasy relations with the Communist government, and the Soviet Union did not send in the tanks, as it had done in Czechoslovakia in 1968. However, the economy deteriorated, while the Soviet government was concerned about the impact on other Communist regimes and on geopolitics: Poland was the link between the Soviet Union and its forces on the Iron Curtain frontline in East Germany. As a result Poland was strategically far more significant than the Communist mavericks: Romania, Albania and Yugoslavia. Strikes in Poland threatened the link.

The Soviets, who had only deployed a relatively small part of their army to Afghanistan, were pressed to act against Poland by the Communist leaders in East Germany and Czechoslovakia, who were concerned about the example being created. Indeed, in October 1980 the East German government imposed travel restrictions with Poland and stepped up *Stasi* activity. The Soviet leadership was also fearful that what it saw as the revisionists of Solidarity would lead Poland to become another Yugoslavia. The Soviets, however, were warned not to intervene by President Reagan. The defence minister, Dmitriy Ustinov, supported intervention, but his colleagues were reluctant to do so. By not intervening with its own forces the Soviet Union ensured that the Polish crisis did not become more serious, and this, in the context of super-power hostility over NATO's plans to introduce medium-range nuclear weapons in Western Europe. This decision not to intervene also prefigured Mikhail Gorbachev's unwillingness to act in 1989 to preserve Communist control in Eastern Europe. The official creed of 'Socialist Internationalism' only meant so much.

In September 1980 Edward Gierek, first secretary of the Polish Communist Party since 1970, stepped down to be replaced by Stanislaw Kania, another longstanding Communist bureaucrat, but he failed to stabilize the situation and was, in turn, replaced by the defence minister, General Wojciech Jaruzelski, who became prime minister in February 1981 and Party secretary that October. He sought to use his personal prestige, an appeal to national patriotism and the threat of force, in order to reach a settlement with Solidarity. Walesa, who shared the wish for a peaceful solution, was ready to co-operate but serious economic problems continued to create discontent and to lead to criticism of the government. Meanwhile, the Soviet Union pressed Jaruzelski to come out in defence of Socialism, which was now overshadowed by Solidarity and by the Catholic Church. Having downgraded the role of the Polish Communist Party, Jaruzelski sought to play off Solidarity against the Soviet Union in order to gain concessions (stability and aid respectively) from each.

In the event Jaruzelski used the Polish army to declare martial law on 13 December 1981, arresting Solidarity's leaders and many others in an effort to end political unrest and strikes. Martial law remained in place until July 1983 and indicated the strength and weakness of the Communist system: it could maintain order, but could not provide the economic growth or popular support that made order much more than a matter of coercion and indoctrination. The percentage of Poles aged nineteen and over in the Communist Party in the mid-1980s was the lowest in Eastern Europe bar Albania, always the maverick. The East German percentage was more than three times that of Poland.

The response in Western Europe to the suppression of Solidarity was largely pusillanimous. The French and West German governments sought stability and were ready to recognize Soviet dominance of

Eastern Europe. If much public opinion took a different view, encouraged by the earlier reporting of Solidarity's activities, the left did not mobilize much of its vigour on behalf of the Polish workers. In West Germany the left was to be more vocal against the deployment of Cruise and Pershing missiles in 1983 than on behalf of the Poles.

GORBACHEV

Dying on 10 November 1982 Brezhnev was succeeded as General Secretary of the Communist Party by Yuriy Andropov, the ruthless head of the KGB Secret Police from 1967. He did not share Brezhnev's complacency and, instead, appreciated the need for improvement, but in his search for efficiency was not willing to make radical changes and was anyway increasingly ill. Dying on 9 February 1984 he was replaced by Konstantin Chernenko, another member of Brezhnev's gerontocracy and, like Andropov, in poor health when appointed; he died on 10 March 1985. An impression of stagnation, if not decay, became more insistent.

Soviet policy, however, changed greatly from the mid 1980s as a response to recognition of Soviet weaknesses. A search for stability also led to arms-control agreements with the USA from 1987. Domestically, Mikhail Gorbachev, the youngest member of the Politburo, who became leader as General Secretary of the Communist Party on 10 March 1985 at the age of 54, sought to modernize Communism by introducing reforms. There was also now a focus on international disengagement, which led to the withdrawal in 1988–9 of Soviet forces from Afghanistan, where they had failed to sustain the pro-Soviet Communist government in the face of American-financed guerrilla opposition.

The sham character of Communist progress, however, helped ensure that the reform policies of the Gorbachev government, the attempt from 1985 to create 'Socialism with a human face', inadvertently destroyed Communism in Eastern Europe and the Soviet Union, as well as the Soviet state. It proved impossible, in yet another stage of encouraging Socialist consumerism and thus winning popular support, to introduce market responsiveness to a planned economy. Moreover, the post-Communist dismantling of the old command economy was to expose the uncompetitive nature of much of Soviet-era industry. Before the deluge, attempts from 1985 to achieve economic and political reform had faced the structural economic and fiscal weakness of the Soviet system, not least the preference for control by *Gossnab*, the State Supply Commission, over any price system that reflected cost and availability. In 1985 Gorbachev dismissed Nikolai Baibakov, a Stalinist who had headed *Gosplan* from 1965, and had earlier served Stalin as minister for the oil industry.

Committed to good relations abroad, Gorbachev greatly defused tension, not least by leading to Soviet disengagement from Afghanistan and Angola. Although a one-time protégé of Andropov, Gorbachev was also willing to challenge the confrontational worldview outlined in KGB reports and the vested interests of the military–industrial complex, transforming Soviet foreign policy as well as the nostrums of Marxist–Leninism. For example, he was convinced that US policy on arms control was not motivated by a hidden agenda of weakening the Soviet Union, and this encouraged him to negotiate. Margaret Thatcher endorsed Gorbachev as 'a man we can do business with'.

The architecture of the Cold War was steadily dismantled. In December 1987 the Soviet government accepted the Intermediate Nuclear Forces Treaty, which, in ending land-based missiles with ranges between 500 and 5,000 kilometres, forced heavier cuts on the Soviets, while also setting up a system of verification through on-site inspection. This agreement pushed the German question to the fore, as West Germany was the base and target for short-range missiles. Gorbachev told the United Nations on 7 December 1988 that the Soviet armed forces would be cut, including in East Germany, Czechoslovakia and Hungary, and that each state should be free to choose its own path. Thus the possibility that Eastern European states would leave the Soviet bloc was presented as part of a new *détente*. The situation in East Germany was most significant as there were nearly 400,000 Soviet troops there and they were important as the final support of the government. Already, visiting Prague in April 1987, Gorbachev had publicly repudiated the Brezhnev Doctrine of intervention in order to uphold Communism, claiming, instead, that 'fraternal parties determine their political line with a view to national conditions'. In 1990

NATO and the Warsaw Pact were able to agree a limitation of conventional forces in Europe, while in 1991 START 1 led to a major fall in the number of American and Soviet strategic nuclear warheads.

In the Soviet Union economic reform, in particular *perestroika* (restructuring), the loosening of much of the command economy, led unexpectedly to economic problems, including inflation, a major rise in the budget deficit, shortages, a breakdown in economic integration and political change. Furthermore, Gorbachev unintentionally provoked the fall of the Eastern bloc. His attempts to push through modernization in Eastern Europe, which totally surprised the East German leadership who argued that there was no need for reform or openness, left the governments weak in the face of popular demand for reform and for more change.

This demand helped lead to the successive collapse of Communist regimes in Eastern Europe in 1989. They had lacked the necessary flexibility to respond to problems, although there were important differences, with Hungary proving the most flexible. Janos Kádár, its dictator, had played a major role in the brutal repression that closed the 1956 rising, but from the 1960s adopted a less rigid approach. Indeed, Hungary had become a member of the International Monetary Fund and the World Bank in 1982. The home of 'Goulash Socialism', Hungary had offered its people small freedoms that were welcome in the 1970s but insufficient in the late 1980s and Kádár himself was replaced as General Secretary of the Communist Party in May 1988. Gorbachev was also unwilling to use the Soviet military to maintain the governments of Eastern Europe. They had totally failed.

The intellectual crisis of Marxism was not the reason for the collapse of the Communist states, although the failure of what the Soviet Communists under Lenin and Stalin had fashioned and presented as the Marxist model for an economic system joined its political to its intellectual crisis. The collapse of Communism was largely due to the specific political and economic circumstances of the 1980s. Moreover, the possibility of a different trajectory was exemplified by developments in China where capitalism proved compatible with the Communist rule that was maintained by the use of force. In Eastern Europe intellectual matters were not the key issue, except in the form of the serious and debilitating failure of economic planning. The commitment of much of the population in Communist countries to Marxism as the basis for understanding themselves and their world was, anyway, limited, and debate among intellectuals was of scant relevance to them. Furthermore, the relevance of these intellectuals was limited as the political authorities were in control of the educational process. The crisis of Marxism as a viable theory was not of great relevance for Communist governments. The sense of change as necessary owed far more to pragmatic considerations.

Linked to this was the modest impact of the dissidents, especially in the Russian Federation, the major part of the Soviet Union. Dissent there did not gather pace to become opposition, which was a reflection of the nature of Russian public culture, the dominant role of the Communist Party in education and among workers, the effectiveness of repression and a degree of anti-intellectualism that included anti-Semitism. There was certainly no comparison with the impact of the opposition intelligentsia in Czechoslovakia, let alone Poland. The situation, however, was different within the Soviet Union in some of the non-Russian republics, where nationalism provided a more popular and inclusive language and form for dissent. This was often specific in its grievances, for example about the role of Russians, which was an issue in Kazakhstan among other republics, whereas dissent within the Russian Federation lacked such focus. Russian nationalism was not the theme of dissent there, in part because the Soviet system acted as the protector of Russian interests.

That the sense of change as necessary was widespread in the élite helps explain why Gorbachev was not assassinated or removed in a coup. He saw liberalism as essential for a stronger Soviet Union and was willing to argue the case publicly, pressing for a 'Socialist pluralism' in 1987, and persuading the Party Conference the following year to support truly contested elections for a legislature independent of the executive. These elections entailed Communists able to compete with each other and to do so pushing different policies, which was a rejection of the Leninist idea of democratic centralism in favour of what Gorbachev called, in 1990, 'political pluralism'. Gorbachev's support for real checks and balances and his backing for the rule of law both broke with the authoritarian legacy of Communist rule. So did his sweeping relaxation of censorship, which made it far easier to question Marxist-Leninism. Unused to such attacks Party ideologues were pushed onto the defensive, and this was important both to a fundamental split within the Communist Party and to the loss of its legitimacy. Supporting *glasnost* (openness) Gorbachev was confident that the Soviet Union and the Communist Party would not only be able to survive these challenges, but would also be mutually strengthened by them. He was to be proved completely wrong.

TRANSFORMATION IN EASTERN EUROPE

Across Eastern Europe the Communist states were weak, as demonstrated in Poland by the activities of underground Solidarity and by the serious strikes that began in April 1988. The Polish government grudgingly sought to widen its support by negotiating with other elements but it wished to exclude Solidarity. The Catholic Church, however, refused to create a co-operative Christian labour movement as the government wanted, preferring to leave Solidarity as the key body for negotiations. The Communists were opposed to trade union pluralism but, as a sign of movement, the amnesty of 1986 had freed political prisoners.

The 1988 strikes in Poland discouraged the Party leadership and demonstrated its failure to find a solution to the country's problems. Combined with Gorbachev's renunciation of intervention on behalf of Communism this failure encouraged the leadership to move toward yielding its monopoly of power. On 30 November 1988 there was a televized debate between Walesa and Alfred Miodowicz, the chief of the official trade union federation and a member of the Politburo and on 6 February 1989 Round Table talks between government and opposition began, with the Church playing an important mediatory role. Under an agreement signed on 5 April 1989, reached against a background of widespread strikes, elections were held on 4 June. Only 35 per cent of the seats in the lower house, the Sejm, were awarded on the basis of the free vote, the remainder going to the Communists and their allies, but all of these seats were won by Solidarity. Communist cohesion collapsed, not least with the Communist Party being abandoned by its hitherto pliant allies. Strikes and other protests meanwhile continued. The new government was headed by Tadeusz Mazowiecki, a member of Solidarity and a Catholic intellectual.

East Germany, apparently the most successful Communist regime, although with its economy wrecked by ideological mismanagement, was on the edge of bankruptcy in the autumn of 1989. It had only been able to continue that long thanks to large loans from the West. Gorbachev's *glasnost* and *perestroika* intensified East Germany's loss of legitimacy. By September 1989 this supposedly model regime was dissolving as people left in large numbers. Hungary's opening of its Austrian border on 2 May enabled large numbers of East Germans to leave for West Germany. They were abandoning not only economic failure but also the lack of modern civilization in the shape of free expression, tolerance, opportunity and cultural vitality. East Germany, indeed, had experienced continued dictatorship since 1933. Hungary refused to heed pressure from East Germany to stem the tide and Gorbachev was unwilling to help. In the first nine months of the year 110,000 East Germans resettled in West Germany. Others took part in mass demonstrations, notably in Leipzig from 4 September, with steadily larger numbers demonstrating: 1,200 then, but 500,000 on 6 November. A sense of failure and emptiness demoralized supporters of the regime and West German consumerist democracy proved far more attractive to the bulk of the population, not least because the East German government could not finance its social programmes.

The terror state, moreover, no longer terrified. Indeed, it had suffered a massive failure of intelligence, with a serious inability to understand let alone anticipate developments. All its intercepted letters availed the *Stasi* naught. Force without adequate intelligence was a flawed method of control, especially as the regime did not wish to rely on force while the East German army was unwilling to act. The demonstrations were peaceful, which helped remove the option of repression from a government that did not want to compromise its domestic and international reputation. The lack of a central leadership for the demonstrators also lessened *Stasi* options. Erich Honecker was deposed by his colleagues on 16 October 1989 but, under pressure from popular action, they could not gain control of the situation, nor even produce an impression of control. The entire government and Politburo resigned on 7–8 November but Honecker's successors, Egon Krenz and Gregor Gysi, could not provide the reform from above they sought to ensure stability.

The Berlin Wall was opened on 9 November and this was seen as a symbol of a new age. The Fall of the Wall, which was soon demolished, became a totemic act, like that of the Bastille in Paris at the outset of the French Revolution in 1789. The real consequences were certainly greater in 1989. Whereas only a few insignificant prisoners were freed from the Bastille, large numbers of East Berliners poured over the border on 9 November 1989.

From the opening of the Wall, pressure for reform was increasingly supplemented by demands for German unity, although the majority in the citizens' movement wanted a liberal East Germany, not unification. Meanwhile government authority collapsed, with the *Stasi* headquarters in Berlin occupied on 15 January 1990. On 1 February Hans Modrow, the prime minister, unveiled a plan for a German–German confederation as part of a United Fatherland. Communist one-party rule was followed by multi-party politics and free elections on 18 March 1990.

In a sense Communism was democratized, which was why it allowed itself to pass from the scene. If, as has been argued, the events of 1989–91 were 'anti-revolutions', marking the end of 'Enlightenment revolutionism', they were certainly welcomed by the bulk of the population, who were politicized by the crisis, particularly by the citizens' movement. In the elections the East German CDU led by Lothar de Maizière, who became prime minister, won 48.1 per cent of the vote, compared to 21.8 per cent for the SPD. Currency union took effect on 1 July 1990, East Germany came to an end as a separate state on 3 October and the all-German elections followed on 2 December 1990.

East Germany had been seen as the leading Soviet client state and the fall of Communism there was followed by its unravelling elsewhere in Eastern Europe. Changes in Hungary (where Kádár was replaced in May 1988) and Poland had in many senses been a prelude to developments in East Germany, both in terms of popular protest and with reference to shifts in government policy toward reform. The

Round Table idea used in Poland was copied in Hungary. In each case the crisis in East Germany helped encourage the move to free elections.

The same was true elsewhere. In Czechoslovakia, which had remained more authoritarian than Hungary, there were mass demonstrations and an end to Communist rule in the Velvet Revolution of November 1989, the creation of a largely non-Communist government that December, the adoption of a new constitution the following April and free elections on 8–9 June 1990. On 29 December 1989 the dissident Václav Havel was chosen president by the Czechoslovak Assembly. The escalating pace of the change that seemed graspable was indicated by a slogan of the Velvet Revolution, 'Poland – ten years, Hungary – ten months, German Democratic Republic – ten weeks, Czechoslovakia – ten days'.

In Romania the situation was more violent, and Nicolae Ceauşescu, abetted by the secret police, resisted reform. He was overthrown, however, in December 1989 after mass demonstrations and the army was responsible for his execution on Christmas Day. Nevertheless, Ion Iliescu, a protégé of Ceauşescu until 1971, who succeeded him as president, winning elections in May 1990 and October 1992, presided over a government that represented a high degree of continuity.

The public nature of the pressure for change was important, as it could be captured by a domestic and international media no longer under state control. Scenes of East Germans travelling west were followed by those of the demolition of the Berlin Wall and, later, by demonstrators in Bucharest booing Ceauşescu. These scenes showed that existing regimes were collapsing.

As an instance of a different trajectory to that in East Germany, in Bulgaria the key development was not that of people power but rather of a crisis in the Communist Party, as the elderly leader Todor Zhivkov no longer enjoyed the confidence of many of his colleagues nor of Gorbachev. By 1988 Zhivkov, who had once been associated with reform, was now distant from reform circles and in November 1989 opposition by politburo colleagues led to his resignation. A pro-Gorbachev group took power but found itself under pressure from public expectations, while in 1990 the Communist Party changed its character, accepting democracy and separating itself from the state. The first post-Communist elections, held in June 1990, led to the former Communists winning power but their inability to deal with the serious economic crisis and strikes led to the formation in December of a coalition. The new constitution promulgated in July 1991 was that of a democratic state and, in December 1992, an association agreement was signed with the EU.

Far from having being made redundant by the advance of Communism, nationalism re-emerged publicly as a powerful force, both in Eastern Europe and in the Soviet Union. Indeed, in Yugoslavia the serious economic problems of the 1980s had already exacerbated nationalist tensions and encouraged a politics of envy and grievance. This was also true in Bulgaria where there was longstanding pressure on the Turkish minority, accentuated in 1984 with an attack on Turkish ethnic identity, with all Turks required to adopt a Slav name. This policy was presented as an attempt to regenerate the true Bulgarian identity of those who had been Turkified in the past but, in part, it was a response to the higher Turkish birth rate and to concern about Islamic assertiveness. Those resisting were killed. In 1989 fresh protests led to permission being given for ethnic Turks to leave for Turkey: 370,000 did so, hitting the economy hard. This is a reminder that the large-scale movement of people in 1989 was not restricted to East Germans travelling west. Eventually, over 40 per cent of these ethnic Turks were to return because they did not find Turkey the land of opportunity, while the Bulgarian wish for the friendship of Turkey in what was an increasingly volatile Balkans ensured that care had to be taken of the minority. In marked contrast to the situation in Yugoslavia the Turks in Bulgaria gained a parliamentary voice as well as an expansion of educational and broadcasting facilities. More generally, the new order in Eastern Europe was seen with the disbanding of Comecon and the Warsaw Pact in 1991.

SOVIET EXIT

The fall of the Soviet Union was an important stage in decolonization for, however much it was in theory a federation, it also rested on a powerful degree of Russian as well as ideological imperialism.

However, the growing weakness of the Soviet state and the division and confusion of the government's response to nationalism was accentuated by the strength of nationalist sentiment from mid-1988, especially in the Baltic republics, the Caucasus and western Ukraine. There was no protracted attempt to use the extensive military resources of the Soviet state to prevent this collapse. Counter-reform attempts by the Soviet military, keen to preserve the integrity of the state, led to action against nationalists in Georgia (1989), Azerbaijan (1990), Lithuania (1991), Latvia (1991) and Moldova (1992) but they were small-scale, and there was no violent supporting action by the 25 million Russians living within the Soviet Union but outside Russia. Gorbachev wanted to preserve the Soviet Union, if necessary as a loose confederation and, when the Baltic republics (Estonia, Latvia and Lithuania) declared their independence, he supported the attempt to maintain the authority of the Soviet Union by sending troops into the republics in January 1991, leading to clashes in Riga (Latvia) and Vilnius (Lithuania). These moves did not intimidate the nationalists.

Nationalism meanwhile culminated when Yeltsin in effect successfully launched a Russian nationalist movement against the remaining structures of the Soviet Union. The Russian republic had had no institutions of its own until 1990, being instead conflated with the Soviet Union. To Yeltsin this was unacceptable. Russian sovereignty was declared in June 1990 but the greater Soviet Russia which protected Russians living in the other republics was thus replaced. As so often in history, personalities played a major role, in this case Yeltsin's unwillingness to co-operate with Gorbachev. So also did the staples of nationalism, which undermined the Soviet Union as it had earlier done the Austro-Hungarian Empire in the 1910s, and of the strain of international competition.

There was an attempted coup in Moscow by hardline Communists in August 1991 but they were unable to prevail. This boosted the prestige of Boris Yeltsin who had been elected President of Russia in June 1991. Unlike Gorbachev he had played a prominent public role in opposing the coup. The failure of the coup was followed by the marginalization of hardline Communists and their power-centres. The KGB was abolished on 11 October 1991.

In late 1991 nationalism in the republics led to their independence. The Ukrainean referendum of 1 December, which saw a 90 per cent vote for independence, was decisive. A week later Yeltsin, as President of Russia, and his Belarus and Ukrainean counterparts announced at Minsk that they were forming a 'Commonwealth of Independent States' in place of the Soviet Union and invited the other republics to join. Gorbachev protested the next day but he was now without consequence. On 21 December at Alma Alta the heads of all the republics, bar Georgia, Estonia, Latvia and Lithuania, endorsed the step taken on 8 December, joined the Commonwealth of Independent States (CIS) and declared that the Soviet Union had ceased to exist. Gorbachev resigned on 25 December as president of the Soviet Union. The agreement dissolving the Soviet Union and establishing the Commonwealth of Independent States was seen by Yeltsin as leading to a truly federal system but this was not to be the case as far as, crucially, Ukraine was concerned, and most other republics followed its example.

THE EEC IN THE LATE 1980S

Turning to Western Europe, there were also significant developments, although none as dramatic or transforming as those in the East. The nature of the EEC changed in the late 1980s, with aspirations for a move beyond the existing pattern of links and joint authorities. Economic developments also played a role, with economic growth boosting the apparent prospects for integration. Yet it was unclear whether this was to mean a federation or an enhanced confederation.

In large part the change in the nature of the EEC also reflected shifts in French politics, namely the failure of Mitterrand's initial policies of economic autarky. To many French politicians Europe seemed an alternative way to give effect to their visions and on their terms. In 1985 Jacques Delors, a French Socialist who had been Mitterrand's Minister of Economy and Finance from 1981 to 1984, became President of the European Commission, and revived the policy of European integration, seeing it as a complement to the enlargement of the 'nine' to the 'twelve': Greece joined in 1981 and Spain and Portugal in 1986.

These entries themselves revealed the horse-trading that was so important to EEC institutions but also to politics elsewhere, for example Japan and the USA. In particular French determination to ensure that their interests were protected, not only within France itself but also in the EEC as a whole, was made abundantly clear. The prospect of Portuguese and, even more, Spanish entry was seen as a challenge to French agriculture as both countries produced similar products, especially wine, olive oil and fruit, but more cheaply. Moreover, the challenge was strongest to parts of France near Spain, notably Languedoc, a major producer of indifferent wine. This challenge led to successful demands from France for increased EEC support payments to its farmers as well as a long 'transition period' before their exports were admitted to European markets on equal terms. In turn the new member states gained compensating payments, not least subsidies under 'Integrated Mediterranean Programs'. This agreement increased the net cost of the EEC and notably the burden of sectional and regional social welfare in the form of support for less competitive sectors. On the plus side this support may be seen as helping anchor the new member states as democracies, although that argument presupposes a crude causal relationship that may not be appropriate, while such payments were not necessary for French farmers. Moreover, the challenge of and to 'anchoring' was in part posed by EEC internal protectionism in the form of regulation, slanted markets, notably in agriculture, and insufficient mobility, particularly for labour.

Payment in return for political support was in line with the internal political practice in many states, a practice encapsulated in the trade-offs that marked the establishment and sustaining of coalition governments, but such interest politics created patterns of dependence as well as constituencies of co-operation, while these patterns also seriously distorted economic markets and were a key aspect of a systemic lack of international competitiveness. A particular beneficiary was Greece, a member state since 1981, which received proportionately more than any other EEC state in the late 1980s. While this aid helped in the development of Greek infrastructure, it was far from clear that it encouraged the degree of change that both the Greek political system and its economy required.

To Delors, who was President of the European Commission until 1994, a stronger Commission and a weaker national veto were crucial if progress was to be made; indeed, he used the Commission to provide a driving force for integration, a position it lost in the early and mid-2000s as national governments came to play a more active role in what by then was the EU. Delors also saw Europe as a new forum for the advancing of what were presented as worker rights. Mitterrand, who backed Delors, meanwhile sought to rebuild relations with West Germany, demonstrating anew that irrespective of political shifts national interests for both countries were seen as including a European system that was very much a Franco–German project. Delors had the big advantage of being backed by Kohl and Mitterrand: the Bonn–Paris axis. Indeed, he was the only strong President of the Commission the EU has ever had.

Yet more than French politics and Franco–German relations were involved. Big business, including the important American presence in Europe, was in favour of closer integration. The Single European Act was signed in 1985, following a Solemn Declaration by heads of government in 1983 committing them to a future EU. The decision to move to qualified majority voting was designed to lessen the problems caused by the earlier requirement for unanimity. National vetoes had to be restricted if a larger EU was to work or, at least, to confront challenges other than by spending money. It was also agreed that there should be a single internal market in goods and services by 1992. But the birth of the euro, although envisaged by Brussels, was a central bankers' project, which is why it has a different consistency to most other EU innovations.

The energy of the French left was strengthened in 1988 when Mitterrand was re-elected as president, defeating Chirac in the second round. Barre, the candidate for the centre, had been eliminated in the first round. Moreover, the victory of the right under Chirac in the National Assembly elections on 16 May 1986 was reversed in 1988, after the presidential election, with the victory of the left in new elections to the National Assembly. Michel Rocard, the Socialist most acceptable to non-Socialists, became prime minister, but was to be dismissed by Mitterrand in May 1991, a victory of the president's preference for feline manipulation.

France's ambitions for the EEC were accentuated when German unification became an option, as deeper European integration seemed a way to contain Germany, just as the original establishment of the EEC had been seen as a way to anchor West Germany. Mitterrand, who met Gorbachev in Kiev in November 1989, agreed to unification on condition that West Germany accept French plans for a 'closer' EEC and one under Franco–German control. A Europeanized Germany was the solution, not a Germanic Europe, and to the French this meant a Germany under French guidance. West German policymakers, such as Hans-Dietrich Genscher, the foreign minister, claimed that German unification would serve the interests of Europe and the entire process was eventually put in a European framework. Kohl remarked that 'A good German is a good European'. To win Soviet support, Genscher was willing, in January 1990, to exclude East Germany from NATO, which was unacceptable to the USA, but this did not prove necessary.

The outside powers, including the weakening Soviet Union, were not able to control the process. Thatcher opposed unification, fearing that Germany would become too powerful and might insist on regaining the territories lost in 1945, which indeed was a goal held out by some of the refugees of that era. Although with strong links to Kohl's Christian Democratic party, they, however, were unable to direct German policy, not least due to international pressures. The strong fears that were held about a reunited Germany turned out to be misplaced. Thatcher herself was isolated, as the USA strongly supported unification, with President George H.W. Bush referring to 'partnership in leadership' between Germany and the USA.

In a significant instance of the marginality of the EEC the key moves and decisions were made by a member state acting on its own initiative, West Germany, by two other member states pursing their own national interests, Britain and France, and by the super-powers. The crucial roles were played by West Germany, the USA and the Soviet Union, with Kohl's visit to Moscow on 10 February 1990 particularly important. Kohl met Bush at Camp David on 24–25 February and agreed a common strategy, with the USA taking the lead on the international and security fronts while West Germany handled the national and economic levels. The EEC as an institution played no significant role. With Kohl and Mitterand determined to have a united Germany anchored in the West, the USA keen to ensure the same result, and East Germany collapsing, the Soviet Union was unable to prevent a united Germany in NATO: there was to be no equivalent to the neutralization of Austria. Gorbachev accepted the point in a summit in Washington on 31 May 1990. Thus the post-war international order collapsed in Europe.

Kohl was determined on unification, and on the West German model, which entailed the end of any prospect not only for an independent East Germany (a distinctive German state like Austria), but also of a different former East Germany within a united Germany. The citizens' movements that had spawned the mass demonstrations of late 1989, such as New Forum, were thus not to serve as the genesis for a new vision of German society, but that reflected more than simply the external pressure and financial prospects deployed by Kohl. The movements, which did not compare to Solidarity, lacked unity, while the pressures of practicality, not least of responding to economic failure, undermined any mass enthusiasm for a different path to that of the West German model. German unification arose from more than just the strength of West Germany but the latter was a key element in ensuring that no other options appeared really viable. This unification was then to help define power in post-Communist Europe.

Chapter 8

Politics, 1992 to the Present

Rolling countryside east of Paris, 1992. 'A cultural Chernobyl', a reference to the nuclear disaster of 1986? Hardly, but the new 'Disneyland Paris' captures the receptiveness of France to global branding and, indeed, American cultural imperialism. The challenge to static conceptions of national identities and markets is clear.

EUROPEAN UNIFICATION?

German unification provided an opportunity to rethink the power politics of the EEC. The Maastricht summit of European leaders held in December 1991 brought a commitment to greater integration as part of what was presented as a relaunch of Europe. The word 'federal' was excluded from the Maastricht Treaty but that was more a victory of style than substance, although it enabled British politicians to refuse to be frank with the people. Indeed, the Treaty on European Union, signed at Maastricht on 7 February 1992, created the EU, the new term an indication of the new prospectus. Every citizen of an EEC member state was to be a citizen of this Union, with certain rights in every EEC country.

The treaty also extended the scope and powers of the EEC over its members and announced that 'a common foreign and security policy is hereby established'. The scope of the EEC's executive branch was extended over more areas of policy, including transport, education and social policy, the last a very vague concept. In pursuit of 'a high degree of convergence of economic performance' member states were required to accept the fiscal discipline demanded by the Commission and the Council of Ministers. In addition, the ability of national ministers on the Council of Ministers to exercise a veto on behalf of their national interests was restricted by qualified majority voting, while the powers of the European Parliament over legislation were extended.

The criteria for convergence toward European Monetary Union (EMU) were also outlined, with an agreement that the national debt of participant countries should not exceed 60 per cent of GDP, and the budget deficit 3 per cent of GDP, a significant restriction of national independence in fiscal policy and one designed to contain borrowing and inflation. These criteria, which were to be adopted for the Stability and Growth Pact agreed by finance ministers in 1996, were to be assessed in 1997 as a basis for EMU in 1999. Referenda in France and Ireland supported the treaty but it was rejected by a narrow majority in Denmark in 1992. Denmark then got four exclusions from the Treaty: Denmark is not part of the defence co-operation within the EU, is not a member of the EMU, is not included in the stipulations about EU citizenship and does not participate in the supranational legal co-operation. In 1993 a new referendum in Denmark found a majority in favour of accepting the Treaty with these exclusions. Britain also achieved opt-outs, notably from the euro and the Social Chapter.

In a television address on 29 March 1993 Mitterrand, ever-keen on hyperbole, declared 'Without a common monetary system, there is no Europe'. As a key part of the EMU process the ERM, within which currencies were supposed to be aligned, was the prelude to the European currency, the euro, which was the logical consequence of the single economic market, as the Americans had argued at the time of the post-war Marshall Plan.

Meanwhile expansion of the EU continued. East Germany was admitted in October 1990, when it was reunited with West Germany, and Austria, Finland and Sweden all joined in January 1995, although Norway voted 'no' (52.5 per cent on a 89 per cent turn out) for the second time in 1994, while Sweden only voted 'yes' by 52.3 per cent. That Austria, Finland and Sweden joined was a product of the end of the Cold War, because neutrality had been enjoined on the first two by Soviet pressure. It was a condition of the State Treaty of 1955 under which four-power occupation of Austria ended (whereas, in East

Germany, Soviet troops did not leave until after the unification of 1990). Thus Austria did not decide to seek membership in the EU until 1992. By then, despite earlier concerns about the impact of competition from Western Europe, Austria was determined to move rapidly to avoid being consigned to the same category as the former Communist states.

The accessions of new states to the EU helped ensure that, alongside the end of Communist one-party states, the unification of Germany, the collapse of the Soviet Union, and the creation of the EU, the early 1990s was very much a period of new constitutions. This extended to the tiny Pyrenean state of Andorra where, in place of the near total power of the Governors representing the two sovereigns, the new constitution of 1993 brought democracy, permitting the establishment of political parties, extending the franchise and ensuring that the Assembly gained legislative powers.

There was considerable reluctance within the EU towards rapidly extending membership to the countries to the east that had rejected Communism. In particular there was widespread anxiety about the impact on EU funds of the relative poverty of Eastern Europe, and concern about the extent of likely migration. From the perspective of the late 2000s it is easy to overlook these concerns and, instead, to present a seamless passage from the fall of the Iron Curtain to the extension of the EU. Indeed, such an account can be employed in order apparently to justify the EU. Yet the emphasis on the beneficial stabilization neglects the extent to which not only initially was there a marked reluctance to support expansion, or at least rapid expansion, to include Eastern Europe, but the latter was made to feel unwelcome, which was the very opposite of stabilization. Ideas of a two-tier EU were advanced, notably by France, in order to contain the Eastern Europeans in a secondary and dependent role, while the core was to press ahead with a degree of integration that would further underline its status as the core. The Maastricht Treaty and the drive for the euro made it more difficult for Eastern European countries to meet the criteria for membership, as their public finances so obviously failed to match the requirements.

This situation left Eastern Europe in a no-man's land of more liberal trade agreements with the EU and, if lucky, associational status.

Western complacency, however, was hit by the crisis in Yugoslavia, which led the EU summit held in June 1993 to hold out the prospect of the associated states becoming EU members, but this was not to be a rapid process, in part because the EU concentrated for the rest of the decade on the measures that led to the euro. From the perspective of a Yugoslavia collapsing into civil war this emphasis seemed somewhat bizarre, and it certainly reflected the degree to which the EU relied on NATO, and therefore the USA, for its security. Indeed, the Maastricht process had been conceived on the assumption that Eastern Europe would remain Communist, and the EU's inability to adapt the process must be considered a major defect. Once the euphoria about the collapse of Communism was over, Western leaders looked at what appeared to be the chaos further east and decided that they were not going to risk their precarious prosperity in order to lift up these countries to which they felt scarce commitment. This impression was confirmed when the others looked on the situation in Germany, where West German transfers of vast funds to the former East Germany dragged public finances down for years.

While British politics were convulsed by the difficulties of getting the Maastricht Treaty through parliament, Germany focused on the consequences of unification. Key issues included the choice of the capital (Berlin), the reconstitution of the *Länder* (regions), the restitution of property, land-ownership, the law on abortion and the consequences of currency revenue. Meanwhile in Italy *Tangentopoli* (Bribe City), the name given to a large-scale criminal investigation of corruption spanning business, politics and the Mafia, helped create a crisis in the established political system, with the collapse and dissolution of the Christian Democratic Party. Prominent individuals charged included two former prime ministers, Giulio Andreotti and Bettino Craxi. The latter fled to Tunisia, being sentenced in *absentia* in 1994 to eight and a half years' imprisonment. More generally, the early 1990s was a period of economic crisis, which in many states, such as Finland, was severe, and this absorbed much government attention.

There were also serious fiscal problems. The ERM buckled under pressure, with Britain unable to sustain sterling within it in the agreed currency band. As a result Britain, like Italy, left the ERM in 1992.

Portugal and Spain also faced difficulties, although they were able to remain in the ERM. Moreover, Greece produced very questionable figures in order to qualify for euro membership. These problems were also seen in what presented itself as the European core. France's ability to meet the convergence criteria rested in part on the sleight of hand involved in selling French Telecom, while the German budget for 1997 revealed a very serious fiscal crisis. Earlier the need to reduce government expenditure had led Alain Juppé, the conservative prime minister appointed in 1995 by Chirac (when he succeeded Mitterrand), to propose cuts in expenditure. These, however, resulted in mass demonstrations and helped in 1997 to lead to the defeat of his government at the election, forcing Chirac back to 'co-habitation' with the Socialists, a system that did not work well and that exacerbated Chirac's preference for gesture politics, particularly in foreign policy, rather than for addressing systemic problems in the economy.

The sleight of hand involved in selling French Telecom can be linked to the more general character of much European government. This involved the concept and reality of what Helmut Schmidt, Chancellor of West Germany from 1974 to 1982, termed the 'political class', a notion that can be seen as integral to the practice of government in Europe. Reliance on an 'élite' of professional politicians is common across the modern world, and European states are not alone in having this élite able to limit its exposure to popular pressures, but much of Europe was certainly different to the USA in tempering adversarial politics as a consequence. Thus in France a small élite of graduates of the *grandes écoles*, particularly the Ecole Polytechnique and the Ecole Nationale d'Administration (ENA), established in 1945, dominated government, politics and business through a system of *pantouflage*. Chirac was an ENA graduate, as was Valéry Giscard d'Estaing and prime ministers such as Fabius from the left and Juppé from the right. As an indication that the democratic deficit was a problem in member states as well as at the level of the EU the Juppé government introduced the measures intended to cut government spending by decree and not via the National Assembly. The role and impact of ENA politics are important to France's current national identity crisis and Sarkozy (who did not go to ENA) and his network self-consciously see themselves as a break with them.

From a different direction Austria had defied the consensus in 2000 after the right-wing (to its critics far-right) Liberal Party, under its iconoclastic leader Jörg Haider, one of the key figures in European right-wing populism, won 27 per cent of the votes in the October elections and became part of the governing coalition with the mainstream conservative People's Party. The EU, in response, quarantined Austria, restricting its role in EU institutions.

In November 1998 the simultaneous Eurozone interest rate cut, by what were eleven still-autonomous central banks, suggested that common policymaking was possible and acceptable, and that the euro would work. The political context was propitious. Narrowly re-elected in 1994, Helmut Kohl had ran out of steam after unification and he lost the German Chancellorship to the SPD candidate, Gerhard Schröder, in September 1998. However, there was no question of Schröder rejecting the policy of concerted policymaking and going for one-nation reflation, as Mitterrand had sought to do in France in 1981. The euro was launched as a trading currency on 1 January 1999. Notes and coins followed in 2002 when earlier currencies such as the deutschmark were retired. There were initial problems. A sharp initial fall in the euro's value was followed in the autumn of 2000 by another major fall. Moreover, in 2001 failure by the European Central Bank (ECB), particularly in its obligation to focus on fiscal stability (especially fighting inflation) rather than economic growth, was blamed for the recession across much of the Eurozone, as it was to be anew by French politicians in 2008.

Furthermore the responsible fiscal management decreed by the Stability and Growth Pact did not work out. The Pact laid down that budget deficits were not to exceed 3 per cent of the nation's annual GDP, and that the national debt must be limited to 60 per cent of GDP. Failure was to lead to sanctions by the ECB, and national accounting was to be monitored from outside. These provisions, however, did not stand the pressure of economic and budgetary problems in the 2000s, and the political will to maintain them, both nationally and at the level of the EU, was lacking. Portugal breached the 3 per cent deficit ceiling in 2000, followed by Germany and France in 2002, Greece in 2004 and Italy in every year from 2002 to 2006. By early 2005 the Greek deficit was about

5.3 per cent of GDP. That Germany and France repeatedly flouted the Pact was serious due to their prominence in the EU.

The EU Commission was poorly placed to respond to the problem. The imprint of the Delors era was such that all the big nations decided 'never again'. After the Maastricht process was completed a big swing back to national capitals set in and 'subsidiarity' developed as an idea justifying decision-making at the national level. Conversely, the very need to refer to 'subsidiarity' reflected the difference Delors had made and sought to make. He even set in motion notions of a European defence policy, an aspiration, however, rapidly crushed by events in the shape of the 2003 Gulf War, a conflict that revealed major differences between leading EU states. As Commission Presidents, Jacques Santer, Romano Prodi and José Manuel Barroso lacked the political backing Delors had received. Indeed, quite the opposite, as demonstrated by the bitter rivalry between Prodi and Silvio Berlusconi, the Italian prime minister.

There were other limitations. In 2000 the Danish government had sought to abolish Denmark's exclusion from the EMU by holding a referendum, but the idea was turned down by the Danish electorate and so the euro was not introduced there. It was also not introduced in Britain and Sweden.

The early phases of the euro were difficult and were accompanied by much small-business-driven inflation in some countries. Moreover, the measures judged necessary to ensure stability and growth proved hard to swallow. The confusion of the EU over the issue was captured by Romano Prodi, the president of the European Commission from 1999 to 2004, who in November 2002 declared, 'The Stability Pact must be respected in all aspects but in such a way that economic recovery is promoted. We can consolidate the Pact by interpreting and implementing its rules in an intelligent way', a remark that indicated the lack of consistency in the implementation of policy by the EU.

The Pact itself was seen as a challenge to national sovereignty in policy making because of the centrality of public expenditure in economic and social policy. The tensions that arose were demonstrated in 2004, when the French prime minister, Jean-Pierre Raffarin, a Chirac protégé, responded to the French failure to respect the rules over deficits limits for the third year, by insisting that his 'prime duty' was to fight unemployment, not 'to produce accounting equations ... so that some office or other in some country or other is satisfied'. In short there was a tension between fighting unemployment at the national level and containing inflation at the national and international levels.

The precariousness of the national level, which in other words is that of national democracy, was indicated by the French elections of 2002. In the first round of the presidential election Jean-Marie Le Pen, the candidate of the far-right, got more votes than the Socialist candidate, Lionel Jospin, prime minister since 1997. Jospin suffered from a lack of personal charisma, from divisions on the left, including within the fratricidal Socialists, and from the unpopularity of the Socialist government. Amidst misleading talk of the rise of Fascism in France there was a second round run-off between Le Pen and Chirac, who had done best in the first round and who won the second handsomely: by 82 to 18 per cent. He benefited from the determination on the left to defeat Le Pen and a consequent willingness to vote for Chirac. Victory for Chirac also provided him with an opportunity to bring co-habitation (president from one party, National Assembly majority from another) with the Socialists to an end.

In Germany that year Gerhard Schröder, the unpopular chancellor, unexpectedly won re-election on 22 September, but by only 10,000 votes. In large part this re-election was due to two unexpected events. First, Schröder's opposition to Anglo-American policy over Iraq won him support, particularly in formerly Communist East Germany. Second, serious floods in what had been East Germany won Schröder more backing as he responded promptly with substantial financial assistance. Moreover, Schröder's opponent was a Bavarian and a Catholic and regional and religious factors matter greatly in Germany.

Alongside tension about the Stability Pact in countries that breached its provisions, successive breaches of the deficit ceilings also helped ensure that opinion in states that did observe the ceiling, such as the Netherlands, Sweden and Finland, was very critical. This criticism was a result accentuated by the bullying nature of German responses to the situation.

The very nature of EMU, in particular a one-fit interest rate, also created problems. It had a deflationary effect on Germany and thus damaged economic growth in the Eurozone. The overall impact of ECB monetary policy has always been deflationary. If, however, this hurts some a lot more than others it is, at least in part, a transfer to the Eurozone level of the previous system of national disparities within particular states.

The economic and financial problems were particularly acute in Italy, leading in 2005 to unsuccessful pressure there for devaluation and to calls for a change in EU fiscal policy or for withdrawal from the euro, although a revival of the lira (the pre-euro currency) would have had no chance of success. By indicating that economic pressures would be blamed on the EU this crisis helped demonstrate one of its major weaknesses: its policies were not fundamentally grounded in consent. At the same time the Italian situation underlined another weakness: in the absence of economic convergence, the euro project was vulnerable to developments in individual states, particularly if they lacked fiscal discipline. The ability of any system to cope with the degree of economic heterogeneity that will remain, in the context of nation-states retaining democratic politics, is unclear. Italian public finances improved in 2007 in part because it proved possible to bring some of the many who had never paid tax into the tax-paying bracket but, that year, the Italian public debt was still 105 per cent of GDP and in December 2007 Italy forecast growth of 1.3 per cent, continuing its underperformance of the Eurozone. The Italian economics situation deteriorated in 2008.

The Italian political system certainly found it difficult to confront the country's problems. The Maroni law, settling the retirement age at 60, only came into effect in 2008, having been postponed for three years, while the Biagi law, permitting employers to offer more flexible contracts, was also watered down. Although in 1993 the electoral system was reformed in order to produce a strong past-the-post element, this was replaced in 2005 with a proportional correction to the new system, with a reward for the parties with the higher percentages. Combined with low thresholds for individual parties this helped move Italy back towards a more unstable situation.

Italy provides a key instance of the issues facing modern Europe and also the problems of offering a judgement. In 2008 the economy remains the sixth industrial power in the world. Society hangs together at a pinch, albeit, as elsewhere, much tried by immigration. Moreover, the sense of national pride and identity comes not from military power, political leadership, institutions or scientific inventions but from events like winning the World Cup, the Formula One World Championship and the world motorcycle championship in the space of two years. All of these have important economic and prestige consequences in what is sometimes seen as a postmodern world.

On the other side in Italy is the pitiful performance of the huge political class, the inefficiency and lack of legitimacy of the institutions, the conspicuously Third World character of the South and the fact that half of those polled feel that the state should guarantee everyone a job. The same year that Italy won the World Cup (2006) there was a huge corruption scandal in Italian league football. Limited confidence in Italy in institutional forms and a strong role for tax evasion were suggested by the percentage of total personal consumer expenditure spent in cash in 2007: 38, compared to 18 for Britain and 22 for France. The Italian right has failed to produce a decent governing élite and the left to offer a convincing reforming one; there are very few moments when Italy has made any positive impact on developments in the wider European scheme; the country punches well below its weight on the international scene and the character of national humour and confidence suggests a perception that this is a very bad period.

Spain, in contrast, was more successful, with rapid economic growth, an absence of a sense of malaise and a peaceful transition of power from the tired Socialists to the conservative Popular Party under José Maria Aznar in 1996. The situation was less happy in 2004 when train bombings by Muslim extremists in Madrid on 11 March formed the backdrop to a contentious Socialist victory. Economic problems became more pressing from 2007 although by then the ability of Spanish companies to take over much of the British airport system and a major British bank were arresting signs of a shift in economic power.

Whatever the problems at the national level and, indeed, encouraged by them, federalism meanwhile was pushed forward in the mid

2000s by the EU's attempt to introduce a European constitution. It was drafted by the Convention for the Future of Europe under the chairmanship of Valéry Giscard d'Estaing, who had his own ambitions to be a president of Europe. Federalism, moreover, appeared one response to the enlargement of the EU to include much of Eastern Europe in 2004. The alternative of a looser system that made more allowance for national differences was antipathetic to the culture of the groups that directed and profited from EU institutionalization.

The Constitution was accepted in June 2004 by the European summit in Dublin. It represented a major shift towards recreating the EU as a quasi-state. Article I-5 required member states 'to facilitate the achievement of the Union's tasks and refrain from any measure which could jeopardize the attainment of the Union's objective'. Furthermore the implications in particular areas were striking. In the field of foreign policy the individual member states were expected to comply with EU policy: 'before undertaking any action on the international scene or any commitment which could affect the Union's interests, each member state shall consult the others within the European Council'. This was a comment on the very divided stance of the EU states in 2002–3 over the Iraq crisis, with France ready to veto a Security Council mandate for war, talk of a hostile Paris–Berlin–Moscow axis and, in contrast, an open letter of 30 January 2003, the 'letter of the Eight', demonstrating Eastern European backing for Anglo-Spanish support for action.

Under the Constitution the European Court of Justice would gain jurisdiction over foreign and security policy. Furthermore the codification of the primacy of EU law would have led to the European Court of Justice that would in practice become a European Supreme Court. Detailed provisions were even more intrusive and, in effect, left national governments with limited functions. This was a rejection of the theory of subsidiarity outlined in the Maastricht Treaty of 1992 as well as of many of the claims of compatibility between the EU and a major role for such governments. The Commission's duty under the Constitution to 'co-ordinate economic policies' created a right to end what would be seen as national variations. 'Public health' was also established as an EU competence under the Constitution, which provided for 'supporting, co-ordinating or complementary' action in health, education, vocational training, culture, youth and sport, a process of extension that provided opportunities for recasting much of the fabric of sociability.

Provisions for the EU's 'area of freedom, security and justice' and for a European Public Prosecutor, as well as the European Arrest Warrant which came into force in 2004, were intimations of a federal police and justice system. The Constitution decreed 'approximation of the laws and regulations of the member states' in criminal matters having 'a cross-border dimension'. In light of such provisions it was ironic that fraud was an endemic aspect of the EU, with the European Court of Auditors repeatedly refusing to approve the EU accounts. Much of the fraud focused on the CAP, which is not only a serious structural flaw in EU finances and policy but also a source of more widespread corruption. Fraud is also more wide-ranging. In 1999 nepotism in the Cresson affair led to the resignation of the Santer Commission and in 2003 fraud within Eurostat, the Commission's statistical body, hit the Prodi Commission.

By making the provisions of the European Charter of Fundamental Rights compulsory, the Constitution's guarantees, for example of the right to strike, to paid leave and to limited working hours, also strengthened the regulatory nature of the provisions. As part of what is often termed the 'European social model', this emphasized the welfare state, rather than the state as the facilitator of individual freedom and liberties. The Constitution was also intended as the departure point for a new process of institutional expansion. A Fundamental Rights Agency was to ascertain if rights endorsed in the Constitution were being defended. In light of such proposals it was scarcely surprising that Miguel Angel Moratinos, Spain's foreign minister, remarked 'We are witnessing the last remnants of national politics'.

In 2005 Spain voted in favour of the Constitution in a referendum, while France and the Netherlands rejected it in May and June respectively. Aside from the unpopularity of the national governments that supported the Constitution there was also a popular concern that individual countries were losing control of their destinies. European centrality in France was less desirable than French centrality in Europe.

Furthermore, in its ongoing process of intergovernmentalism and supranationalism, the EU represents a transfer of power to government (both ministers and bureaucrats), and away from the scrutiny of legislatures and thus the popular political process. This situation is most pronounced when ministers reach agreements at summits, and then present them to domestic legislatures as *faits accomplis*. At the same time similar points about a transfer of power could be made about national governments, such as the Blair government in Britain from 1997 to 2007. Moreover, a popular political process of sorts can be seen in scrutiny in the media.

The referenda of 2005 might seem to indicate the failure of the EU's plans but in 2007 most of the provisions of the Constitution (without the name) were agreed at a new summit in Lisbon. After the upsets of 2005 there was a deliberate avoidance of referenda, with promises to hold them being ignored most prominently by the Labour government led by Gordon Brown in Britain. Ireland rejected the Lisbon agreement in a referendum in 2008 only to be put under pressure to reverse this verdict.

The euro, already the world's second largest currency, expanded. At the start of 2008 Cyprus and Malta took the number of countries using it to fifteen. It now appears that the euro can survive and even flourish despite the failure of strict adherence to the requirements of the Stability and Growth Pact. Contrasts with serious fiscal developments in the USA and Britain in 2007–8 suggested that the euro's life-raft function seems to be working better than its critics had argued, and the Sarkozy government in France considers it a success.

The euro is a challenge to national sovereignty but not as great as globalization, the issues posed by which, by 2008, included oil at the unprecedented sum of over $140 a barrel and a vast outsourcing of jobs. Possibly more serious than the euro's challenge was that the collective responsibility aspect of the currency helped weak and feckless governments, such as that of Silvio Berlusconi in Italy, repeatedly to avoid the fiscal consequences of their actions. In Italy, only the separatists of the Northern League, a small party, adopted a critical note toward the euro, and they were rounded on by all parties. The Northern League seeks a 'Europe of regions', not of states, but support for the EU in Italy has always been almost total. The major sign of concern there was tied instead to the inflationary effect of the introduction of the euro, especially in the first few years of the currency.

More positively, the safety net offered by the euro was more indicative of the value and values of European co-operation than were outbursts such as that in the European Parliament, when Berlusconi, then Italian prime minister, criticized Martin Schulz, the self-important German leader of the Socialist Group, by comparing him to a Nazi concentration camp guard. In practice such tensions were of declining significance in Western Europe, although the process of post-Communist adjustment in Eastern Europe led to a disruptive upsurge of publicly expressed nationalism.

By 2007 there had also been a major change in the politics of Western Europe. The leading politicians of 2005 had been replaced by a new group. In Germany the Social Democrats were rejected by the electorate in 2005 after a crisis of government. Both electorate and politicians had found it difficult to face up to the need to keep the economy competitive and to look at the costs of social welfare. Schröder attempted to change course but lost approval step-by-step. The electorate had become used under Kohl to a major reform bottleneck and substantial structural deficits. In 2002 the Social Democrat and Green coalition had been re-elected in Germany as the less radical choice, but this government then acted like a small version of the EU, with political division and unpopularity greeting the attempts that were made to reform the economy, not least in order to provide the growth necessary to help the 4.7 million unemployed. The government's 'Agenda 2010' economic reform programme was rejected by left-wing critics within the government, as well as by the large number of often poorly skilled, elderly manual workers who felt challenged by it, and the Social Democrats lost control of North-Rhine Westphalia, its key electoral stronghold and Germany's most populous province. In July 2005 Schröder deliberately triggered a parliamentary vote of no confidence in order to prepare the way for a general election a year early. His speech in the Bundestag spoke more generally to the political failure not only of Germany but also of the Stability and Growth Pact and, in some lights, the EU: 'The steady confidence that I need to carry out my reforms is no longer present even within my own coalition government. Dissent and criticism of my policies are on the increase. This is a high price to pay for reform'.

In the event the Christian Democrats became the foremost party in the elections held on 18 September 2005, although with a smaller lead than they had hoped: the CDU/CSU won 35.2 per cent of the vote compared to 34.2 per cent for the SPD. This result led to a Grand Coalition with the Social Democrats, with CDU leader Angela Merkel elected chancellor on 22 November 2005. In part the Grand Coalition was a response to the growing strength of the far-left which caused an earthquake in the German political system. Winning seats in the national election as a result of the unpopularity of Schröder's Agenda 2010, the Party of Democratic Socialism (PDS), the heir to the Socialist Unity Party of East Germany, had made it impossible to establish a more natural coalition of either the SPD and the Greens or the CDU/CSU and FDP Liberals. In 2007 the Die Linke (the left) party was formed by an alliance of the PDS with the Electoral Alternative for Labour and Social Justice, the West German left-wing party. According to recent opinion polls this is now the strongest party in eastern Germany and an indication of former East Germans' disaffection with developments since unification. With coalition members in eastern German state parliaments, Die Linke has also established itself in four western German state parliaments. Germany therefore now has a five-party political system, with all the headaches this brings.

Better public finances stemming from economic growth enabled the Grand Coalition to avoid the consequences of its limited ability to introduce structural economic reforms. Looked at less benignly, the opportunity for reform in Europe's most powerful economy presented by the creation of this coalition was thrown away and now cannot be recovered. The government seemed only able to find new solutions on a limited basis. More generally, Germany's federal system creates far too many important state elections, voting in which is inevitably in part influenced by current national politics. Thus politicians on the national level are in danger of spending too much time campaigning and watching the opinion polls and not enough on long-term policy planning, which reflected a failure of leadership also seen in other aspects of German policy, notably that of their unwillingness to use force in NATO and EU missions. Thus there was a curious interplay among other European states, both a fear of German hegemony and a concern that the Germans did not make due use of their power and position. The Germans have proved reluctant to limit Russian influence in Ukraine, just as in the early 1990s there was a lack of commitment to NATO expansion into Eastern Europe.

In Italy legal charges against recent leaders such as Giulio Andreotti, Bettino Craxi and Silvio Berlusconi are suggestive of a political culture mired in self-interest and institutionalized corruption. The extent to which this is a product and cause of a society that is more generally characterized by a corruption that is inherent to its corporatism is unclear. The willingness to change the law in order to help Berlusconi to avoid trial on false accounting charges underlined the problems of ensuring probity in public life. The corruption associated with Berlusconi sapped confidence in politics, contributed to widespread cynicism and became a subject of the arts, as in Nanni Moretti's film *Il Caimano* (The Cayman). Yet although Berlusconi abused the constitution and, in 2008, held out the prospect of mass action in order to ensure his right to power – 'if we do not get the vote [in a general election] I believe millions of people will go to Rome to demand it' – he was not a Mussolini, the fascist dictator from 1922 to 1945. Indeed, the contrasts between the ways in which these two showmen gained and wielded power said much about shifts in European politics, more particularly the move away from gaining power through force and intimidation.

As another obvious contrast with Mussolini Berlusconi was overthrown in 2006 as a result of electoral failure: the elections of 10 April, the results of which, having been contested by Berlusconi, were confirmed by the judiciary on 22 April. In place of his disjointed coalition another, from the left, was established under Prodi, but that in turn was weakened by division and had a precarious existence, not least because attempts at reform exacerbated its divisions. Prodi managed to stabilize the fiscal situation, but at the price of growth. In 2008 Berlusconi returned to power after victory in the elections.

In France the Chirac years came to an end in 2007 with a combination of political impasse and a high level of suspicion about political ethics that involved both Chirac and his prime minister and destined successor, Dominique de Villepin. Outmanoeuvering Villepin to become the candidate of the right, Chirac's successor Nicolas Sarkozy, who had been first interior and then finance minister under Chirac, in part campaigned for the presidency as an outsider to the mores of the Chirac years, and promised change, indeed a rupture with the past. Although France faces nothing like the problems encountered by Italy, Berlusconi and Sarkozy have similar electoral support, particularly from the old, a rapidly increasing constituency, the professions and the self-employed.

As with attempts at reform during the Chirac years, reforms under Sarkozy led to opposition in the form of strikes and demonstrations. Sarkozy, however, initially proved more robust than Chirac, who was prone to turn back in the face of pressure, notably in 1995. The extent to which France has moved beyond earlier divisions was also suggested by the contrast between the 2007 transport strikes and earlier direct action. Strikes, while highly disruptive to an integrated economy, have less impact in a society in which public-service unions have become less important. There is also, in a more complex society, a greater unwillingness to think in terms of a Marxisante clash between social blocs. Communism has declined in France as an attitude and a tendency as well as a party, while far-left trade unions, such as SUD-Rail, in practice have relatively few members. Yet with his conviction of the value of the state Sarkozy is less of an Anglo-American style neo-liberal than his critics claim. The success of the Socialists in municipal elections in March 2008 revealed that the Sarkozy honeymoon was very short term.

If some would-be revolutionaries think in terms of past episodes of direct action, the French state has little need to consider the willingness of the military to act as De Gaulle conspicuously did in 1968. Indeed, the role of the military within European states has markedly declined, not least in Portugal where, until 1982, they retained through the Council of the Revolution a veto right under the 1976 Constitution. Thus the prominent role of the military in Turkey makes it appear non-European.

As with Sarkozy an emphasis on change was also pushed hard by the new British prime minister, Gordon Brown, as he sought to distance himself from his unpopular predecessor, Tony Blair, whom he succeeded, without election, in 2007. That Blair was questioned by the police in a corruption enquiry underlined the extent to which the funding of political parties in an age of mass media and of large-scale political machines was a key problem. Paying professionals, rather than relying on volunteers, parties preferred to follow a high-cost path of organizational growth and development. The specialized skills required to sell goods in the consumer markets were applied to politics. Brown's government was also affected by corruption claims, although far less so than the Berlusconi and Chirac governments had been. Indeed, in 2007 Chirac was formally charged by magistrates with embezzlement while Mayor of Paris, a position he had held until 1995. More seriously, Brown proved unable to push through necessary reforms in order to recreate an incentive economy, nor even to manage the public sector or public finances adequately.

EASTERN EUROPE

In the ex-Communist world, economic disruption and problems affected political stability, although there were also the difficulties of establishing and bedding down new political and legal systems and practices. The usual basis for successful democracy, including an earlier history of democratic politics notably of acceptance of the legitimacy of opposition, as well as the existence of a large middle class, intermediate institutions and a well-developed urban culture, was absent. More controversially, democracy benefits from a high degree of social consensus, from a commitment to reform or change through peaceful means and from an understanding that large-scale dependency on the state is of limited value.

All of these factors varied in Eastern Europe, with Hungary, Poland and Slovenia, each of which had strong civil societies and pre-1989 reform movements, in a more benign situation than other, especially Balkan, states, particularly when the latter were affected, as with Serbia, by bitter divisions over the definition of the nation as well as the boundaries of the state. The latter were also problems, for example, for Estonia and Latvia, each of which had a large Russian minority.

Powerful populist parties linked to a politics of grievance proved a major problem in the ex-Communist bloc, notably in Serbia but also, for example, in Bulgaria. Difficulties were compounded in a number of countries including Bulgaria and Romania by endemic corruption. These problems were accentuated by the self-interested rule of a number of leaders, not least Boris Yeltsin who proved only too willing to manipulate the Russian constitution.

It was scarcely surprising, given the attempted coup in 1991 and the violent political crisis of 1993 and the marked revival of the nationalities question, that Russia's international influence declined. The Russian government under Yeltsin had sought to create a single army for the CIS that was established by some of the former Soviet republics and Russia, Armenia, Belarus, Kazakhstan, Kyrgyzstan, Tajikistan and Uzbekistan agreed to pool their forces under CIS control. This arrangement was not sustained, however, as the other states, angered by Russian dominance of the CIS command system, created their own independent forces. Security pacts, nevertheless, were signed in 1992 by some of the states, and Russia, Armenia, Kazakhstan, Tajikistan and Uzbekistan agreed to allocate troops for peacekeeping.

Significantly, the Baltic republics and Ukraine refused to be part of this process, and indeed the former joined NATO while from 1994 Ukraine was given US money under military co-operation programmes and by 2008 was pressing to join NATO. The failure of sustained military cohesion was important to the process in which the Soviet Union having ended it proved impossible to replace it by a voluntary federation. The contrasts between the former republics were also demonstrated in 1996, when Kazakhstan and Kyrgyzstan entered into a close economic union within Russia while Belarus entered into a close political and economic union with her. Other former republics did not seek comparable links.

YUGOSLAVIA

The crisis in the ex-Communist world was most acute in the Caucasus, Moldova and the former Yugoslavia. The last was affected by many of the same problems as the Soviet bloc in the 1980s, including economic stagnation, nationalist feeling and uneasiness about the position of the prime power, in this case Serbia instead of Russia. Croatia and Slovenia, the wealthiest of the Yugoslav republics, were unwilling to accept reforms that might strengthen the federal government's ability to address economic powers, in part because they were concerned about the influence of Serbia at the federal level. In turn tension within Serbia, which in 1987 included large-scale strikes against a wage freeze and falling living standards, led to growing nationalist assertion by some of its politicians, but their nationalism took the form of an attempt to use Yugoslavia for their concept of Serb interests. Serb assertiveness within Yugoslavia was accompanied by assertiveness against the minorities within Serbia, notably the Kosovars, and in July 1990 provincial autonomies were abolished.

That year free elections in Croatia and Slovenia helped to strengthen their opposition to Serb assertiveness, and in 1991 they declared independence. The Yugoslav army sought to regain control of Slovenia, but about 70,000 men out of a population of only 2 million Slovenes mobilized in order to resist these attempts. The Serb-dominated Yugoslav army did not push the issue to widespread conflict but it made a far greater effort in Croatia, which, unlike Slovenia, had a border with Serbia and also contained a large Serb minority. Franjo Tudjman, the authoritarian president of Croatia from 1991 to 1999, used nationalism to provide both identity and rationale for his power, just as Slobodan Milošević did in Serbia. In the summer of 1990 Serb militias had been established in Croatia. They were armed by the Serb-run Yugoslav National Army, which also confiscated Croat weapons. The army owes a significant responsibility for the move to war. In 1991 the brief conflict in Slovenia spread to Croatia, which was able to confirm its independence in 1992.

The Serb–Croat conflict spilled over into Bosnia, a part of Yugoslavia that suffered from both Croat and Serb expansion and that was ethnically mixed, with large Croat, Serb and Muslim populations. Outside factors played a role in the outbreak of conflict in Bosnia but so also did the earlier collapse of its government's authority, in part a product of the failure to manage economic problems. This collapse exacerbated ethnic divisions and each of the communities in Bosnia formed an army. The Bosnian Croat and Bosnian Serb forces co-operated with the armies of Croatia and Serbia, pursuing both their own and joint objectives. The Muslims wanted an independent Bosnian state but Croatia and Serbia sought territorial gains. In the subsequent conflict the Bosnian Serbs conquered much of the territory but lost the struggle for international support. The conflicts in Yugoslavia were brutal, involving the deliberate targeting of civilians, and troubling the rest of Europe. The nature of the conflict was also limited. War involved demonstration and negotiation, a politics by military means that was intensely political and a mixture of sudden and brief brutality, truces and convoluted strategies of diplomacy.

Western intervention to end the conflict was undermined by a combination of American reluctance to act, not least from the military leadership, and European weakness. Nevertheless settlements were eventually imposed in Bosnia in 1995 and in Kosovo in 1999, at the expense of the expansionism and ethnic aggression of a Serbian regime that unsuccessfully looked for Russian sponsorship. Although the West played a major role, with 3,515 sorties flown in Operation Deliberate Force in 1995 (the first NATO combat mission), the ability of Serbia's opponents, especially the Croats, to organize military forces capable of mounting credible opposition in the field was important in preventing Serb victory. This ability was seen in the autumn of 1995 when the Croats and the Bosnian Muslims, who had been brought together in large part by American pressure, were able to mount successful offensives against the Bosnian Serbs. Combined with NATO air attack and diplomatic pressure this pushed the Serbs into accepting the Dayton peace agreement which created a federal Bosnian state composed of three ethnic republics. That the agreement was reached in Ohio was symptomatic of the eventual geopolitics of the conflict, with America most prominent, Western Europe secondary, the EU inconsequential and Russia insignificant.

Subsequently, in order to suppress separatist demands and to destroy support for the Kosovo Liberation Army, itself a largely thuggish group, the Serbs also used the tactics of ethnic cleansing in Kosovo, part of Serbia with a majority ethnic Albanian and Muslim population. The Western response in 1999 was coercive diplomacy, which became a forceful humanitarian mission. The air assault caused far less damage to the Serb military than was claimed, although it did help lead to the Serb withdrawal and the Serb acceptance of a ceasefire. Moreover, the devastation of Serbia's infrastructure, in the shape of bridges, factories and electrical power plants, was important, not least because it affected the financial interests of the élite as well as their morale and the functioning of the economy. The Russian inability and unwillingness to help the Serbs also played a role.

Thereafter the continuing isolation of Serbia in a form of economic and financial warfare (sanctions) helped cause serious problems, an erosion of support for Milošević and his fall in the face of Serbian popular action in 2000, which led to the electoral victory of pro-Western parties. He was arrested in 2001 and sent to stand charge before the International War Crimes Tribunal in The Hague on charges of genocide, the first head of state to be tried in this fashion. Serbia and Montenegro, which had formed a Federal Republic of Yugoslavia under Milošević's leadership in 1992, separated in 2003. This was crucial to Montenegro's determination to normalize its position and avoid the isolation of Serbia, and Montenegro's subsequent economic growth underlined the wisdom of this policy.

The precarious nature of the Balkan settlement led to long-term military commitments by Western peacekeeping forces in Bosnia and Kosovo, which ensured that most refugees returned home, including about 750,000 of the 800,000 displaced Kosovan Albanians by the close of July 1999: most had fled to Albania. The disadvantage of the NATO role, however, was an expensive, long-term commitment to Kosovo, which became in effect independent. The disturbed situation in the Balkans also led to a Western commitment in Macedonia in order to end an insurrection by Albanians there. In 2001–2, a force was provided in order to monitor an amnesty that was the background to elections held in 2002.

In contrast to the Balkans, territorial disputes were no longer an issue between states in Western Europe, although in 2004 Spain complained about the celebrations for the tercentenary of British rule over Gibraltar.

Problems in the Balkans distracted attention from the more promising situation elsewhere in Eastern Europe, where the transition to non-Communist governments willing to contest power at the ballot box was managed without military intervention, as was the division of Czechoslovakia in 1994 into the Czech Republic and Slovakia. Eastern European militaries were transformed into bodies under the control of democratic governments and with their structures, tasking, doctrine and weaponry no longer determined by membership of the Warsaw Pact, a process eased by the absence of challenges from Russia. In November 1994 Yeltsin delivered a menacing 'cold peace' speech in Budapest, employing threats to try to prevent NATO expansion into Eastern Europe. Subsequently, an aggressive stance in the Caucasus and toward Ukraine was adopted. Yet this approach was not sustained by Yeltsin, in part due to a lack of regional support and in part to severe economic problems in Russia in 1998. In 1999 there was a wave of Eastern European accessions to NATO, the result of a shift in American policy in 1994–5 from initial reluctance to support for expansion.

In political terms transition from Communist rule was also a successful process and far more so than the transition to democracy in many parts of the world. In some respects the constraints of Westernization and entry to the Western-dominated global economy proved more effective controls than those of the Communist bloc. These constraints were particularly effective in the shape of the requirements for entry into Western institutions, particularly but not only the EU and NATO, and also in terms of the demands of international lenders. The EU's requirements, the *Acquis Communautaire*, comprises 80,000 pages of laws and guidelines, while NATO expects burden-sharing, civilian control of the military and the professionalization of the latter. Combined, and within a context of an emphasis on submission rather than mutual accommodation, these requirements provided a structure that lessened options for Eastern European states and thus the significance of tensions within individual countries. Ten states, Estonia, Latvia, Lithuania, Poland, the Czech Republic, Slovakia, Hungary, Slovenia, Malta and Cyprus, joined the EU as full members in

May 2004, followed by Romania and Bulgaria, which joined in January 2007. Earlier ideas, in particular of Václav Havel, president of Czechoslovakia from 1989 to 1992 and of the Czech Republic from 1993 to 2003, of an Eastern European 'third way' between Communism and consumer capitalism had gone nowhere.

An account of accessions to the EU, first as associate and then as full members, can lead to an underrating of problems that had been prefigured by the major difficulties in bringing prosperity and stability to the former East Germany. Moreover, reflecting in part the degree to which the revolutions of 1989 had involved or led to negotiated solutions in which there was significant continuity in personnel, the continuing influence of former Communists was a major issue in politics in Poland, Romania and elsewhere in Eastern Europe. This, indeed, proved an important contrast between politics in the two halves of Europe, a contrast that was slighted in the West. In Eastern Europe factionalism, ideology, corruption and populism were all aspects of this issue and ensured that the pressure to make a clean break with the Communist past was heavily politicized and deeply controversial.

The break with the Communist past was pushed hard in East Germany, which was in effect taken over from 1990 by the more populous West. The Constitutional Court played a key role as did the *Treuhandanstalt*, the body created to arrange the privatization of industry. There was a purging of university institutes and academics in order to ensure that education would be outside Communist hands and West German academics were sent east, although some preferred to use the new nationally integrated rail system to commute from former West Germany, for example from Munich to Jena. The GDR army was dissolved and some of its personnel were incorporated into the *Bundeswehr*, now the army of Germany as a whole. Another aspect of this break was provided by the collapse of East Germany's former Communist-era economic and cultural links within the Soviet zone. Such links now appeared irrelevant.

Further to the east the contrast between the anchoring of Poland in the Western world and the uneasiness of its political culture was readily apparent. This uneasiness reflected a populist disquiet with what was seen as the continuation of Communist influence. The 1989

Roundtable Talks between Communists and non-Communists had led to a degree of continuity that was consolidated in the 1997 constitution, only to be rapidly rejected by close to half of those who voted in a referendum. This populist tendency emerged victorious in the 2005 parliamentary and presidential elections. The Law and Justice Party-based coalition which then governed Poland sought to foster a Catholic, national, and anti-Communist identity for the country. However, in turn the populists fell out and were rejected by the electorate in 2007.

The transition to a more grounded democracy varied by state, not least with reference to the state of politics prior to the collapse of one-party Communist rule and the nature of this transition. A key moment in post-Communist politics was when a transfer of power took place, which was the case in Bulgaria in 1997 when the Communists (now the Bulgarian Socialist Party) lost the elections to the Union of Democratic Forces; Romania, where the same process occurred in 1996, and Slovakia where the autocratic rule of Vladimir Mečiar was rejected by the electorate in 1998. In each case, especially in Slovakia, a measure of liberalism followed, although endemic corruption remained a key problem in Bulgaria and Romania.

Across Eastern Europe as a whole the division of what had been the liberal opposition movement, such as Civic Forum in the Czech Republic, should, however, be seen as a sign of political maturity en route to multi-party democracy. The relationship between these developments and economic circumstances was far from automatic but the more prosperous states such as Hungary and Slovenia proved better able to engender democratic processes and liberal politics and this owed much to the extent to which they had developed, at least in part, a market economy with light industry and advanced technology.

In the most obscure Communist state, all-too-forgotten Albania, the Hoxha regime collapsed in 1990–2: Hoxha himself had died in 1985, in 1990 an opposition party, the Democratic Party of Albania, was permitted, and in March 1992, under Sali Berisha, it won the elections. The ensuing speedy transition to a post-Communist world proved painful. Dissatisfied citizens destroyed large segments of the Communist-built infrastructure (although vastly more destruction occurred during the riots of 1997). In the main the transition from Communism focused on politics and the cities but it also extended deep into the fabric of the country. Collectivization was comprehensively reversed – in some cases by the villagers themselves. The re-privatization of the land and flocks of collective farms led to the rapid building of walls to separate the new farmholdings. Old tribal customs and allegiances, never neglected, were reasserted.

RUSSIA

No longer running the show but still an ominous presence, Russia appeared an unpredictable element. The authoritarianism of Vladimir Putin, who was elected president in March 2000, brought a measure of stability in Russia, although at the cost of the failure of attempts to build up a democratic infrastructure. These had suffered badly in the Yeltsin years, when the government devoted lip-service to the idea of a liberal, free-market democracy, while preferring the pursuit of power and profit, which were linked in corruption and peculation. Putin, who had allegedly promised Yeltsin that he would protect him and his family from retribution for their corruption, betrayed the authoritarian and manipulative inclinations to be expected of his secret service background. It is also claimed that he had responsibility for explosions attributed to Chechen extremists, as well as for an Islamic militants' attack on Daghestan.

Putin certainly suppressed opposition, ended freedom in the media and centralized government authority. The effective autonomy of the business 'oligarchs' in the now-privatized industries, as well as that of provincial governors, was brought to an end. His government, nevertheless, was reasonably popular, not least as a result of offering apparent stability, while the brutal resumption of the war against separatist Chechnya launched in 1994 was presented as a defence of national greatness. The difficulties of the 1990s, moreover, weakened the appeal of democracy to at least part of the Russian public. Real wages, in contrast, have doubled under Putin. The favourable electoral results in 2007 largely reflected Putin's popularity. However, at the same time the treatment of both electorate and, even more, the opposition reflected an inherent authoritarianism which was also pronounced in the rapidly oppressive imposition of control over television and the press. Aside from gravely limiting freedom of speech Putin destroyed movements for human rights. Systemic features of Putin's Russia include the large number of officials appointed by the president, which helped ensure that the KGB came to control the country, not least *Gazprom*, a key source of power and funds.

Russia's influence was accentuated by the increased value of its raw materials, particularly oil and natural gas, and their supply was used for political ends by Putin, who had gained state control of them, in part through legal manipulation. Russia is the largest exporter of natural gas and the second largest of oil. Russia's alliance with China, which led to the Shanghai Co-Operation Organization of Russia, China and the Central Asian republics, has also increased the challenge it poses. Thus having lost its bloc in Eastern Europe Russia is now central to an essentially non-European bloc. Russia, of course, not as potent in relative terms as it was during the Cold War, was not able to impose anything during the Kosovo Crisis of 1999, and there are serious limits to the Russian ability to project its power anywhere much outside its own backyard. Yet Russia retains national pride, however misplaced, as well as the ambition reflected in Putin's Annual Address to the Federal Assembly in 2005 in which he described the end of the Soviet Union as the 'greatest geopolitical catastrophe of the last century', and, moreover, the capacity to take an aggressive stance towards its neighbours. This is particularly so in the Caucasus region and Central Asia.

This ambition and capacity may produce a new, smaller version of the Cold War, one in which the ideological tension is different, but the power politics are still focused on competition via protégés, although a comparison with Russia's role in Balkan power politics in 1875 or 1912 may be more pertinent than the Cold War. Geopolitics, indeed, has come to the fore in Russian strategic culture. It was always there but the ideological overlay is now largely absent or rather is presented in terms of an assertion of national sovereignty. Russian policy over both the Iraq war of 2003 and Iran's attempt to develop a nuclear capability was hostile to American views and, in the latter case, to those of Britain, France and Germany as well. So also was the use of *Gazprom* for power projection.

Russian policy also kept matters on the eastern borders of Europe unsettled, which ensured a zone of tension in what to certain commentators was part of Eastern Europe, to some a sort of Far Eastern Europe and to others, especially critics concerned about the burdens of EU enlargement, beyond Eastern Europe. Russian pressure played a role as did the difficulties of creating democratic practises. In Georgia the 'Rose Revolution' of 2003 brought democracy but Russia intervened in Georgian politics and supported a violent secessionist movement in Abkhazia, part of the state. In Ukraine the 'Orange Revolution' of 2004, directed against a rigged presidential election, also led to democracy but, again, not the stability hoped for. Russian intervention exacerbated political and regional rivalries within Ukraine, notably between the more pro-Russian east and the more hostile west of Ukraine. It was also directed against Polish and other attempts to anchor Ukraine in the West. Indeed, in 2004 Lech Walesa travelled to Kiev to offer himself as a mediator in the contested presidential election.

Moreover, in Belarus, Alayksandr Lukashenka revealed the serious drawbacks of an attempted stability born of repression. Russian support for Lukashenka, not least after the rigged presidential election in 2006 and anti-democratic meddling in Ukrainian politics, was accompanied by Putin's pressure on Estonia. This included a cyber-attack on its economy in 2007, which was matched by pressure on Finland not to come to Estonia's assistance, which it tried to do through the EU. Authoritarianism at home co-existed naturally with bullying abroad. Both prior to the crisis of 1999 and subsequently Russian support for Serbian nationalism made a settlement of the Kosovo issue difficult, although the root problem was Serbian refusal to accept the separatist inclinations of the ethnic Albanian majority and, instead, a commitment to the 120,000 Serbs in this territory of 2 million people. The Kosovars declared independence in 2008.

EUROPEAN GEOPOLITICS

The relationship between national issues and international bodies seen in both Western and Eastern Europe indicates the degree to which national concerns are advanced within such bodies, particularly today the EU and NATO. In some respects there are parallels with the international alliances that existed a century earlier as security and the furtherance of interests were then seen to lie in co-operation. Despite the elements of collective security and deterrence this, however, led to the First World War, not so much because there were two competing alliances but rather in large part due to the willingness of German, Austrian and Russian decision-makers to resort to war. After 1945 competing alliance systems again nearly took Europe to war, most recently in 1983. The end of the Cold War, in contrast, was followed by the extension of the Western security system to incorporate most of Eastern Europe and there was a high degree of optimism about the security situation. The position, however, has been transformed by the revival of Russian strength and aggression, as this has made it apparent that the politics of rival blocs has been recreated. There is a major tendency to seek to ignore this but the treatment of neighbouring states by Russia has forced the issue to the fore.

One approach is to adopt a Russia versus Europe scenario and to see Europe as a set of values incompatible with Russian authoritarianism. This view represents another iteration of Cold War attitudes and justifiably so. It is also necessary, however, to note the degree to which Russia does not accept this equation any more than its allies in Serbia do: Putin, who controls the largest army in Europe, sees Russia as a world and European power with an agenda of its own to pursue within Europe. Moreover, the ability of the EU to confront the challenge posed by Russia is unclear. These issues may not mean much to British readers but the situation seems very different in the Baltic states and Ukraine. This led to concern about European leaders such as Schröder and Berlusconi who were regarded as overly compliant to Putin's wishes. Similarly, in April 2008 France and Germany successfully opposed the American-backed proposal for NATO accession by Georgia and Ukraine. Despite reassurance in terms of limited Russian military expenditure and signs of interdependence the sense of a Cold World reborn was an unsettling vision of an unchanging past and of the vitality of geopolitical pressures. So also with the Balkans and ethnic–nationalist interests.

Yet as an indicator of change there was also a new political dynamic created by the interaction in the EU of two powerful currents: regionalism and supranationalism. EU institutions, which were responsible for the Council of European Regions established in 1985, found the development of regionalism particularly attractive as it provided them with a role that was not dependent on national governments. This, however, required an institutional formulation. A sense of regional distinctiveness and a call for regional autonomy was insufficient. Instead, there was a need for regional government agencies to seek and spend money, crucial as the direct regional arm of the EU was modest. Such agencies also fulfilled the goals of regional politicians who were newly active as decentralization attracted increased favour as a goal of many national governments. This decentralization had very different results in particular countries, being stronger in Belgium, Italy, Germany and Spain than in Britain (until 1997) or, despite legislation of the 1980s, France.

Aside from the institutional framework regionalist politics were very different, in context, tone and goals, not only between but also within states. Thus in Spain the separatism of Catalonia contrasted with the more violent situation in the Basque Country and both were different to the pressure for autonomy in Andalusia. More generally, regional demands varied greatly, with differing political, religious and linguistic goals. These demands lessened, even weakened, national ties and, if they did not lead to a more clearly European consciousness, the emphasis on the regions transformed the situation by encouraging multiple loyalties. Multiple identities and loyalties were linked to multiple layers of governance, which encouraged politics as business and business as politics. The cost and corruption of governance sapped the integrity of the EU but, more seriously, also made coherent reform more difficult. Political legitimacy was not offered in the shape of enthusiastic consent because the nature of European government was administrative not democratic.

CHANGING SOCIAL POLITICS

As another level of change, the social politics of Europe was changing, not least with the breakdown of previous electoral alignments, particularly between the male working class and the left and the middle class and the right. As Chapter 4 suggested, class became far less secure as a definition of identity and interests, not only because of the crumbling of class identity but also due to the rise of other demands. These were expressed in terms not only of interests, but also of cultural pulses. Generational in origin and character, the latter divided social groups. For example, the anarchical punk rock music of the 1970s might appeal to some of the young and might, in part, parrot radical dissidence in its lyrics, but neither appealed to the older generations. Indeed, the absence of trans-generational cultural styles, which was exacerbated by media obsession with the 18–35 age group, was a major challenge to a sense of cohesion in a period in which interests were increasingly understood in cultural terms or at least with cultural references. This sense of cohesion was also challenged by the rate of immigration and the unwillingness of many immigrants to integrate.

Fragmentation in goals was a powerful political consequence of social and cultural trends. Single-issue policies were pushed hard by groups who were not interested in social allegiance as a basis for defining interests. These policies sometimes conformed to traditional political agendas, such as in taxation, but frequently related to consumer or moral issues that were not so readily explained. The extent to which state regulation was a factor in economic life encouraged consumer politics, while a sense of flux arising from 1960s and post-1960s social liberalism was responsible for the politics of morality.

Consumer politics and the politics of morality were also linked. The interplay of consumption with regulation, or rather the extent to which consumption should lead to regulation, was a key issue and reflected a concern with behaviour that in part was an aspect of a more affluent society. Issues of production, such as state ownership of industry, while still significant were less dominant in personal expenditure, group politics and government policy than they had been in the 1950s. The concern with behaviour was both counter-cultural, not least in the shape of pressure for environmental reform and also for libertarian choices, but also from the right, with an anxiety about social breakdown. The latter anxiety was less articulate than among American conservatives but was nevertheless a factor. Links between cultural concerns and established political movements were often loose or indirect but were nevertheless important. These issues do not exist in a vacuum. The discussion in earlier chapters of environmental change, demographics, social dynamics, cultural identities and economics are not separate. Instead, political tensions interact in what is a situation of great flux.

Chapter 9

Current Issues

The definition of Europe is a key issue because the end of the Cold War in 1989–91 and the subsequent enlargement of the EU to include most of Eastern Europe have pushed it to the fore as a subject of practical politics. In addressing issues of definition Europe can be treated geographically. This is the most common approach, although, once more precision is sought than the statement that it is located between Asia and the Atlantic, such a treatment is open to debate. For example, although the Ural Mountains have conventionally been seen as the eastern physical border of Europe they are neither a barrier nor a frontier, being located as they are within the Russian Federation. Moreover, as an example of the various geographies on offer, in the preface to the second edition of the influential French *Larousse Encyclopedia of World Geography* (1967), Pierre Deffontaines pressed for the unity of the Mediterranean basin and also argued that the Eurasian plains from the Oder to the Pacific should be treated as a single unit. The argument for a united Mediterranean basin, seen in 2008 in Sarkozy's plan for a Mediterranean Union, was frequently made in southern Europe, especially when EU funds were sought for North African states on the grounds that their stabilization, particularly that of Morocco and Algiers, would alleviate pressures such as immigration in Spain and France. A colonial overhang by both powers was also at stake, as also with Italy in Libya, although the latter was far less pressing than the fraught relationship between France and Algeria. Yet such calls for action and aid also reflected the bogus nature of the suggestion of a Mediterranean unity, for they drew on the idea that there was a difference that had to be stabilized in order to contain the serious challenge to Europe posed by immigration and Islamic consciousness.

Alongside geography, indeed, Europe can also be treated as a value system, a goal or an ideology, ideas linked today to the notion of European 'soft power' as opposed to the 'hard power' of American force. This emphasis on a value system, for example the Copenhagen Criteria laid down in 1993 as preconditions for countries acceding to the EU, may suggest a lack of stability if not real meaning as values change and are not held by all. Looked at differently, the emphasis on a value system implies a polyvalent and multipolar character within an entity that lacks fixed borders and has more than one functional system, with contrasts most obviously between the areas based on currency (the Eurozone) and border controls (the Schengen zone). The Copenhagen Criteria, established at a European Council meeting in 1993, were stable political institutions, the guarantee of human rights and the rule of law, economic stability and an acceptance of EU law. An earlier instance was of Hans-Dietrich Genscher's claim in a speech at the United Nations on 27 September 1989 that East Germany risked 'de-Europeanization' if it turned down the opportunity for reform. Gorbachev had already referred to the 'European home' but that implied the co-existence of different systems, which was not the viewpoint of Western European politicians.

Contrasting ideas about Europe were focused with the question of Turkish entry to the EU, an issue that revealed unease as well as uncertainty. In 2002 Edmund Stoiber, the prime minister of Bavaria, who narrowly lost the election for the German chancellorship to Gerhard Schröder, argued that Turkish accession would be an excessive fiscal and therefore economic burden. Frits Bolkestein, an EU commissioner critical of Turkish accession, in September 2004 compared the large-scale immigration that he predicted would follow accession with past political challenges from the Ottoman (Turkish) Empire, declaring 'the liberation of 1683 will have been in vain', a reference to the defeat of the Ottoman siege of Vienna. Given the allocation of political weight within the EU on the basis of population the issue of Turkish entry also accentuated the problems posed by the earlier entry of poor states. Turkey has ten times the population of Sweden but a national product that equals it. In the eyes of critics this was tantamount to putting the Turks in charge of the wealth earned by the Swedes, in short an act of robbery.

In December 2004 the Commission, however, decided to recommend opening accession talks with Turkey. This was a contentious issue the following year as the consent of some states, such as Austria, was only obtained with considerable difficulty. Such an accession would take Europe to the borders of Georgia, Armenia, Iran, Iraq and Syria and bring in a society whose average income is considerably lower than that of the rest of Europe. The nature of Turkish society is also an issue, not least with the role of Islam. In 2005 the European Commission warned Turkey that a draft law on religious institutions did not meet EU standards on religious freedom. Indeed, in some respects Turkey represented the antithesis of the public culture sought by the EU, not only because the latter was really Catholic in its inception in the 1950s but also due to the secular character of much of European society.

This antithesis was doubly the case because of the authoritarianism associated with the central role of the Turkish military, which offered an apparent echo of the systems rejected in Spain and Greece, and because of the role of Islam in Turkish life. The restrictions on freedom of expression in the Turkish constitution appeared particularly unwelcome. The possibility of defining the EU in terms of difference, a possibility also presented by Russia, was, however, compromised by the contrasting policies of individual EU member states, including a willingness in some cases to support Turkish membership. Britain, under Tony Blair, backed this essentially in order to try to stabilize the Middle East by consolidating Western support in Turkey but this policy rested on a failure to consider what the EU meant and how extendable it might be.

The demographic dimension made this clear. The population of Turkey – about 71 million – and its high growth rate when contrasted with the lower growth rate of Germany, whose population is now about 82 million, is such that if admitted it would become the most populous EU state by about 2020, with only the possibility of Russian entry able to dispel this. Demographic strength would be accompanied by voting rights. Although the EU has ruled out accession for the North African members of Euromed, Muslim demographic weight will be further accentuated if Albania and Bosnia join the EU. These accessions would lead, depending on Turkish growth rates, to Muslim-majority states having about 122 million people out of an EU population of about 587 million and the latter will also include the approximately 15 million Muslims in the 25 states of the 2005 EU. Moldava and Ukraine have both expressed a wish to join the EU, which will lessen the Muslim percentage but only modestly.

The value of anchoring the lands to the east of the bulk of the EU in terms of democracy and stability is apparent but it is far less clear that membership by countries such as Albania, Belarus, Bosnia, Russia, Turkey, Ukraine and Kosovo would pose anything less than very serious problems for the EU. The issue also reveals the saliency of tensions in Europe's borderlands, tensions that are an important part of its politics. Cyprus provides a good example. In August 2005 Dominique de Villepin, the recently appointed French prime minister, who was looking for a reason to take forward France's opposition to Turkey's membership of the EU, declared that it was 'inconceivable' that Turkey could begin accession talks without recognizing Cyprus. This was a reference to the fact that when, as a condition of accession talks, the Turkish government signed a protocol extending its customs union with the EU to the new members that had joined the EU in 2004, including Cyprus, it issued a statement that this did not imply recognition of the Greek-Cypriot government. In 1974 a successful Turkish invasion followed by Turkish 'ethnic cleansing' of Greeks had led to the creation of a *de facto* independent Turkish-Cypriot statelet in the north of the island. This statelet has since been sustained and there has been no unification to match that of Germany, understandably so as the divisions in Cyprus run more deeply.

In April 2004, in a referendum, the Greek Cypriots voted heavily against a UN reunification plan that had been seen by the EU as important to accession by Cyprus. The Turkish Cypriots, in contrast, voted in favour. In 2004, however, the EU accepted the accession of Cyprus in terms of the Greek-Cypriot government part of the island. It adopted the euro in 2008. The EU saw this government as the sole legitimate representative of the island and, in light of the wish to speed Cypriot accession, allowed it to accede accordingly without having first reached a settlement with the Turkish-Cypriot statelet. This was not intended as a bar to Turkish accession to the EU and Turkish recognition of Cyprus was not selected as a precondition for Turkish accession talks. Instead, the status of the island was 'parked' by being left to discussion under the auspices of the United Nations. The French requirement, however, which was not supported in the EU's 2005 negotiations with Turkey, indicated the extent to which issues on the periphery interacted with the policies of the key EU states.

To approach the Mediterranean in terms of Cyprus and Turkey is to underplay the crucial role of the older-established EU states and to focus, as is so often the case with the EU, on becoming rather than on already established practices, in short on future possibilities and not established issues. If, however, the shape of the EU is a key issue because of the questions for European identities and interests posed by Turkish membership, that serves as a reminder that politics is not extraneous to deeper rhythms set by more fundamental changes such as those of demography and the environment.

EUROPE AND THE WORLD

Demography and the environment are the leading issues, for demography suggests a major change in the identity and age structure of the European population, as well as its relationship to the rest of the world. The linkage between population numbers and politics might not mean much in a postmodern world concerned with image and discourse, but this linkage is an important aspect of the relationship to the rest of the world, a point that reflects a return to an earlier stage of concern about numbers. As the EU is really a 1950s institution with 1950s solutions, population numbers will always matter to it. The concern about population numbers is very varied across Europe, with the political anxiety foremost in Russia, whereas in parts of Europe the anxiety focuses on the number of workers, not least because of worries about the fiscal and social aspects of dependence: insufficient taxpayers and not enough people to provide social services.

Environmental changes are far from specific to Europe but the consequences are central for its nature as a place to live. The situation is most acute in southerly areas affected by hotter and drier conditions, especially Spain, but is also a factor elsewhere. Furthermore the consequences of the environmental crisis link into politics through issues of public policy, although the ability of Europe to affect global environmental changes is put into perspective by the large-scale economic expansion occurring in China, India and elsewhere, and its major consequences for the environment.

Global warming represents yet another instance of the process by which Europe is centrally involved in and by global changes and ideas, not least concepts and practices of modernity, identity and sovereignty, many of which have a strong American element. Whether affected by Chinese imports or the pressures leading to the rise in the price of oil, by American geopolitical interests or the flows of global migration, Europe cannot detach itself from world events. The EU appears the necessary response to these problems, not least for the smaller European states that otherwise have no chance of having their voices heard. China does not have the time to listen to the 27 members of the EU individually. Britain, France and Germany can expect to be listened to separately but this is not true of the other powers and with the shift of world power to East and South Asia this becomes a more serious issue for these smaller states. When Europe was the fulcrum of the Cold War and, subsequently, when the fate of Eastern Europe and relations with Russia were central concerns, the attitudes of Poland, Romania, Sweden etc. might have seemed of importance, not least as Russia sought to play off individual states, but such importance is far less the case from the perspective of China and India.

The possibility of a European response was indicated in the winter of 2007–8 by united pressure on China from the Eurozone for an appreciation of the renminbi, the Chinese currency. At the same time there are very divergent views within the EU on how best to respond to imports of Chinese goods and Russian energy. The former issue exposes differences between European producers and consumers while the latter exacerbates political fault-lines within Europe and also reveals acute vulnerability. The European level also appears the most important when addressing environmental change, first in order to press for appropriate policies within Europe and second for negotiating more effectively at an international level, in particular for considering how best to take forward the Kyoto process. But the hope that the EU will serve as a great life-raft on the turbulent seas of globalization may well be misplaced, as the idea that aggregating influence by participation in the EU will contain, even solve, problems is possibly more optimistic than realistic. Indeed, alongside the success of the EU in creating a vast, functioning judicial space and in acting as an enabler for democratic modernization in southern and Eastern Europe, its ability to generate solutions and negotiate successfully on crucial issues, such as energy dependence on Russia and trade with China, is unclear.

The emphasis on political integration in the EU is a response to the pressures of globalization, although also to the challenge posed by the degree to which national governments, such as France under Sarkozy, rediscover the temptations of nationally oriented business protectionist policies. Much of this text has been critical of the EU but it is also true that national governments have frequently acted in a reprehensible fashion. For example, EU members in Eastern Europe have only slowly grasped the level of commitment they are expected to show to their own citizens as much as to the EU. Indeed, in the end Europe, in part, is what each member state makes of it and the idea that decades of membership have made France or Italy less French or Italian just is not borne out by reality. The contrast between Merkel and Sarkozy is particularly instructive for the persistence of different national styles. Had the EU been as powerful as sometimes alleged, then episodes such as the Naples refuse disaster in 2007–8 would have been less likely. As a reminder of national traditions, possibly this text exemplifies a British contribution to the debate on and process of integration, namely the readiness to criticize centralist and *dirigiste* approaches and stress, instead, liberal values.

At the same time, it is important to remember that Europe is about more than just the EU. Many European states are not in the EU, while much of the European heritage is being developed in a variety of ways outside Europe. Moreover, if Europe is far less prominent than it used to be, that does not simply mean that it is the recipient, even fag-end, of global pressures and processes. If the nature of the future relationship between Europe and these processes is far from clear, then that is an integral part of the present story.

Selected Further Reading

There is an extensive literature on this subject and this brief list largely restricts itself to books published since 2000. Earlier books should be approached through the bibliographies and footnotes in these books.

P. Albanese, *Mothers of the Nation. Women, Families and Nationalism in Twentieth-Century Europe* (Toronto, 2006)

D. H. Aldcroft, *The European Economy, 1914–2000* (London, 2001)

N. Andjelic, *Bosnia-Herzegovina: The End of a Legacy* (London, 2003)

T. G. Ash, *In Europe's Name: Germany and the Divided Continent* (London, 1993)

E. Bacon and M. Sandle, eds, *Brezhnev Reconsidered* (Basingstoke, 2002)

M. Barke, J. Towner and M. T. Newton, eds, *Tourism in Spain: Critical Issues* (Wallingford, 1996)

D. S. Bell, *Presidential Power in Fifth Republic France* (Oxford, 2000)

—, *François Mitterrand* (Cambridge, 2005)

P. M. H. Bell, *Twentieth-Century Europe. Unity and Division* (London, 2006)

I. T. Berend, *An Economic History of Twentieth-Century Europe* (Cambridge, 2006)

S. Berstein and J.-P. Rioux, *The Pompidou Years, 1969–1974* (Cambridge, 2000)

M. Bess, *The Light-Green Society: Ecology and Technological Modernity in France, 1960–2000* (Chicago, 2003)

R. Bessel and D. Schumann, eds, *Life after Death: Approaches to a Cultural and Social History of Europe during the 1940s and 1950s* (Cambridge, 2003)

B. W. Blouet, *The EU and Neighbors. A Geography of Europe in the Modern World* (Hoboken, NJ, 2008)

G. W. Breslauer, *Gorbachev and Yeltsin as Leaders* (Cambridge, 2002)

E. D. Brose, *A History of Europe in the Twentieth Century* (Oxford, 2004)

T. Buchanan, *Europe's Troubled Peace, 1945–2000* (Oxford, 2006)

F. W. Carter and D. Turnock, eds, *Environmental Problems of East Central Europe* (London, 2002)

M. Castle, *Triggering Communism's Collapse: Perceptions and Power in Poland's Transition* (Lanham, MD, 2003)

M. Cioc, *The Rhine: An Eco-Biography, 1815–2000* (Seattle, 2002)

C. Clemens and W. E. Paterson, eds, *The Kohl Chancellorship* (London, 1998)

R. Clogg, ed., *Greece, 1981–1989: The Populist Decade* (Basingstoke, 1993)

M. Dennis, *The Stasi: Myth and Reality* (Harlow, 2003)

J.-P. Dormois, *The French Economy in the Twentieth Century* (Cambridge, 2004)

R. Drake, *The Aldo Moro Murder Case* (Cambridge, MA, 1995)

K. Dyson, ed., *European States and the Euro: Europeanisation, Variation and Convergence* (Oxford, 2002)

J. L. Gaddis, *We Now Know: Rethinking Cold War History* (Oxford, 1997)

V. P. Gagnon, *The Myth of Ethnic War: Serbia and Croatia in the 1990s* (Ithaca, NY, 2005)

T. W. Gallant, *Modern Greece* (London, 2001)

S. George and I. Bache, *Politics in the European Union* (Oxford, 2001)

M. Gilbert, *Surpassing Realism: The Politics of European Integration since 1945* (Oxford, 2003)

R. Gildea, *France Since 1945* (Oxford, 2002)

J. Gillingham, *European Integration, 1950–2003* (Cambridge, 2003)

P. Ginsborg, *Italy and its Discontents: Family, Civil Society, State, 1980–2001* (London, 2001)

D. S. Hamilton and J. P. Quinland, *Partners in Prosperity: The Changing Geography of the Transatlantic Community* (Washington, DC, 2004)

M. Hilson, *Scandinavia* (London, 2008)

W. L. Hitchcock, *The Struggle for Europe: The History of the Divided Continent Since 1945* (London, 2004)

C. Joppke, *East German Dissidents and the Revolution of 1989: Social Movement in a Leninist Regime* (New York, 1995)

T. Judt, *Postwar: A History of Europe since 1945* (London, 2005)

R. Kedward, *La Vie en bleu: France and the French since 1900* (London, 2005)

P. Kenny, *A Carnival of Revolution: Central Europe 1989* (Princeton, NJ, 2002)

—, *The Burdens of Freedom: Eastern Europe since 1989* (London, 2006)

L. R. Klein and M. Pomer, eds, *The New Russia: Economic Transition Gone Awry* (Stanford, CA, 2001)

G. Kligman, *The Politics of Duplicity. Controlling Reproduction in Ceauşescu Romania* (Berkeley, CA, 2000)

J. Kornai, *Evolution of the Hungarian Economy, 1848–1998: Paying the Bill for Goulash Communism* (New York, 2000)

K. Larres, ed., *Germany since Unification: The Development of the Berlin Republic*, 2nd edn (Basingstoke, 2001)

J. Lévesque, *The Enigma of 1989: The USSR and the Liberation of Eastern Europe* (Berkeley, 1997)

M. McDonald, *'We Are Not French!' Language, Culture, and Identity in Brittany* (London, 1989)

J. McCormick, *Environmental Policy in the European Union* (Basingstoke, 2001)

M. Malmborg and B. Stråth, eds, *The Meaning of Europe. Variety and Contention within and among Nations* (Oxford, 2002)

D. R. Marples, *The Collapse of the Soviet Union, 1985–1991* (Harlow, 2004)

B. Marshall, *Willy Brandt* (Basingstoke, 1997)

—, *The New Germany and Migration in Europe* (Manchester, 2000)

K. Maxwell, *The Making of Portuguese Democracy* (Cambridge, 1995)

R. Maxwell, *The Spectacle of Democracy. Spanish Television, Nationalism and Political Transition* (Minneapolis, MN, 1995)

R. C. Meade, *Red Brigades: The Story of Italian Terrorism* (Basingstoke, 1990)

A. S. Milward, *The European Rescue of the Nation State*, 2nd edn (London, 2000)

A. J. Nicholls, *The Bonn Republic. West German Democracy 1945–1990* (London, 1997)

R. Okey, *The Demise of Communist East Europe: 1989 in Context* (London, 2004)

A. Paczkowski, *The Spring Will be Ours: Poland and the Poles from Occupation to Freedom* (College Station, PA, 2003)

P. Pavlínek, *Environmental Transition: Transformation and Ecological Defence in Central and Eastern Europe* (London, 2002)

V. M. Pérez Díaz, *The Return of Civil Society: The Emergence of Democratic Spain* (Cambridge, MA, 1993)

P. Pesonen and O. Riihinen, *Dynamic Finland: The Political System and the Welfare State* (Helsinki, 2002)

R. Rohrschneider and S. Whitefield, eds, *Public Opinion about the European Union in Postcommunist Europe* (London, 2005)

C. Ross, *The East German Dictatorship: Problems and Perspectives in the Interpretation of the GDR* (London, 2002)

M. E. Sarotte, *Dealing with the Devil: East Germany, Détente and Ostpolitik, 1969–1973* (Chapel Hill, NC, 2001)

R. Service, *Russia: Experiment with a People from 1991 to the Present* (Cambridge, MA, 2003)

L. Shevtsova, *Yeltsin's Russia: Myths and Reality* (Washington, DC, 1999)

T. B. Smith, *France in Crisis: Welfare, Inequality, and Globalization since 1980* (Cambridge, 2004)

T. Snyder, *The Reconstruction of Nations: Poland, Ukraine, Lithuania, Belarus, 1569–1999* (New Haven, CT, 2003)

C. Sowerwine, *France since 1870: Culture, Politics and Society* (Basingstoke, 2001)

G. and N. Swain, *Eastern Europe since 1945*, 3rd edn (London, 2003)

R. Tőkés, *Hungary's Negotiated Revolution: Economic Reform, Social Change, and Political Succession* (Cambridge, 1996)

R. Vinen, *A History in Fragments: Europe in the Twentieth Century* (London, 2000)

R. Wakeman, ed., *Themes in Modern European History since 1945* (London, 2003)

S. L. Woodward, *Balkan Tragedy. Chaos and Dissolution after the Cold War* (Washington, DC, 1995)

P. Zelikow and C. Rice, *Germany Unified and Europe Transformed: A Study in Statecraft* (Cambridge, MA, 1995)

J. Zielonka, *Europe as Empire: The Nature of the Enlarged European Union* (Oxford, 2006)

—, *Democratic Consolidation in Eastern Europe* (New York, 2001)

Index